Papa, PhD

Papa, PhD

Essays on Fatherhood by Men in the Academy

Edited by Mary Ruth Marotte, Paige Martin Reynolds,
and Ralph James Savarese

RUTGERS UNIVERSITY PRESS
NEW BRUNSWICK, NEW JERSEY, AND LONDON

Library of Congress Cataloging-in-Publication Data

Papa, PhD : essays on fatherhood by men in the academy / edited by Mary Ruth
Marotte, Paige Martin Reynolds, and Ralph James Savarese.
    p. cm.
Includes bibliographical references.
ISBN 978-0-8135-4878-4 (hardcover : alk. paper) — ISBN 978-0-8135-4879-1
(pbk. : alk. paper)
1. Fatherhood. 2. Father and child. I. Marotte, Mary Ruth. II. Reynolds, Paige.
III. Savarese, Ralph James.
HQ756.P365 2010
306.874´208631—dc22

                                                                    2009053395
A British Cataloging-in-Publication record for this book is available from the
British Library.

Visit our Web site: http://rutgerspress.rutgers.edu

Manufactured in the United States of America

For Jeff, Ethan, Olivia, and Simon
For Bert and Anna
For D.J.

Contents

Thinking Stiffs: An Introduction / ix

PART ONE *Fathers in Theory, Fathers in Praxis: Merging Work and Parenting*

Disney Dad AMITAVA KUMAR / 3

Gaining a Daughter: A Father's Transgendered Tale
LENNARD J. DAVIS / 7

Gifts from the Sea DAVID G. CAMPBELL / 16

The Luck of the Irish F. D. REEVE / 26

Shifting the Tectonic Plates of Academia JERALD WALKER / 29

Hair-Raising Experiences JOHN W. WELLS / 34

A River Runs through It: Queer Theory and Fatherhood
JOSEPH GELFER / 46

On Writing and Rearing DAVID HAVEN BLAKE / 50

Doing Things with Words IRA L. STRAUBER / 55

On Fecundity, Fidelity, and Expectation: Reflections on Philosophy
and Fatherhood J. AARON SIMMONS / 59

Sheathing the Sword GREGORY ORFALEA / 66

PART TWO *Family Made: The Difference of Alternative or Delayed Fatherhood*

Weighed but Found Wanting: Ten Years of Being Measured and
Divided ROBERT MAYER / 73

Vespers, Matins, Lauds: The Life of a Liberal Arts College Professor
RALPH JAMES SAVARESE / 83

How White Was My Prairie MARK MONTGOMERY / 88

Meniscus ROBERT GRAY / 95

Once Was Lost JOHN BRYANT / 100

Shared Attention: Hearing Cameron's Voice MARK OSTEEN / 110

Accidental Academic, Deliberate Dad KEVIN G. BARNHURST / 116

Late Fatherhood among the Baptists ANDREW HAZUCHA / 128

Being a Dad, Studying Fathers: A Personal Reflection
WILLIAM MARSIGLIO / 135

Single Dad in Academia: Fatherhood and the Redemption of
Scholarship ERIC H. DU PLESSIS / 141

Superheroes STANFORD W. CARPENTER / 150

PART THREE *Forging New Fatherhoods: Ambitions Altered and Transformed*

Maybe It Is Just Math: Fatherhood and Disease in Academia
JASON THOMPSON / 159

Dreaming of Direction: Reconciling Fatherhood and Ambition
MIKE AUGSPURGER / 168

Making a Home for Family and Scholarship TING MAN TSAO / 176

Change Is Here, but We Need to Talk about It: Reflections on Black
Fatherhood in the Academy JEFFREY B. LEAK / 184

Vocabularies and Their Subversion: A Reminiscence
JOHN DOMINI / 188

Balancing Diapers and a Doctorate: The Adventures of a Single Dad
in Grad School CHARLES BANE / 196

It's a Chapter-Book, Huh: Teaching, Writing, and Early Fatherhood
ALEX VERNON / 201

Pitcher This: An Academic Dad's Award-Winning Attempt to Be in
Two Places at Once COLIN IRVINE / 207

Odd Quirks CHRIS GABBARD / 217

The Precarious Private Life of Professor Father Fiction Chef and Other
Possible Poignancies GARY H. MCCULLOUGH / 224

Notes on Contributors / 231

Thinking Stiffs: An Introduction

A Marxist literary critic at Disney World, a biologist swimming with sharks in the Amazon, a political-scientist-turned-administrator in a prop-filled death-and-dying classroom—each is a contributor to this volume. Working stiffs, or perhaps we should say thinking stiffs, they, along with their fellow contributors, map out the terrain of academic dads. What difference does contemplative fatherhood make? How might the setting of academia facilitate more vigorous involvement with one's children? What kinds of vigorous involvement might it facilitate? Are Papa, PhDs at the vanguard of alternative family-making? Do they have something to tell us about reformulated masculinity? About ambition? About egalitarian politics in the home? These are just some of the questions this collection addresses.

In an era when Promise Keepers on the Right and President Barack Obama on the Left exhort men to meet their parental responsibilities, when memoirs like *Big Russ* and self-help manuals like *Better Dads: How Fathers Can Guide Boys to Become Men of Character* capture the popular imagination, when shifting cultural attitudes about women and the hard facts of divorce and economic exigency (i.e., the need for two incomes and, thus, the less than perfect availability of Mom) compel men to be more active in raising their children, fatherhood is at once commanding attention and provoking debate. Academic fatherhood is no exception.

In some ways, it is just catching up to academic motherhood. In 2007 Rutgers University Press published a collection of essays entitled *Mama, PhD: Women Write about Motherhood and Academic Life*. Coedited by Caroline Grant and Elrena Evans, the collection gave voice to the enormous frustration of women in the academy as they try to balance, and in part reconcile, the two roles that the book's title wittily conjoins. Not every contributor was frustrated, of course, but many felt that the academic workplace was hostile to the parental obligations of women. A good number wrote of soldiering on, while some wrote of opting out of academia altogether.

This volume differs considerably, even provocatively, from its companion volume. Although male academics can be seen increasingly at the library during story time, at the doctor's midday with a sick child, and at the grocery store picking up food for dinner—"They're like reintroduced wildlife!" a well-known scholar once quipped—*Papa, PhD* doesn't register the same sort of guilt or anxiety as *Mama, PhD*. Indeed, many of the essays in this collection register no guilt or anxiety whatsoever. One even pointedly laments that the birth of the author's child might harm the author's vocation as a philosopher. Other essays recount, as previously mentioned, adventures at Disney World and in the Amazon, but also in Moscow and Lima. To be sure, there are pressing concerns here, including divorce, economic distress, professional disappointment, cultural prejudice, and disability, to name just a few. There is also lots of thoughtful reflection.

But why the lack of intense frustration? An appeal to the professional literature offers possible explanations. In her book *Redefining Fatherhood*, Nancy Dowd says simply that though "fathers are more engaged in the care of children than ever before . . . father care remains rooted in the assumption that the mother will be the primary caregiver."[1] Such an assumption enables not only perceptions of women as less valuable in the workplace, she argues, but also notions of masculinity that privilege the father's role as provider over that of nurturer. Hence, while the condition of a working woman's motherhood is subjected to intense scrutiny—by herself, her colleagues, her family, and the culture in general—a working man's fatherhood is, in contrast, almost entirely ignored.

James A. Levine and Todd L. Pittinsky, authors of *Working Fathers: New Strategies for Balancing Work and Family*, believe the very phrase "working mother" connotes an insoluble bind. They write, "For many people, *working mother* has come to symbolize conflict. When a woman works outside the home, our society assumes she must feel a constant tug-of-war between her 'job self' and her 'parent self.' But *working father* is a redundancy, isn't it? . . . The prevailing assumption is that men do not feel that tug-of-war between their 'job selves' and their 'parent selves.'"[2] Men, in other words, might feel just as torn as women, but they are encouraged to keep quiet. Levine and Pittinsky note, for instance, that some men will admit to being afraid of speaking about their "domestic responsibilities" because it might have a negative impact on their job security or future opportunities.

Watching "male colleagues [be] lionized for heroic efforts that defy family needs" only works to seal men's lips ever more tightly.[3]

In short, a man may acknowledge his family in the workplace as the beneficiary of his provision but not as a distraction from his work. Levine and Pittinsky cite the example of "colleagues, coworkers, and bosses [who] view a family photo on a man's desk as a sign of stability and commitment . . . rather than as a picture of real people whose real needs could tear him away from his desk."[4] "Hey, cute kid," a man's supervisor might say. "Can you stay late tonight?" Even in the comparatively flexible setting of academia, men are often reluctant to prioritize parental obligations. In a recent blog post in the *Chronicle of Higher Education* entitled "In Support of Academic Dads," Mary Ann Mason suggests that "while many academic fathers want to be more involved parents, they're reluctant to ask for accommodations, out of fear that they'll be stigmatized as 'less committed' by their departments."[5] Either you're up for attending a lecture on the Lost Boys of Sudan or you could soon be watching every last one of your own lost boy's pee-wee soccer games.

And so, while men may enjoy a certain freedom from culturally induced guilt, those who want to do their fair share of parenting (or who must do it) suffer from the pervasive stereotype that these authors critique. "I need to get my son at school" still sounds different coming from a man than from a woman; there's simply less cultural preparation for it. Add to this paradoxical quandary ideologies of ambition, which posit success at work as more important than success at home and which code the former as masculine and the latter as feminine, and it isn't any wonder that male academics often resist asking for accommodations and almost never opt out of the profession—unless the profession itself, as is the case in the current market, fails to cough up a sufficient number of decent jobs.

It may also be that men are more reluctant to talk about their feelings of conflict and anxiety when it comes to work and parenting than are women, especially in a forum like this collection. They have been taught not to. Indeed, a few potential contributors either declined to write a piece or withdrew what they had written, citing just such a reluctance. Untenured professors were especially reticent. When women in the academy voice their frustrations, they can appeal to a vigorous tradition of feminist critique, which holds that the personal is political. So-called personal criticism is a direct legacy of second-wave feminism. For men to be personal in this way seems, in the words of Stephen Kuusisto, like an "invitation to be nude in public."[6]

Just as important, many male academics believe that they are tremendously privileged, what with flexible schedules, job security after tenure, long vacations, and the opportunity to do meaningful labor. To complain would seem, well, unseemly. Of course, this relative privilege is, like everything else in American society, unevenly distributed, so one has to be careful with generalizations such as "academic dads." A man without tenure who teaches a 4/4 load for $38,000 a year is a lot less privileged than an endowed chair with tenure who teaches a 2/1 load for $150,000 a year.

Our point is not to bemoan the lack of guilt and anxiety in this collection or to rant about persistent inequality and a tougher burden. Clearly a reflection of the predicament of working mothers generally, *Mama, PhD* seemed to be rooted in the disappointments of academia specifically. What to the public at large often appears inscrutable and bizarre to young scholars appears as a kind of utopian space: a space of alternative thinking and possibility. The AAUP will tell you that this space is becoming less utopian by the second as the values of corporate America intrude ever more decisively, and perhaps it was never that utopian to begin with, especially for women. But the gap between the subversive rhetoric that the space typically produces, at least in the humanities and social sciences, and the labor practices that structure it appalled many an academic mother.

Papa, PhD is a different rhetorical arena with different rhetorical possibilities. One of its overarching themes is the project of joining work and fatherhood. Instead of "Bring Your Child to Work Day," imagine "Bring Your Child to Work Every Day"—or even "Bring Your Work to Your Child Every Day." Many of the contributors reflect less on how to do it all than on how to do both simultaneously, as when a father accepts a teaching appointment at a foreign university or brings his daughter with him to do fieldwork. Just as many reflect on the way that progressive concepts in one's discipline can shape how one parents. Writing well and thinking critically aren't just values in the liberal arts classroom; they're values in the liberal arts home. The fathers in this collection seek to expand their children's horizons, to give them the gifts of better topic sentences and a cosmopolitan sensibility. They seriously consider the implications of gender theory and queer theory—even Marxist theory. Why raise children so that they become stereotypical men and women? Does the world need more unthinking consumers? At the same time, what are the dangers in making childhood explicitly ideological—that is, an object of parental critique?

These aren't the fathers of *Two and a Half Men* or the now defunct *Everybody Loves Raymond*, shows in which befuddled breadwinners haven't a clue how to parent responsibly and well. Nor are they the fathers of that current critical darling *Mad Men*. The series depicts a bygone age in which men had little to no interaction with their children other than to pat them on the head when returning from a day's work. How not to interpret this show's popularity as at least in part nostalgia for a simpler time, a time replete with much more clearly differentiated gender roles? The notion of father as provider and disciplinarian receives a slick and intelligent sheen in *Mad Men*, but it no longer obtains in contemporary America. Mythic simplicity gives way to ineluctable complication.

The contributors to this collection do not look back; they look forward to new parental and professing synergies. They welcome ambiguity even as they're sometimes clobbered by it. The method of their madness is a reinvention of significant terms: fatherhood, family, ambition, success, and masculinity. A second overarching theme concerns precisely the reformulation of kinship ties—whether through adoption, foster care, disability, divorce, remarriage, or alternative parental arrangements. What difference does difference make? More than one might think. While parenting in many ways remains the same in these varied contexts, the diversity of experiences puts pressure on any basic notion of family. It asks us to reimagine what family, and thus fatherhood, might be like beyond the shibboleth of blood relations or lifelong heterosexual unions. How might we pursue the social organization of feeling and responsibility? How might we do this across racial, ethnic, class, gender, sexual, and body lines?

The simple fact of heterogeneity compels consideration of fathers whose children or partners have significant disabilities. What accommodations should they be entitled to? Or fathers whose children are of a different ethnicity or race? Why the assumption of, or insistence on, familial sameness? We increasingly live, after all, in what Adam Pertman calls "adoption nation." This is especially true of academia, where many put off having children and, as a result, encounter fertility problems but where some intentionally endeavor to make that thing we call family differently. How about the situation of single fathers? Or gay fathers? Or gay fathers of lesbian couples' children? While sometimes hard on kids—we still live in a normative society—these alterative arrangements are themselves instructive, perhaps even a kind of critical pedagogy. They remind us: The world can be otherwise. It can be better, fairer, more open to difference. Think of some of the contributors in this collection as not only living deliberately, in Thoreau's phrase, but doing kinship deliberately, which is not to say always with complete success. Thoreau, after all, regularly had difficulty at Walden Pond with far more mundane concerns such as dinner and laundry.

A third overarching theme involves the challenge, on the one hand, of amending ambition when the circumstances of one's life and employment demand it and, on the other, of actively constructing new fatherhoods in what is still a relatively privileged profession. Behind the projects of joining work and parenting and of reformulating kinship ties exists the daily challenge of juggling multiple obligations and constituencies. To be an academic father, at least an engaged one, is a bit like serving as a triage nurse in an emergency room. Which obligation and constituency should be addressed immediately? Which can wait? The contributors to this collection wish to be both responsive and responsible: responsive to their children, partners, students, colleagues, and their own intellectual work; responsible for their performance in each sphere. They seek to leverage the flexibility of academia to make dynamic engagement possible and to rewrite dominant cultural scripts—an especially daunting task for African American, Asian American, and Arab American fathers, as the collection shows.

But no two jobs in academia are the same, and the profession itself is brutally competitive. In the field of English, it takes the average applicant 3.92 years to secure a tenure-track job, and that job might come with a heavy teaching load and a low salary. How to leverage this academia to be responsive to competing constituencies and obligations? Among other things, scholarly ambition might have to be sacrificed. Even prized jobs with lower teaching loads and higher salaries can be uncooperative, foiling the fondest of fatherly hopes as young scholars strive to publish at all costs. Two-career families create their own challenges. A man who follows his wife or partner to her new job may have the script of more vigorous fatherhood thrust upon him whether he entirely wants it or not. Single fathers with joint custody enjoy a portion of the week in which they can be devoted academics, but otherwise they must scramble. And single fathers with sole custody—how do they get anything done? It's a terrific irony that professional disappointment and divorce can just as easily serve as fatherhood's facilitators as its impediments.

Whatever the varied and various particulars, new fatherhoods have begun to emerge, and the mood is generally upbeat. To borrow a geological metaphor from one of our contributors, the tectonic plates are shifting—the plates of both fatherhood and academia, the latter not entirely positively. Who knows what the globe will one day look like, with once discrete continents having merged; others, separated. The point is, the dishware of our social relations is shaking on our very shelves. Grouping the essays in this collection according to the three overarching themes, we have allowed this commotion to unsettle any easy conclusions. What we present are assertions and counterassertions and, finally, questions, lots of questions.

In the first section, entitled "Fathers in Theory, Fathers in Praxis: Merging Work and Parenting," many of the contributors make relevant theoretical connections between their work and the less abstract, more pragmatic, world of fathering. Ira Strauber, for example, writes about the intersection of parenting and professing in the use of words, that most basic of instructional tools. F. D. Reeve and David Campbell detail one of the rewards of academic parenting: the frequent travel and exposure to people and places that offer rich experiences for children as they mature. The enthusiasm with which Campbell integrates his daughter into his globetrotting life as a marine biologist and Jerald Walker integrates his son—in the form of pictures and stories—into the literature classroom differs profoundly, though, from Joseph Gelfer's uneasiness at incorporating queer theory into his "less than queer" life in the suburbs of Australia. While Walker notes how bringing one's children to work can glorify the male academic but undermine the female one, Gelfer struggles to respond to his child's desire to suckle at *his* breast. Similarly, Lennard Davis expresses qualms about marrying theory to real life when his son announces that he is transgendered, though Davis speaks boldly of "gaining a daughter." How easily some of these men have merged the realms of fatherhood and academia does not register at all in J. Aaron Simmons's essay, which candidly explores hesitations about impending parenthood and a fear that caring for his son will compromise both his teaching and scholarship.

Some of the essays in this section reflect the challenge of keeping the roles of parent and teacher/scholar distinct. Though deeply critical of American consumerism, Amitava Kumar does not want his daughter's innocence to be tainted by high theory and political activism, at least not while she's very young. This well-known Marxist not only agrees to go to Disney World but finds that he enjoys it. In a hilarious and self-effacing narrative, John Wells contests the hope for such separation by recounting the unavoidable and sometimes explosive fusion of his roles as administrator and father. By imagining that every young boy wants to grow up to be a provost, he reveals the occasional absurdity of academic perspectives in the home. David Haven Blake favors fathering through a shared love of writing, relating to his children by "seeking the right words" as often as engaging with them in more traditionally paternal activities. As scholars unaccustomed to failure, having had success in publication as well as teaching, these writers confront parenting situations that sometimes seem insurmountable. Gregory Orfalea, for example, writes of the struggle to let go of the son he has raised, even as that son appears to make questionable choices. Part of letting go involves *not* bringing to bear a traditionally masculinist approach to the problem.

The second section of the book, "Family Made: The Difference of Alternative or Delayed Fatherhood," foregrounds scholars who have chosen, or found themselves on, a parenting path that deviates from the norm. Perhaps what resonates most emphatically throughout this section is the astonishing range of forms that fatherhood can take, and certainly for these men, alternative fatherhood has sometimes caused aggravation. How to chase a progressive idea when it is trapped in an archaic institution? Andrew Hazucha reflects upon his apprehension at being the son of an "older" father, only to find himself in a similar position at the age of forty-eight and ready to reap the difficult rewards. William Marsiglio, a prominent expert on fatherhood, reveals the satisfaction he has gained in a new marriage promoting his young son's development. Bittersweet, however, are the gifts of a second chance as he recalls his less than vigorous involvement with his now adult first son.

Ralph James Savarese relates the toll that his career has taken on his wife, and he laments that the attention he would direct toward his autistic son is sometimes subsumed by the pressing needs of his students and scholarly deadlines. With the pressing needs of a significantly disabled child, a radical idea—adoption as a first resort—can reproduce a centuries-old sexist arrangement. Similarly, Mark Osteen writes of the difficulties coordinating his professional and personal lives and, ultimately, of the harrowing decision to put his autistic son in a residential school. Also redefining ideas about fatherhood and family, Mark Montgomery, white father to adopted African American and African sons, candidly discusses his relationship to race and racism. "How white is my prairie?" he asks when engaging with students at a midwestern college and with members of his community. Robert Gray depicts his experience as the gay father of a lesbian couple's child, and Kevin Barnhurst, gay father of three, recounts the guilt he felt when leaving his marriage because it also meant leaving his children. Both Gray and Barnhurst make clear the obstacles to modifying standard fatherhood. In some ways, the proverbial wheel must be reinvented.

In his essay about adopting the adopted Chinese daughter of a colleague who passed away suddenly, John Bryant reveals just how flexible are the conventional boundaries that have long constituted "family." At the same time, he calculates the point of emotional elasticity for a middle-aged man with grown daughters who begins an unanticipated second round of fatherhood. We find Bryant searching unsuccessfully in the rain for his new daughter's dog: symbol of everything she has lost and an unwanted omen. Robert Mayer recounts his experiences with his diverse family of three sons—two adopted and one biological—finding that the hopes and disappointments of parenting resonate with those of teaching. What to do when your children are disengaged—when they don't like, and seem psychologically unable, to study? Eric du Plessis argues from the standpoint of a single father of two that the customs of academia—impromptu meetings, increasing publication requirements alongside ever-increasing course loads, for example—should be reevaluated because the vulnerability of children and the immediacy of their needs demand it. Du Plessis speaks of the "redemption of scholarship," clinging admirably to an intellectual commitment while somehow fulfilling his fatherly duties. Stanford Carpenter, too, relates his experience as a single father, but as an African American man in a contentious custody battle, he must wrestle with cultural stereotypes that could well determine the extent of his future relationship with his daughter.

In our final section, "Forging New Fatherhoods: Ambitions Altered and Transformed," the contributors challenge traditional norms by actively questioning the status quo. They labor to create new forms of fatherhood by exploiting the flexibility of academia and at the same time responding to forces beyond their control. Ting Man Tsao, for instance, critiques not only traditional gender roles in parenting but also deeply embedded cultural notions about work and childcare. Tsao was the first stay-at-home dad that his traditionally minded Chinese father had ever known, which was at once a progressive achievement and a financial necessity. Like Tsao, Jeffrey Leak critiques prevailing models of fatherhood but goes one step further to understand how African American fathers might resist notions of white American manhood. These models, he argues, inhibit men from diverting from the typical path of ambition. Colin Irvine notes, with some irony, the difference between fully experiencing fatherhood and simply writing about it, as he does in this collection. Even after the security that tenure should bring and winning a Father of the Year award, he finds himself falling short of maximum engagement.

This failure might seem a luxury to those for whom the profession has been, at least in part, a disappointment or for whom life circumstances dictate more strenuous involvement at home. Mike Augspurger admits how altering his ambition for the sake of his wife's career and growing family has not been accomplished without significant discomfort on his part, and Chris Gabbard reports that in order to meet the needs of a son with a significant physical and cognitive disability, he redefined his ambition; he literally had no choice. Gabbard cannot travel to conferences because only he can physically lift his son, placing him in, or taking him out of, his wheelchair. His wife's neck injury and the cost of assistance compel this arrangement. Certainly John Domini's sense of ambition has been recast in his failed quest for a tenure-track job; the market doesn't always—or even regularly—bow to the dreams of its degree-holders. As a divorced and distant father, he struggles to help a troubled daughter whom he sees only intermittently.

Charles Bane's story of being a graduate student and father of three with no promise of a tenure-track position and Jason Thompson's story of believing academia to be a ticket out of poverty but of still not reaching the middle class due to mounting medical bills—his wife has MS—extend the altered ambition theme. Each man might be frustrated by his occupational situation, but each dramatically rewrites caregiving narratives. In contrast, Gary McCullough and Alex Vernon depict the academy as allowing the time and flexibility to become more involved fathers, fathers who will watch their children grow, who will cook for them, who will know their favorite games.

While exhibiting obvious differences, these essays coalesce in their dedication to revising tired definitions of "father" and "scholar." What the contributors have accomplished, though, still seems unclear, as the titles of their works suggest. The revisions are in progress—aware of a precarious balance, charting new directions, carving out new interactive spaces, and embarking on grand (and sometimes perilous) adventures. Meanwhile, the plates continue to shift; the institutions on top of them shake. New fault lines appear.

We are pleased by the range of experience represented in this collection. The contributors are as diverse as the kinds of fatherhood they describe and espouse. They hail from the disciplines of art history, biology, communications, economics, English, French, philosophy, political science, Russian, and sociology. They are white, black, South Asian, Asian, and Arabic. They are gay and straight, married and divorced. They are tenured and untenured, at research-one universities and at community colleges. Some write from the beginning of their careers and some from the end.

We are also pleased by the writing, which, though treating academic issues, eschews an academic form in favor of the personal essay, or what now goes by the name of creative nonfiction. The essays are, in a word, readable—pleasurably so. A good number of the contributors are nonfiction writers in addition to traditional scholars; hence what they present has a professional finish. The collection, while thoughtful, while thinking, is anything but stiff. For several of the contributors, the act of writing presented the first opportunity to reflect on what it means to be a father in the academy today—or what it meant ten, twenty, or thirty years ago—and they rise to the occasion with admirable verve.

We hope that we have captured something of value here: scholars meditating on fatherhood and its connection to their work. We have learned a great deal while conceiving of this project, while editing these essays, and while corresponding with these men. We have been inspired to take our children to the Amazon (though we'll probably not swim with the sharks); we have sampled Gary McCullough's Tomato Basil Risotto with Scallops, and it is both easy to prepare and stupefyingly good; and we have embraced Disney World for the fleeting happiness it can bring to young children, even as we wait for their appreciation of all things Jane Austen and Fredric Jameson. Perhaps most important, we have fostered a discussion about our work and our families that is now more complete.

Notes

1. Nancy E. Dowd, *Redefining Fatherhood* (New York: New York University Press, 2000), 86.

2. James A. Levine and Todd L. Pittinsky, *Working Fathers: New Strategies for Balancing Work and Family* (San Diego: Harcourt Brace & Company, 1997), 17.

3. Ibid., 30.

4. Ibid., 29.

5. "In Support of Academic Dads," 27 February 2009 <http://chronicle.com/blog Post/In-Support-of-Academic-Dads/883/>. The writer of this blog posting on the *Chronicle*'s Web site cites Mary Ann Mason.

6. Stephen Kuusisto, *Planet of the Blind* (New York: Dell Publishing, 1998), 100.

PART ONE

Fathers in Theory, Fathers in Praxis

MERGING WORK AND PARENTING

Disney Dad

AMITAVA KUMAR

In a recent blog post on "Mama PhD," Libby Gruner tells us of her little daughter rewriting the story of Beauty and the Beast; in the revised version, Belle refuses to marry her ugly beau, making her intentions clear by saying, "You're not my boss. I'm going to put you in the zoo." Hurrah.

Let's suppose you've labored long in the salt mines of academia, carrying out in your arms small signs of criticism in the classroom, treasures exchanged for torn fingernails and what sometimes seems to be quickly liquefying flesh. In that situation, statements like those made by the Gruner child can bring great cheer.

You can tell yourself that your labors will be less in vain in the future. The consumers of mass culture have stepped out of the medieval darkness of mindlessness. ("Kids are just smarter and more political these days.") You can even delude yourself that your pedagogy has unexpectedly found fertile ground.

There's such pleasure in proclaiming victory. No more slavery in the mines! The beloved utopia is here! The only salt on your hands from now on will be from the drying water as you make a pleasant trudge back to your towel on the beach!

But I have no right to such fine expectations. And not only because I struggle with sentimental notions and would rather have my daughter show greater compassion to the Beast, particularly to his painful shyness about his ugliness. The plain truth is that my six-year-old daughter, Ila, has shown no critical distance to Disney narratives. Her world is populated with princesses. One of her most valued possessions is a photograph taken at a restaurant in Disney World: A young blonde in a yellow gown, a tiara poised on her coiffed head, has put her white-gloved hands around Ila's shoulder. For my child, meeting Belle, if you'll pardon my use of the cliché endlessly touted by Disney, is a dream come true.

I complain about this situation all the time. I am embarrassed about my child's embrace of reactionary cultural practices, and I sometimes ask myself why I accommodate at home what in the classroom I would clearly oppose. All of this can be put in the form of a question: Am I a better teacher than I am a parent?

Nearly two years ago, Ila and I went to Disney World. My wife, who is an economist, refused to come with us. She said something like "It is a corrupt consumerist trap; you cannot possibly take Ila there."

But I did and enjoyed the trip very much. I had taken two or three books to read; I never got the chance to open any of them. From morning to night, nervous about a thousand things, I took my child in a rented stroller from one overpriced ride to another. There was tea with Sleeping Beauty. There were endless encounters with people in cute, but no doubt hellishly hot, stuffed-animal costumes. We met patient princesses who held their smiles while parents of the kids standing next to them figured out how to use a simple digital camera. In the evenings, the fireworks were spectacular. And in the mornings, a parade would emerge from nowhere, and the songs that were being sung by the marching bands were recognized and taken up immediately by the visiting throngs. I couldn't join in; to me all of it was new. But I keenly felt the happiness of the people around me. It seemed that they were being returned to their childhood. And they had paid too much to complain too much.

Ila was cheerful throughout, and if her face ever lost its smile it was only when we went into a souvenir store and she couldn't decide what she should buy. I had told her beforehand that I wouldn't get her an expensive gift. But what is an *expensive* gift? I saw her looking at the princess costumes for a long time, and then I noticed that she seemed to be swallowing something. Her gaze turned to other objects. She walked to the cart with trinkets. Heaps of little bracelets with Mickey or Cinderella or Winnie the Pooh on them. Ila looked up at me tentatively. Were *they* affordable? What was one to do in this giant, glittering island of cute, tawdry, reduce-Dad-to-poverty commodities? It shamed me that I had put my child in that difficult position. I might have hated Disney a little then, but I certainly hated myself a lot more.

A colleague of mine, a historian of modern Europe, recently took her daughter to Disney World. When she came back, she said to me, "How come you didn't go crazy? Everything there is set up for merchandise. The whole thing is cloaked in consumerism." But had her daughter enjoyed the visit? "Yes," she replied, "but it also confused her. She didn't know what she wanted."

I was reminded of what I had experienced with Ila, and I wondered why it is that as academics we expect our pleasures to be pure. I bring this up because I had mixed motivations for visiting Disney World. In the pages of the *New York Times*, Thomas Friedman had written that post–September 11 America had become hostile to visitors and our government was exporting fear, not hope; more specifically, Friedman had complained, "If Disney World can remain an open, welcoming place, with increased but invisible security, why can't America?" Now, ordinarily I wouldn't trust Friedman on anything, but I was writing a book on the war on terror, and his remark had sparked my curiosity. I suddenly felt that I could excuse my extravagance. Once there, I noticed that bags were searched before entry, but there wasn't much more research that I could do. It wasn't as if while rushing from the Caribbean Beach Resort to the Magic Kingdom, I could touch Sleeping Beauty's elbow and ask, "Say, where are the hidden cameras?" Not only that. Even if I had found the answer to that question, perhaps all I'd have wanted to find out next was whether the cameras would reveal where the lines for the rides were shorter.

A part of me believes that my child, at four or six or ten, is a child and should be treated as one. When she's older, I hope she'll read Virginia Woolf and, if she's interested, Eve Kosofsky Sedgwick. But I'm quite happy that she isn't a young critic right now. And that she doesn't mimic the thoughts and actions of her parents. I don't want to sound smug when I say this, but I've never sent her to school in a -T-shirt that says "Stop Deportation Now" or "U.S. Out of My Body." But some of her friends in preschool come to class clad in those slogans, and I wonder whether the children have any idea about those words. Would it really make any difference to them if they wore to school a shirt that said "Free Pizza"? Perhaps there'd be more conversation with others. "Hey, Ernie, are you giving away free pizza?" is perhaps easier to say than "Hello, Lola. Have there been deportations taking place around here?"

I'm being flippant. The parents who dress their children in the right sentiments ("Clean Water, Clean Air," or maybe even "Clean Water, Clean Air—for Everyone on this Planet") are, I'm sure, ready to engage in a conversation with their kids about these issues. *They* are being good teachers, and thereby also good parents.

If I were to look back on my nearly two decades of teaching, I think I might have been of greatest use to my students when I was being more like an indulgent parent. When I was starting out in academia, I once took my students to a local high school to teach poetry to the younger kids there.

That one course taught me a crucial early lesson. The best classes are those where the students and the teacher get the chance to do something adventurous and fun.

I haven't always done that; I have often sought critical rigor and confused teaching with rectitude. As a parent, I recognize how futile such an attitude can be, especially when dealing with a young child. Patience and playfulness are two crucial attributes in a parent as well as an instructor in a classroom; and I admire my child's teachers for adhering to those principles much better than my colleagues. I should perhaps answer here the question I raised earlier: The point isn't whether I am a better teacher than I am a parent—the real issue is whether, both at home and in the classroom, I allow the parent to keep the teacher in check and vice versa.

Many years ago, Charles Bukowski wrote in a letter, "Study yr keeds. Kids. There are a lot of poems there. But don't write about yr kids. Write about the human, what's left of him, where he's going, what he dropped on the floor." So here's a story not about Ila rewriting a Disney narrative, but about your humble author drawing a line through three words on the very first page of our copy of *Cinderella*. The first sentence of the story introduces the reader to a "wealthy widower" and his daughter, Cinderella. We are told of his remarriage to a woman with two young daughters who were about Cinderella's age. And then the line: "Sadly, the gentleman died soon after, and Cinderella discovered that her stepmother was a cold, cruel woman." The book is open in front of me: Over "died soon after" I have written "went away." I'm not ready to face a future where my child is without me.

Ila was two when she got the book as a Christmas gift from her teachers; I substituted those three words the very first time I read the story to her. But I wrote the words down so that my wife would do the same. Kids are good at remembering the stories and can easily spot changes. ("Uh-oh, Dad, you forgot something . . .") But I needn't have worried; Ila had no idea about the meaning of the phrase that I had changed. I discovered this accidentally, a year or more later, when she said to me that Cinderella's mother had "dived." Dived? "Yes, it means that you are not well, and you go away to never come back." This is the human that Bukowski wants: Mine is a body no longer young, conscious of its age in the company of my daughter's sweet young life, wanting to offer something valuable to children, mine and others', not ready yet to take the dive. Charlie, keed, keep me afloat longer.

Gaining a Daughter

A Father's Transgendered Tale

LENNARD J. DAVIS

I look around and find myself, strangely enough, in the women's lingerie section of the Kmart in an upstate New York town. I am with my nineteen-year-old son, who is comparison shopping for a pair of black tights. Some farm ladies are regarding us with dubious glances. My son asks if I think medium is too large for him. He stands at about five feet eleven inches. I really have no idea what will fit him. Trying to be helpful, I suggest that he might want to wear the fishnet stockings, which seem to me a bit more goth, but he sticks with the regular ones. Then we move on to the cosmetics section for lipstick and hair dye. As I help him pick out a L'Oréal shade called Parisian Black, I wonder to myself how I got here.

How indeed? A few days earlier, my son had arrived back from his first year at college. The following morning, he sat me down at the kitchen table and announced that he had a big thing to tell his mother and father. My wife was on the telephone, and as we waited for her to finish talking, my son whispered, "I'm getting married." Then he added, "No, just kidding." He was jumpy with nervous intensity. When my wife sat down, he spoke: "I've been thinking about this for a long time, and I wanted to tell you— I'm transgendered!" He looked pleased with himself and somewhat triumphant. My wife and I looked at each other, confused and horrified.

He must have sensed that we were nonplussed. So, being of an academic bent, as we are, he began pulling out of his backpack books with titles like *My Gender Workbook* and *Gender Outlaw*, reading us long passages like the following, from Leslie Feinberg's *Transgender Warriors*:

> Both women's and trans liberation have presented me with two important tasks. One is to join the fight to strip away the discriminatory and oppressive

This essay originally appeared in the *Chronicle of Higher Education*, March 24, 2000.

values attached to masculinity and femininity. The other is to defend gender freedom—the right of each individual to express their gender in any way they choose, whether feminine, androgynous, masculine, or any point on the spectrum between. And that includes the right to gender ambiguity and gender contradiction.

It's equally important that each person have the right to define, determine, or change their sex in any way they choose whether female, male, or any point on the spectrum between. And that includes the right to physical ambiguity and contradiction.

As he talked, I tried to listen but could not escape the sensation that I was in someone else's movie. I thought about this young person and wondered if there was something I was missing. He had always seemed to be a very masculine guy—interested in girls—who never once could have been mistaken for a female. He wasn't effeminate in the least, and there seemed to be no apparent prehistory to this moment. Later, though, I recalled the many comic strips and zines he had written featuring female main characters. They seemed, in retrospect, to have been his alter egos.

My wife and I both consider ourselves progressive academics. We have been willing to accept virtually any behavior from our children—from their experimentation with marijuana to having their sexual partners sleep over at our house. We are a poster family for permissiveness and have cruised fairly comfortably from grunge through swing to goth. I've seen my kids' hair go from brown to blue to green, as mine has gone to gray. I followed my son as he crossed a police line and grabbed a bullhorn at City Hall to protest budget cuts in education; worried as he came back late from punk-rock clubs; trembled a bit as he explained that he might be arrested for defacing (or reconstructing, as he would say) corporate billboards. We are feminists against homophobia. And I teach courses with titles like "Women, Nation, Empire" and "The Different Body." Could anyone be more of a political ally than I?

Had he announced, "I'm gay," my wife and I would have been relatively prepared to say, "Great! Who's the lucky guy?" But transgendered? I didn't have much of an idea then what the word meant. We asked some predictable questions. "Are you gay?" My son laughed, "No, I love women. I'm completely heterosexual." "So, do you want a sex-change operation?" "No, I like my body the way it is." "So, what does this mean?" "It means I'm a girl. I want to wear dresses, makeup, and challenge the whole patriarchal, bourgeois idea of gender."

My mind raced. We were having Stanley Fish and Jane Tompkins over for dinner that night. I imagined my son swirling down the stairs, arriving at dinner like Loretta Young in flowing chiffon. How exactly would I explain such a phenomenon to my guests over hors d'oeuvres? As it turned out, our son dressed neutrally and got into an argument with Stanley over Bosnia, not biology.

Over the next few days, my son continued to explain his metamorphosis to us: "Michel Foucault says that gender is socially constructed. So does Judith Butler." Foucault! Butler! Those were the names of scholars I teach, now being hurled like grenades at my feet. Those theoreticians believe, as I do, that such seemingly fixed and essential things as gender or disability are really pliable and plastic. It had seemed fine to accept that gender was a social construction, but now here was my child before me, attempting to carry out in principle what I had been teaching only theoretically in my courses. I suddenly felt rage toward those ivory-towered theoreticians who glibly spout gender theories. Now I was going to have to pay in humiliation and pain, in seeing my son in a dress. Thanks, Judy!

The next few days were pretty intense for my wife and me. As we sat up late discussing this alteration in our family life, we quickly passed through the phases associated with getting a fatal illness. First was denial, followed by the willing accomplices of rage and despair. Acceptance kept its reserved distance; the sticking point was the issue of wearing dresses. I thought I could logically argue my son out of that penchant. "If women are oppressed and femininity is a construct, why should you essentially reinforce or parody the feminine? Isn't that giving in to patriarchy? Reinforcing the gender binary?" As a litigious academic, I could in a pinch come up with a cogent argument. Knowing my rhetorical strategies only too well, my son replied that to break down the binary, we had to be able to dress as we wished. In our culture, women could wear men's clothing without any opprobrium, but men could only wear women's clothing at their own peril. If a woman wears a tuxedo she's an icon, as Marlene Dietrich knew, but if a man wears a dress he's comic. Just ask Tony Curtis or Jack Lemmon.

He was right, no doubt, but no matter how rational our discussion was, the dress became an eternal stumbling block. As some friends of ours said later, our son had picked the one thing that we, as progressives, couldn't accept. I continued trying to argue, "How would you feel if you saw me wearing a dress and makeup?" He replied, "I'd be so relieved." I countered, "What would your roommate think?" I was figuring that his Japanese friend, who was obsessed with technology, would be horrified. "Oh, he's

saving up his money for a sex-change operation." My last round of arma-
ments was quickly being depleted. One last salvo: "Well, you say you like
women. What will they think of you wearing a dress?" He smiled like a
cat with a canary in his maw and confided, "It's the greatest way to meet
women," and winked knowingly. What could I say?

By now, I was beginning to understand a bit about this transgender
issue, although I'm far from an expert. My son says that a transgendered
person is anyone who breaks the rules of the gender binary. By his definition, people who are gay, lesbian, or bisexual are not necessarily transgendered, since they define themselves by their sexual preference, rather than
their gender crossing. They would be transgendered only if they attempted
to break from the gender they were assigned at birth, by redefining their
identity through an act of philosophical or political awakening, hormonal
or surgical intervention, or choice of clothing.

My son says that it's all about a person's right to choose. He defines
himself as a "transgirl." Some women may choose to define themselves as
men. And other folks may head for the shifting middle ground of gender
"variants," who like to keep things ambiguous. Inhabiting the transgender territory are drag queens and drag kings, "transgirls," "transboys," and
those who vote for their identity with anything from estrogen to haircuts.
A heterosexual male could be considered transgendered if he were a cross-
dresser, although a cross-dresser is not necessarily transgendered if he only
likes to wear women's clothing but doesn't consider himself female or a
gender variant.

The possibilities are mind- (and body-) boggling. There are relatively simple variations along the transgender continuum, including male-to-female
"post-op" transsexuals, such as Deirdre N. McCloskey, the noted economist,
or female-to-male transsexuals such as Feinberg. Then there are those who
adopt hormonally and surgically the secondary sexual characteristics of the
other gender while keeping the genitalia with which they were born. There
also are bearded women, like the well-known circus performer and gender
activist Jennifer Miller. Intersexuals—formerly known as hermaphrodites—
whose parents "corrected" their gender, walk side by side in this movement with those who managed to retain their congenital organs. Then, on
the genetic level, there are women who, according to their chromosomes,
should be male (they have female genitalia, but they can't reproduce). The
old gender binary begins to look pretty Procrustean when confronted with
this welter of permutations.

My son is part of what might be called a "fourth wave" in gender activism. The first wave was clearly the feminist movement, followed by the next tsunami, as gays, lesbians, and bisexuals established their identities as individuals and communities. Then came a surge of queer activism, which challenged even gay notions of what was normal. But to my son and his peers—who are mostly under thirty—those three sea changes now seem merely to be part of a conservative undertow. This generation believes that earlier activists, while challenging various kinds of gender abuses, still clung to the notion of the criticality of gender per se. First-wave feminists, for example, never doubted that being a woman was essential to their mission. Likewise, although gay men, lesbians, and bisexuals challenged the notion of mandated or "normal" sexual preference, they saw their identity as defined by a ratio of one's gender to one's sexual choice. That is, a lesbian could only be defined as a woman who chose another woman as a sexual partner. Even some conservative post-operative transsexuals cling to the gender binary, saying, "I was born the wrong gender, and now I've become the right one." Members of the fourth wave, who like to call themselves "trannies" (perhaps in solidarity with sixties "hippies"), see challenging the fixity of gender as their most important goal. My son reported to me that gender is so complex that there are a hundred genders, and that we can morph through twenty of them in a single morning. He indicts the quotidian norms that force people to subscribe to one gender, to be legally identified as having one, and to be forbidden to use certain social spaces by that specific aspect of identity. Indeed, the International Bill of Gender Rights, drafted and adopted in 1993, lists as fundamental the prerogative to define one's gender identity, control and change one's own body, and have access to "gendered space."

When my wife and I asked my son why he thinks he is transgendered, his snappy retort was "I don't know which bathroom to use." When he is wearing a dress, should he use the men's room or the women's room?

The transgendered concept allows for some interesting family groupings. A father in a couple might undergo sexual reassignment surgery and thereby become a lesbian, if he remains with his wife. Or a cross-gendered bisexual can pair off with an intersexual lesbian. A cross-dressing male can live with a post-op male-to-female and appear to fit nicely into the prototype of the typical American family. The possibilities are limitless. They make Ozzie and Harriet look like something from the late Devonian period, and Ellen DeGeneres's coming out seem as staid as that of a debutante.

I understood all this intellectually, but I was taking a fair amount of time to process it emotionally. My wife initially insisted on an N.I.M.H.—Not In My House—policy in regard to cross-dressing. That stance resulted partly from embarrassment and shame about how friends and family might perceive our son if they knew the truth.

Somewhat conveniently, the grandparents had already transmogrified to that genderless beyond, so at least we wouldn't have to explain the situation to them. Our sixteen-year-old daughter thought the whole thing was kind of cool and couldn't understand why we were so upset. "Some boys in my school come to class in skirts or wearing lipstick, and we think they're sexy." My brother, a financial analyst living in the suburbs, was blasé. His college-age son was open-minded, having lived his four university years in a frat house, where he had no doubt seen worse.

We were uncertain about what to say to our friends. The artistic types were intrigued and even offered some fetching outfits, if needed. One male friend was judgmental and said our son was manipulating us. But that same friend sheepishly admitted that when his wife bought new high-heeled shoes, he had to be the first to wear them at home. Another friend, who is part of a gay couple, confessed that his dream was to be married in a wedding gown, something his more conventional partner just would not hear of. In fact, a lot of folks stepped up to our confessional with Oprah-like stories of their own journeys into the backrooms of sexuality, gender, and fashion.

In the midst of all this turmoil, or because of it, my son decided to go to an indie-rock concert in Washington state. He would take a Greyhound bus and camp out. He asked me to help him get organized, which is how I ended up in the Kmart as his shopping consultant. He packed a few dresses into his backpack, along with his other clothing, and left. All of us felt relieved.

We began to get phone calls from bus stations scattered across the country. At first our son was friendly, but one late-night call from Fargo turned angry quickly. "I've been thinking, and I'm really upset that you won't accept me for who I am." My groggy response was that I was doing the best I could. "That's not good enough. I can't believe that you, of all people, who teach about the rights of people with disabilities, people of color, working-class people, can't accept this. These are my people! They are being discriminated against, cast out, and you can't accept it?"

For the first time, I felt that he was completely right. I had no counter-argument. Whether I liked it or not, a disenfranchised and despised group was in need of support; what made it difficult to accept was the fact that my son was in that group. I had to confront my own prejudices and realize that I was a bigot. I, like many of my peers, thought that a man in a dress was either humorous or pathetic, as so many episodes of *Monty Python* or *Benny Hill* have suggested. It was true that I didn't know whether to laugh or cry about my son.

My son asked that I read some of the books he had brought home, and I agreed. I also ordered some books through Amazon.com. (Then, when I logged on, I got helpful messages like "If you liked *Transvestism: A Handbook*, you'll like *Bound and Gagged*.") I not only read through the material, but, since I would be teaching a course in the fall called "The Different Body," I decided then to put some of the books in my syllabus. (It is interesting to me that my reaction, as an academic, was to teach about what was mystifying and edifying me.)

I've just about gotten used to seeing my child in women's clothing. At first I experience a confusing, cognitively dissonant moment, but then I remember that he is the child I've known for years, with the same brio for life he's always had, the same excitement over his ideas, commitment to fairness and justice, and love for us. The only difference is that he's in a skirt. I remember my mother's agony over my long hair in the 1960s— how she asked me not to come to her place of business because she was embarrassed, and how much that hurt me. I knew as a parent, and as an activist, that I could not legitimately reproduce that rejection.

Our life has gone on. My son announced that he wanted to bring his girlfriend, a "bidyke" as he described her, home for the holiday season. I learned that the term "dyke" has now been freed up from its dependence on sexual preference and is an operative word to describe a strong woman. When she arrived, she seemed a bit androgynous, but not remotely butch. And she wore a prom dress out one night. We all liked her, and it was a memorable Christmas.

Meanwhile, my graduate course on "The Different Body" went very well. The body in question was a little more different than it had been in the previous year's version. But the students were barely fazed by the transgendered component of the course. They were not wowed, even when I told them about my son or showed them pictures that I thought were pretty shocking—like a photograph of Tala Candra Brandeis by Loren Cameron titled "Biology Is Not Destiny," depicting a nude person with long, flowing hair, breasts, tattoos, and a penis. It seemed to be all in a day's work for this generation of cultural-studies adepts, brought up as they had been with

RuPaul and *The Adventures of Priscilla, Queen of the Desert*. I shared with the class my son's zine entitled *Boy Is Girl* and gave them his e-mail address so they could converse with him about these subjects. My son was pleased with the correspondence, and the students were, too.

The story is not over. In the months since his announcement, my son's attitudes toward some issues have shifted. He has come into conflict with more conservative elements in the trannie community who do not agree with his radical politics. He has had to deal with the fact that some people within that community do not regard him as truly transgendered, because he hasn't taken hormones or had an operation. He is evolving a position that I have come to respect and from which I have learned a great deal. In many ways, he occupies a similar position to the one I do in disability studies. I am not a person with disabilities, and I have to negotiate that liminal status on a regular basis. In addition, both he and I are against the narrowness of certain kinds of identity politics and see our goal as opening up the question of identity through a notion of the mutability of the body. So we talk a lot about the ways in which our interests intersect. I've helped him with his zines, and he's helped me with my course.

As an academic, my job is to learn from the world. And if that world comes into my house in women's clothing, spouting Eve Kosofsky Sedg-wick, then I have to learn from that. As a father, my pleasure is to love and accept my children. When those two roles come together, in a kind of serendipitous confluence, one must be quick to recognize the opportunity that presents itself. My child and I have grown closer through what might have been a terrible conflict, one that in some families might have been the end of the line. What made a better scenario possible was that same intel-lectual desire to learn, to know, and to encourage that has been behind all my teaching and scholarship.

The other day, my son announced that he wanted my wife and me to refer to him as our "daughter." He asked that we not use masculine pro-nouns or nouns to describe him. I told him that I probably could not find it in myself to call him my "daughter," that my sense of the English lan-guage was that it was not sufficiently flexible, nor was I, to accomplish that gender purification of my linguistic practice. This was finally a moment, I felt, when the old binary dog couldn't learn new transgendered tricks. We got into an argument, and he hurled Judith Butler at me again. She was getting to be my nemesis.

My son knew that I was writing this article, and he approved. But when I told him that it would be impossible for me to write this piece without using masculine pronouns, he was upset. He suggested that I use "s/he" or "ze," and I responded that I was sure the *Chronicle* style sheet was pretty limited in that regard. After some discussion, he said, "OK, but just do it at the end of the essay." So I told her I would. After all, I figured, I wasn't losing a son, I was gaining a daughter.

Gifts from the Sea

DAVID G. CAMPBELL

When Tatiana was four years old her duty was to sing to the bears. She understood that singing was serious work and that she was protecting her family. Skipping down the trail, holding hands with her mom and dad, who swung her across the wet patches and mud puddles, she threaded this melody through the forest:

L'amour est un oiseau rebelle
Que nul ne peut apprivoiser,
Et c'est bien en vain qu'on l'appelle . . .

We were hiking along the right bank of the Resurrection River, just north of Seward, Alaska, on a windswept Indian summer afternoon in late August. The last birches were turning, scattering their big yellow leaf-petals to the wind, and the coho salmon were running. When the coho salmon run in the Resurrection River, all of the grace of the sky seems to be captured in the water: the darting cloud-shadows of the fish surging upstream, the quicksilver flash when one intercepts a fleck of sunlight. Of course the grizzly bears knew about the salmon, too, and came to the river to eat those fish. It was a convergence as old as the Land and the River themselves. We were the newcomers. That's why Tatiana sang to the bears: so that they could hear us first and, being sensible beings, avoid us.

L'amour est enfant de Bohème,
Il n'a jamais jamais connu de loi,
Si tu ne m'aimes pas je t'aime,
Si je t'aime prends garde à toi. . . .

The bears didn't speak French, but neither did Tatiana—although she loved the story of Carmen and would sit on my lap for hours while we listened to the opera and I told her what was going on. She simply la la la'ed the aria, plugging in a word or two when she remembered it. The bears must have gotten the message. We didn't encounter one that day, although we saw their scats and the fresh remains of gutted fish they had ripped open. We got out of that forest intact. The kid knew that she had done a good job.

Tatiana had always been a fearless little girl, determined never to be left behind. This was no easy task, since, as the daughter of two botanical explorers, she spent parts of her childhood in the Amazon forest, the Maya Mountains, and the mangrove forests of the Mekong Delta, not to mention wild lands on four other continents. She was a sensible girl, too. The first time we walked together down a rain-forest trail in Amazonia, she kept a step or two behind me . . . until I told her that the sleeping vipers usually strike the second person, after the first has awakened them. Then she took the lead.

For years the Brazilian Amazon was our summer home. We lived with a group of students and alums aboard a wooden boat of local construction, traveling for thousands of miles on the Rios Solimões, Amazonas, Negro, Branco, and Xeruiní. We adopted the crepuscular behavior of the locals, arising before dawn and setting off in canoes to explore the narrow ox-bows, furos, and igarapés—channels and loops—where the mother ship couldn't go. Ours weren't the gracile canoes of North America but were rather stable broad-bellied two-ton workboats made out of iron-hard maçaranduba wood. Tatiana loved to stand with me on the prow; I wrapped the painter around my right arm and held my daughter with my left. When the sun had risen bright and burning, we'd return to the mother ship, have breakfast, and rest, arising again at dusk and working long into the night. A lot of the work was conducting censuses of animals. This is best done after dark, using a spotlight to search for the reflecting tapeta of the night-creatures: caimans, potoos, iguanas, boa constructors, pit vipers, innumerable spiders (some lofting past us on long strands of silk), and shrimps fidgeting with the algae in the water beneath us. Uncountable eyes . . . all watching us. Tatiana, at my side, loved to hold the light, and when she spotted something new or strange, she'd take a deep breath and grip my arm a little tighter. Now and then a night-flying armadillo wasp flew down the column of light emitted by our torch and stung her. The kid wrinkled her brow and just took it.

We spotted the jaguar on a moonless night, a few minutes after midnight. All evening we had been silently paddling our canoe along the forested shoreline where the Rio Branco weds the Rio Negro, forming a string of white swirls on black water that attracts denizens of both worlds. We had been fishing, not with hook and line but with our spotlights. Like the wasps, the surface-feeding aruanãs were irresistibly attracted to our lights, devoted to them, and launched themselves through the air, slapping us and flailing onto the floorboards. We turned the little ones loose but kept a few big ones, over a meter long, for breakfast. The jaguar had probably come to the shore to catch aruanãs, too. It appeared out of the void. First we saw only the reflection of the cat's eyes, retinas oddly jiggling like Jell-O. Then the tracings of a face . . . a Cheshire cat in reverse time. When it spotted us the jaguar froze . . . staring, sniffing the air, tasting it too, lifting its upper lip in the characteristic cat-grimace (that people often misinterpret as aggression) and rubbing its tongue across its palate, for a hint of who we were. It must have been no more than fifteen or twenty feet ahead of us— and of course, Tatiana and I were closest, standing on the prow. For a few long moments cat and father and child carefully observed each other, each transfixed. Then, like childhood's hour, the moment passed. The jaguar vanished.

The gifts of being an academic's daughter—worse, an explorer's daughter—are unorthodox and mixed. What does a kid say when she comes home to small-town Iowa after spending the summer counting caimans and spotting jaguars in Amazonia, or in grizzly bear country in Alaska?

She fibs.

This duplicity started because of public humiliation. Tatiana had spent the first semester of first grade sailing around the world aboard a floating university known as the Semester at Sea, on which her mother and I were teaching. She was the second-youngest person on that gypsy city of nearly six hundred people; almost all the rest were college students, faculty, and crew. And she missed Iowa terribly, especially Phantasia, her newly adopted black kitten. During a port call in Kobe, the three of us strolled, agog, through a high-rise department store that sold everything from sushi to Toyotas; it was a pagoda of consumerism. Tatiana spotted a black velveteen toy cat with big yellow eyes who seemed to beacon her across the crowded aisles. A surrogate Phantasia; it even had the curled, frostbitten ears of the real thing. And it was forlorn, the last of its kind in a heap of strange toy beasts. Lonely toy; lonely child. To buy the kitty was a rescue mission. Tatiana clung to that toy for the rest of the voyage, and in the years ahead she carried it to all seven continents.

The next semester, back in Iowa, facing the usual childhood problems of integration into a group of strangers, Tatiana was invited to bring something to show-and-tell. She had a lot of choices—a dinosaur egg, a conch shell, a capybara tooth—but of course she brought her fake friend Phantasia, and effusively told the story of how she'd rescued her in the department store and had fallen in love with her at first sight.

"Now Tatiana," her substitute teacher gravely declared in front of the whole class, "we all know that you've never been to Japan. Do you even know where Japan is? We all know that you're fibbing." All the kids laughed at Tatiana's preposterous story. "Geez," they thought, "what a snob!" The poor little kid was crushed.

So Tatiana adopted a double life, a sort of secret agent life. She kept her adventures hidden from her teachers, classmates, even her friends, lest they ostracize her. After one of her trips to Amazonia, she told her friends that she'd been to the Mall of America. After spending the summer in China, she said that she'd stayed at her grandmother's cottage in Michigan.

In the years ahead, Tatiana's secret life shifted to the ragged coastline of Belize, a narrow strand of pineland, mangrove, and sand between the Maya Mountains and the restive Gulf of Honduras. This is Creole country. Descended from just about everybody who ever washed ashore here, the Creoles live in storm-ravaged fishing villages perched on spindly stilts a yard or two above high tide. When the sun sinks behind those western mountains it gets dark fast; there can be no green flashes here. Sometimes, at dusk, a backwash of land air works its way down the range to the shore, bearing the reek of decomposed wood and leaves, hot and moldy. The Creoles call these "undertaker winds," and you know at those moments that there's a jungle out there. But just before dawn the breeze always becomes a sea wind, a "doctor's wind," cool, salted, and refreshing. This is the sea that launches the hurricanes that dumbly ramble ashore every decade or so, splintering the villages and upheaving the pinelands. But those cyclones also keep the coastline forever young, and the swollen rivers bring nutrients back to the sea, a wine of the land that nourishes the mangroves and the coral reefs. The Creoles understand the geomancy of tempest, rain, and river. That's how they survive.

Every spring for six years I took a group of students to Glover's Atoll, about thirty-five miles off the Creole coast, to the marine biology station on Middle Caye. Glover's is the southernmost atoll in Belize. Its eastern edge is a long barrier of broken coral, ephemeral sandbars, and cayes trussed up from the sea, and flotsam sheared off of the coast of Honduras. The flotsam brings the shards of busted-up lives—pirogues, furniture, bassinettes, ship- wrecked plastic toys and dolls, even barbershop poles—and beachcombing there is a creepy experience. But that disheveled barrier shelters a vast lagoon, a still-water aquarium seventeen miles long and five miles wide, in which grow about seven hundred patch reefs. Each is a universe. Every spring Tatiana joined us at Glover's, where for a week she would become an aquatic being, a silkie snorkeling over those patch reefs day and night. She memorized the names of the fishes and corals, sketched them in a notebook, pasted seaweed and shells onto its pages as if it were a Dagwood sandwich.

The harbormaster at Middle Caye is a Creole named Danny Wesby, a mariner whom I trust implicitly to watch over my landlubber students when they're in the sea. Danny spent a lonely childhood on Long Caye, another of the small islands that fringe the atoll. It was a perilous child- hood, too: During Hurricane Hattie in 1961, Long Caye was inundated by a storm surge and Danny's stilt house was swept away. To save his son's life, Danny's father lashed the boy to the leeward side of a coconut tree. The coconut survived the surge and screaming wind . . . and so did Danny.

For years Danny had told us about a crocodile who lived in the lagoon of Glover's Atoll. It had probably been washed out to sea during a storm decades before, and was all alone. Five years in a row we roamed that lagoon in Danny's open boat from north to south, but never saw it. For my students the crocodile became an intergenerational legend, a mythological beast. The lagoon was vast, and there were plenty of places for it to hide. We knew it was out there, and close, too . . . but it never materialized.

Beauty, I've found, ambushes you . . . and you have to be prepared. The inevitable encounter with the crocodile happened during our sixth trip to Glover's. It was our last day, and we had spent a long sun-seared afternoon snorkeling over the reefs near the abandoned lighthouse at the northern tip of the atoll. Exhausted, sunburned, and hungry, we were racing in Danny's boat across the still lagoon to Middle Caye, to a shower, a dinner, and bed. And there it was: the crocodile, sculling across the lagoon a quarter mile to our south—as unexpected as a green flash. Danny spotted it first and im- mediately cut the motor. Voicelessly—not stirring, not bumping an oar— we drifted toward the reclusive animal. When it finally noticed us, it stopped sculling, drooped its body and tail so that only the turrets of its eyes and nose remained above the sea, and waited to see what we would do.

I knew what I would do: In thirty seconds I had donned my mask, snorkel, and flippers and had slipped silently over the side of the dinghy, grabbing a wooden oar to bop the crocodile on its snout if it came too close. As soon as I put my head underwater, I could see it, hanging indolently from the surface. I estimated that it was ten or twelve feet long and about as many feet in front of me. It turned toward me, sculled a little closer, stopped. I held the blade of the oar between the two of us. Each of us stood our ground.

The students, meanwhile, had all crowded to the port side of the dinghy to watch us. Danny was shouting that they were going to tip the boat.

"Keep she level, mon," he ordered, "I keepa tellin you to balance de boat."

What to do? A professor with a boatload of other people's children up to his proverbial ass in . . . well, you get the picture. I declared to my students, my voice laden with responsibility, "Everybody stay on the boat. This is a dangerous animal."

And then I hissed, "Tatiana! Get in the water. This is the chance of a lifetime." I needn't have invited her; she was already at my side, clinging to my left arm.

Naturally, the students refused to stay on the boat. I had no reason to expect them to. Had I not invited my own child to join me? I knew that the crocodile was *probably* too shy to attack us, that my flock was *probably* in no danger. *I knew I had the oar.* Maybe I simply wanted to delay the chaos, to share a few minutes with my daughter and the crocodile before all hell broke loose. And did it ever. Now the students were piling into the sea, slapping their flippers, banging the boat, flailing like a school of hysterical mullets. Danny stayed on board, cussing at them.

The poor crocodile became terrified by all the hubbub and nose-dived onto the sea floor twenty feet below, stirred up a puff of sand, bolted to the edge of a small patch reef, and jammed its head beneath an overhanging shelf of coral. Just its head, mind you . . . the croc was bigger than the reef. The rest of the monster—its dark body, arms and legs, splayed fingers and toes, and long tail—was conspicuously laid out on the pale sand.

"Piaget level number two," I thought. "Preoperational visual denial. The crocodile thinks that if it can't see us, then we mustn't be here." And then I whispered to myself, *"Good thing. . . ."*

Oar in hand, I accompanied the students one by one from the dinghy to the spot where the croc was hiding. Each kid got a good look at the Mesozoic leftover. I figured that as a professor of biology my first duty was to instill a sense of wonder in them. What better way than to introduce them personally to this megafaunal predator? (It seems that my plan worked. Several of the kids told me later that those moments were the high point of their college careers.)

After each student had a turn, I ordered them back to the safety of the boat. Danny stopped cussing and relaxed. Tatiana and I were last. We lingered in the darkling sea, waited until the croc surfaced, watched it take three deep breaths and, sculling its long serrated tail, head north. The three of us, father, daughter, and beast, slowly fluked in tandem through the mercury sea . . . eye to eye to eye.

Throughout her childhood, the Creole coast brought Tatiana surprising gifts from the sea, and she filled one Dagwood sandwich after another. And when she was eight years old, on an enchanted evening of a full moon in May, Tatiana discovered whale sharks. They are the largest fish in the world, formidable animals that grow up to forty-five feet long but, being filter-feeders, are harmless to humans. We had been staying in Placencia, a Creole village that a few years later was practically wiped away by Hurricane Iris. The Gulf of Honduras off Placencia is as moonstruck as any place I've been, and on the night before our encounter with the sharks, we watched that big yellow orb rise over the sea. First it seemed to trickle onto the water; then it climbed through the sea wind, over the lightning storms that roamed the horizon, and floated above the hot ocean that is the forge of tempests.

Full moonrise is an event almost as old as Earth herself. There have been approximately 51 billion of them since the moon was ripped from Earth's side by a collision with some wayward planet. Because of entropy the moon is drifting farther from Earth, abandoning her, and each moonrise has drawn the tide a little less onto the land, for a shorter time, than the previous one. In the Bay of Honduras the full moons of May are the most portentous, presaging food and sex in the warming springtime sea. These are the moons that arouse the cubera snappers, who spend most of their lives hunkered down in the safety of shallow patch reefs, and draw them to Gladden Spit, a sandy promontory in the open sea beyond the barrier, thirty-six miles offshore from Placencia. The cuberas congregate there by the tens of thousands in order to spawn, releasing millions of eggs. This orgy attracts the whale sharks, who for most of the year roam the deep waters of the bay like ancient mariners, to feed on the uncountable progeny of those snappers' unions.

We had contracted Glen Eiley, the chairman of Placencia, to take us to see the sharks. Like Danny, Glen is descended from generations of Creole fishermen, and like Danny, Glen has a preternatural understanding of the sea. Most importantly, Glen knew how to find that place of rendezvous.

Glen's boat was about twenty feet long, open, beat-up, made of fraying fiberglass, and powered by twin Yamaha 150s. The next morning the waters of the Placencia lagoon were so tranquil that we hydroplaned among low mangrove cayes, sandbars, and dark patch reefs. By midmorning Glen had brought us to Eiley's Cut (named after one of his ancestors), a navigable passage through the barrier. But as we approached the cut, the whole eastern horizon turned lumpy. Huge swells were roaming out there, and dying out there, surging over the reef and exhausting themselves on the barrier. Every collapsing breaker made a hollow concussive boom as deep as the abyss: a sea quake.

The snappers were out there, too, waiting for dusk, and that was where the whale sharks were headed. Glen nosed the dinghy through the passage just to see what the conditions were like. They were not good. We became surrounded by roaming walls of water, fractal places tousled, crinkled, and fretted by the wind, a thousand tracings on every sea flank.

Of course, it was not fractal at all. There was pattern and process inscribed, however ephemerally, on those swells, and Glen knew how to interpret this information. The Creole captains call it "reading the sea" and are ever checking the horizon for storms, tasting the wind, marking its direction, noting how rapidly it's cycling around the compass, the extent of its fetch, the vectors of each swell. They also read the tides, both the incoming ocean tide that is full of plankton and the hot scavenged tide that drains the lagoon. They read the long lines of shoestring sea grass that align like compass needles with the tide and currents.

I stood on the prow, grasping the anchor line to keep me steady, amid the hot salt air, the fast warm spray, the turning horizon, the distant, troubling storms and dark mountains. My body became one with the swells, moved with them as if they were inside me. Tatiana, alas, wasn't doing so well and didn't join me at her customary place at my side. She was seasick, lying on a plank with her head on her mom's lap. The poor sea-girl was laid flat by the sea she loved.

I tried to reassure her, saying, "Tatiana, you know, there are two kinds of sailors in the world. Those who *are* seasick, and those who *will be* seasick."

But I knew that my words were of little comfort. I'd been there. We had no recourse but to return to the safety of the lagoon and wait things out. In any event the whale sharks wouldn't arrive until dusk, and maybe by then things would have calmed down.

No such luck. As the sun descended hot and red over the Maya Mountains, the time of rendezvous arrived, and Glen plowed once again into the maelstrom. He pushed his dinghy against the wind but with the tide, over the eastern horizon into the trackless sea. He chased the white Sandwich terns, royal terns, and white-headed noddies (which mimic the white-capped sea itself) that were also heading to the open gulf. The birds knew where the snappers were—maybe they could spot the action from high above—and Glen knew that if we followed them to the edge of the continental shelf we would be over the spit. Now a fleet of bounding yellowtail tuna—so many that their crescent fins shredded the sea surface—and a legion of sun-silvered ballyhoo—airborne among the swells—told us that we were above the moon-spelled place where the sappers were congregating.

It was getting dark and there was no time to waste. Already the whale sharks were breaching; all around us we could see their huge dorsal fins, like triangular sails, and their scythe-shaped tails cutting the sea. Glen dropped a sea anchor.

Tatiana had aroused herself and was gamely looking around. I was astonished to see that she was putting on her mask, snorkel, and flippers.

"Are you still sick?" I asked.

"Yes, but I came here to swim with the sharks," she declared, "and *I will*, Daddy."

I was reluctant. What if she got lost in the swells? I wasn't sure that I, alone, could manage this bounding sea, much less take care of her. What if she choked on her own vomit and drowned?

Glen was watching us, and understood. He took my arm and said, "David, give she to me. I'll take she into de sea. I be keepin her safe, jus as my daddy did for me."

I knew that I trusted this man. I knew that he understood the sea better than I ever would. I sensed that this might be a milestone in my daughter's life. I agreed.

And so we threw ourselves into the swells, become lost in the swells. Glen tucked Tatiana under his left arm and swam away with her. I stayed as close to them as possible, but often I couldn't see them, or the boat, just the green sea and the pale, sandy bottom eighty feet below. The snappers were swarming down there, thousands of them—turning counterclockwise like a prayer wheel—and the whale sharks, six, maybe seven, were all around us, emerging from the void as if the open sea were suddenly turning into fawn-colored flesh, as big as school buses, as big as the swells above. They were indifferent to us—we were too small for them to notice, I presume—and as they slid past, flexing their tails, we tumbled in their wakes.

The vortex of snappers turned faster now, the females rising off the sea floor. At the moment of release, they turned on their sides, exposing their white flanks to the hungry water, and shuddered, ejecting flurries of pink eggs the size of currants. Then they flipped back to vertical and descended into anonymity. The males followed, releasing a pale milt so copious that it made the sea surface slick and momentarily calmed the wind-ripples.

A billion unions of egg and sperm were going on around us; a billion hopeful new cells were becoming beings. Most, of course, died in an instant, swept into the maws of a whale shark, snatched by a tuna, or dipped from the surface by a tern. The whale sharks pushed their big, open mouths—maws as wide as my daughter was tall—through the spawn, filtering and swallowing the billowing caviar. Each shark must have ingested a ton of eggs at the hour of their birth; each must have ingested a reef full of fish.

We snorkeled until dark, and with great struggle managed to pull ourselves into the bouncing dinghy. By the time I came aboard, Tatiana was proudly standing by the helm with Glen. She had earned her sea legs. On the wild night ride back to Placencia she joined me on the prow. By then the wind had shifted westerly, becoming an undertaker wind, and the long fetch of the lagoon pushed up new sea-swells. They were growing fast, breaking over the prow of our boat, and we were in danger of being pushed by one dark wall of water into the next. But Glen masterfully angled the dinghy so that it never took the swells head-on, and the little boat sambaed up and down the flanks of the waves, the props cavitating as we rode the crests.

I wrapped Tatiana in a blanket and held her close. She was shivering, more from excitement, I thought, than from wind or cold. I realized that both she and I had discovered an unexpected courage: she—damn the discomfort—to face the sharks; I to let her do it, to let her go.

Now the wind shifted again, was being sucked toward a tall thunderstorm to the southeast, a column of vapor that drew all the wet energy from the sea and lifted it halfway out of the atmosphere. The hot air raced to die in that frigid vortex, turning counterclockwise as it rose, like the snappers below. All those molecules were dancing around that center . . . so were the fish and the sharks, the little boat, the father and his child.

And the center held.

The Luck of the Irish

F. D. REEVE

"The luck of the devil," says a Republican, and "the luck of the Irish," says a Democrat, both meaning that's how the privileged scion of generations of working-class immigrants got elected president in 1960. Only a few years before that, it was how I got into academia and how, the next year, I got to Russia.

The big step forward in my lucky life was being a pupil of R. P. Blackmur, from whom I learned that the reading and writing of books was a respectable, indeed, a preferable, highly valuable alternative to the middle-class, business-and-banking careers of my conservative family. A few years after I graduated, he introduced me at my first big New York poetry reading. By that time, I had worked on the docks, become a lifelong socialist, and gotten inducted into academia.

Entering academia, like first meeting Blackmur, was "the luck of the Irish." On a final exam in a final MA semester, I penned a fiercely critical evaluation of a course, expecting no reply. To my surprise, the warm, generous, and fair-minded Ernest Simmons called me in, justified his course—and offered me a teaching position in the Slavic Department that fall. Moses Hadas approved me for the Columbia humanities program. I was hooked.

For the next fifty years I got paid for reading and writing. I never really thought of it as a job except as it answered the conventional question, "What do you do?" For me it was—and still is—a way of life peopled by some of the finest, fastest minds of my time and one opportunity after another to see the workings of the world. Of course, I'm biased in favor of culture over commerce and politics. I hate the oppressive natures of American capitalism and Russian communism and ex-communism, but I admire the hard-nosed Nikita Khrushchev for his tactful honoring of Robert Frost, whom I had the chance to escort to the Soviet Union and serve as translator when the two met privately. I bet my students never guessed that they were teaching me more than I was teaching them.

Children were in the picture from the word go. (Never any resemblance to Longfellow's "The Children's Hour" ever.) Daughter Alison was born in Paris, where I was on a Ford grant researching Russian Symbolism for my dissertation. After a bitter cold winter, Helen and I borrowed a friend's baby carriage, packed a duffel, and took a train trip with baby through sunny Italy.

Baby Alison made our stay at the Roman "hotel" recommended to us spectacularly cheerful: With its lovely flagstone patio and cool, wide staircases it had become a bordello, and the beautiful young women doted on the little girl.

The Twentieth Congress of the Communist Party took place that year. De-Stalinization began in earnest. Clemens Heller kindly tried to include me in the French cultural exchanges, but the Russians refused to allow it. Five more years passed before an American-Russian exchange was ratified and I was chosen to go.

Off we sailed on the *Flandre* from New York to Le Havre: Helen, Alison now five, Brock, four, and little Mark, six months. We squeezed into a red VW Bug in Paris—Mark rode on a pile of diapers in the well behind the back seat—passed through Warsaw, and made it to Moscow. We were quartered in a pleasant hotel in Moscow, then in a fancy hotel in Leningrad, then in a new apartment in Moscow. Everyone, but everyone, was affectionate to the children. Even though I was tailed all day every day, ordinary people and academic acquaintances treated us as a normal foreign family in the parks, on the streets, on buses, subway, and trains, and in their homes. Not that we could go very far. Circulation was strictly limited. But the bold people who dared invite foreigners to their houses were warm and delightful, and our children charmed all comers. Oh, even on hot days old ladies in public kept telling Helen to put a hat on Mark, who was having a fine time peeling around in a stroller and excitedly walking as much as he could. But the height of parent-child relations came one morning after we'd been there a couple of months when we heard the three kids, who slept together in one room, talking avidly to each other in Russian, the two older ones fluently, and Mark imitating the sounds. Every morning Alison and Brock made a habit of reading Mark little stories or rhymes read to them some night before. It was a Russian mini-kaffeeklatsch. They were very happy having their own private world imitating the big one.

Back in the States, the Russian lasted for a while, but Alison started kindergarten and the social pressures took the language away, though to this day she remembers a lot (the boys don't) and, as a doctor, has visited Russia several times.

You never know which direction luck will turn you. A few years after that Russian year and after my trip the next year with Frost to meet Khrushchev, during a sabbatical semester I lectured and tutored at New College, Oxford. People were cordial; some were very friendly to Helen and me; Mark, too young for school, played with trucks and conkers on the floor while I wrote lit crit at a table; but Alison and Mark at the local school had a lonely time, rather shunned by other pupils and constantly corrected in spelling and pronunciation. They could imitate the English behind their backs perfectly, but they hated the harassment. The Beatles were just coming on the radio and we all loved them, but the picayune nature of daily school life and the rigidity of class distinctions were so discouraging (especially compared to what positive lives faced the children at home) that when I was invited to apply for the chair in Russian, I declined. No regrets: The recent slug-fest between Ruth Padel and Derek Walcott to become Oxford's professor of poetry documents how petty and pointless the cloistered life can be.

How much did an academic childhood influence the children? All the summers traveling, fishing, sailing; skiing in the winters. All the visitors from near and far always talking about books. Back in second or third grade, asked to identify an obvious church-with-spire façade by selecting the proper word of four from a list, they, who had been in cathedrals and abbeys but never attended church, picked the word "university." During college, Alison earned money as a ski instructor. After college, she spent two years doing research before going to medical school; she is now a distinguished professor of psychiatry at a large university hospital. Brock took an MPhil in classics, taught for a year, disliked it, became a business consultant, acquired an MBA, and now—by the luck of *his* Irish—is the executive director of Harvard's Stem Cell Institute. He's an expert horseman. After graduating from Harvard, Mark earned his JD at the University of Washington, clerked for a federal judge, joined a large firm, and then established his own practice in environmental law and served two terms on the Oregon Environmental Commission and now is a regular consultant to the state on all such issues. He is one of the most skilled fly fishermen in the country. The academic umbrella under which they grew up encouraged them to think freshly, to pay their own way, and to act vigorously in what mattered to them—and they did. I was there to watch.

Shifting the Tectonic Plates
of Academia

JERALD WALKER

When my wife, Brenda, was a graduate student, she was warned by a male professor to not have children if she intended to be a serious academic, or, put another way, an academic who would be taken seriously. That was more than a decade ago; I wonder if this professor still offers the same advice. Perhaps now, as a result of personal growth, he directs young female scholars to have as many babies as they desire, and then to find a reputable hospital where they can be surgically changed to men. This would not be entirely poor counsel, for male academics with babies, empirical evidence shows, are awesome. As an academic and father of two, I am doubly awesome.

What is not so awesome is how female academics with babies are stigmatized, particularly if the babies are illegitimate, which is to say born pre-tenure or, worse, pre-dissertation. The latter was the case with our friend Doris. Before her indiscretion, the faculty in her master's program had viewed her as a rising star, an ascent aided by a highly coveted teaching assistantship, departmental grants, funded conferences, and invitations to faculty dinner parties where martinis and Pinot Grigio flowed as freely as the gossip about her fellow graduate students. "Oh, *that* one will never finish the program," she heard a professor remark one night, speaking of a newly pregnant peer. Sure enough, this pregnant peer did not finish, though some felt this had less to do with her infant than with the financial aid that was reduced at the discovery of her pregnancy, just as Doris's financial aid was reduced at the discovery of hers.

Brenda attempted to have her financial aid reduced as well, but we had difficulty starting a family; by the time our first child arrived, she had completed her PhD. She had also learned that there were precious few tenure-track positions in her field. So she returned to school to earn a master's in library science, and then she worked for a year as a librarian while I—still completing my doctorate, though having no interest in ever actually using it—remained home with our son. When she at last found a suitable teaching position for which to apply, our child was ten months old. He was also still nursing. This fact, as soon as Brenda was invited for a campus interview, raised a terrible dilemma. If in the patriarchal world of academia a mother could not be taken seriously, then a mother with leaking breasts during a presentation would be preposterous. Clearly a disaster was in the making, and as the date of her interview neared, I grew increasingly anxious. Which made Brenda increasingly anxious. Anxiety, of course, threatens milk production. All that had to happen, I realized, was for me to work her into a tizzy by the time she left for her campus interview and, presto, problem solved. I mean, it wasn't as if our son needed to nurse anymore. His cheeks were rosy, his lungs were robust, and his energy was high. A little too high, in fact. Especially between 2:00 and 6:00 A.M. A bit of lethargy on his part, it seemed to me, could do us all some good. So I proceeded with my plan, unleashing a full assault on Brenda's nervous system about a month before she was to fly from Iowa to Massachusetts, where all that stood between her and the ivory tower was a milk-filled mote.

Brenda glanced up from a book she was reading. "Pardon me?" she asked.

"No more nursing," I repeated. I looked at our radiantly healthy son, who was on the floor near Brenda's chair, playing with some wooden blocks. "The bar is closed," I told him. "Capeesh? Hasta la vista, baby!"

Brenda scooped him into her arms.

"Give me the boy," I said, approaching her slowly.

She tucked our son's head under her blouse, where he promptly began a late lunch.

"There's *no* alternative," I explained.

She rose and backed away.

"Remember what your professor told you! Remember Doris!"

Brenda went into the bathroom and closed the door. The lock clicked before I reached the handle.

"This is your dream job," I called to her, and it was true. The position was at a teaching institution with earnest, first-generation students, located near the bustling city of Boston. Brenda, a kind and patient soul, was perfectly suited for such a college, while I, somewhat excitable, longed to live near a city that bustled. I pounded my fists on the door. "They'll never take you seriously!" I yelled, a phrase I repeated regularly over the next several weeks, during which I slept fitfully and developed a twitch in my left eye.

A curious thing happened, though. Brenda's milk production appeared to increase rather than decrease, as if some survival gland had been triggered—every time I saw our son he seemed to be gorging on a nipple. Such was his activity when, a few days before her interview, Brenda phoned a female member of the search committee and threw herself on the mercy of the court, confessing that she was a nursing mom and would need to pump. "No problem," the faculty member said. "We'll set aside time for you."

This was a promising sign. Perhaps the tectonic plates of academia had begun to shift; female professors with children were no longer pariahs. Still, to play it safe, Brenda and I agreed that at every opportunity she should stress that I was a stay-at-home dad, eager to relieve her of all parental responsibility at the drop of a bib. "Tell them you spend so much time in the library being serious," I coached her, "that you often don't see the baby for days."

"That's ridiculous."

"Weeks?"

She did not take this advice, and yet she still landed the job. Her presentation had gone very well, apparently, though I suspected the key to her hiring was her emphasis on my availability to provide around-the-clock care for our son. I was so convinced of this, in fact, that as soon as we'd moved from Iowa to Massachusetts and gotten situated, I suggested we have another baby. I was the primary caregiver, I reasoned, so there would be minimal negative impact on her career, particularly since by the time we conceived, if our first child was any indicator, she would be a full professor.

A month later she was pregnant. She had been teaching for only two weeks. When we hesitantly broke the news to her colleagues, it was at a dinner party, hosted by her male department chair. "Good thing I'm a stay-at-home dad!" I chanted throughout the evening. "Bring on those babies!" What I didn't mention was that the high cost of living in New England was hurtling us toward bankruptcy, and that my stay-at-home days, lest that home become a shelter, would necessarily have to come to an end.

Soon afterward, as luck would have it, the English Department at the college posted a tenure-track position in my field. And so I applied. And so I came to realize my awesomeness.

I got the first glimpse of it during the campus interview. It was a little after 10:00 A.M., and I was in the conference room, where I'd just been drilled about my teaching pedagogy. Now I was waiting to be escorted to my visit with the dean. All of my future colleagues had departed, except for one, a woman I guessed to be in her late twenties. I passed the time with her by telling cute stories about my son, drawn from two years' worth of material. She was impressed. "It's so wonderful when fathers are that involved with their children," she said. I took out my wallet and showed her pictures. Her hands went to her cheeks.

She did not say, "But how are you going to manage a 4/4 teaching load with a toddler?" or "What childcare arrangements will you have?"

She said, "He's precious!"

A short while later, the dean agreed. This was the same dean who'd interviewed Brenda. She had shown him pictures of our son, too, just after stressing, of course, that I was a stay-at-home dad. I put my photos away and gestured over the dean's right shoulder toward a bookshelf, where pictures of his teenage children were proudly on display. "That's quite a good-looking brood you have yourself," I noted.

Beaming, he told me their names before mentioning some of their recent scholastic accomplishments, and then he relayed a few stories about them, working his way back in time to when they were toddlers. "That's such a fun age," he recalled, smiling. "And you and Brenda have another baby on the way?"

I nodded. "Due in June!"

He did not say, "But that's only two months before classes start" or "How will you manage your classes with a newborn and a toddler?"

He said, "Congratulations!" He said it again in a month, when he called to offer me the job.

By the time the fall semester arrived, Brenda and I had arranged our teaching schedules in such a way that usually one of us would be with our sons, though we often had to pass them to one another in the middle of campus. Her department colleagues were pleasantly accepting of her motherhood, but the warning of her professor still haunted her, as well as the horror stories of our female friends in academia who had or desired to have children. So Brenda took the boys to her office only if it could not be avoided. A couple of times, with great reluctance, and fearful of what it might mean for her tenure, she brought them to faculty meetings.

I, on the other hand, experienced no anxiety about having the boys with me at work. Several times a week, I could be found sitting in my office, my two-year-old on the floor happily yanking books from my shelves, or scribbling on stacks of ungraded exams, while my infant cooed in my arms. Colleagues passing my office invariably paused to marvel at my dual roles of academic and father. So, too, did my students. This was especially true of the females, who would sometimes plop down on the floor with my oldest, or pry my youngest from my arms and peer into his eyes, their own eyes seemingly on the verge of tears, as Brenda's had been when she was advised to choose books over babies, publications over playdates. None of my professors had ever warned me not to have children. I know of no male peers whose funding was reduced at the announcement of impending parenthood. I have never had to fear that lactation would cost me a job.

Nor have I had to wonder, as Brenda has had to wonder, if too many references to the boys during class would result in my being viewed as a parent who professes, rather than a professor who parents. My class notes from those first years of teaching were punctuated with marginal comments like "Tell grocery store tantrum story here!" or "Good time to mention projectile vomit episode!" If I happened to go a few weeks without offering a daddy-story, which was rare, students asked for one. And sometimes, as I made my way across campus, a former student would stop me and inquire about the well-being of my children. "I've always wanted to tell you," someone said on one such occasion, "that the way you balance being an academic and a parent is awesome." She aspired, she told me, to one day do the same.

I did not say that academia would not take her seriously. I did not say she should have her gender changed.

I said, "That's wonderful."

And then I advised her to talk to my wife, an academic and the mother of my sons, because she's pretty awesome, too.

Hair-Raising Experiences

JOHN W. WELLS

Nineteen ninety-seven was the year that my son, Garland, and I came into a new life at the same time. He emerged from the warmth of his mother's womb, while I came out of a similar level of comfort as I moved from faculty to administration. Neither of us asked for what we got, and neither of us understood what we were getting ourselves into. Wide-eyed, we would both enter this new world screaming, knowing that the relative ease of the recent past was gone. It struck me that I was given identical advice for my move to administration and for my transition to fatherhood. My advisors, an unlikely pair, were the provost at the college and my shirtless middle-aged neighbor, who never tired of giving me his version of how to be a good father (spank 'em harder). Although they couldn't have been more different, their words were uncannily the same.

The advice started with the provost. Upon assuming the head of the honors program at the liberal arts college where I taught, he called me in to offer his wisdom. "John," he intoned, his left leg bouncing wildly, "taking on administrative responsibilities doesn't mean that you are abandoning your calling as an educator. In fact, it means that you have merely gone from selling education retail to selling it wholesale." I wasn't at all certain what the hell he meant, but I nodded with as much enthusiasm as I could muster. I agreed with the same level of feigned understanding as I did when the doctor explained why my newborn son, whose complexion had turned a deep shade of orange, needed to spend the night under a big heat lamp. "You will be faced with many difficult choices, and you may wind up offending some of your colleagues." This sounded ominous. "You will have to make decisions the likes of which will have a lifelong impact on people, and that is sometimes a heady responsibility. You will need to exercise your power with humility." How else would power be exercised as the honors director at a small liberal arts college in Appalachia? Try as I might,

I couldn't imagine myself as a kind of midlevel college-manager version of Idi Amin. The "welcome to the big leagues" lecture ended with the provost smiling broadly. He pumped my hand and gave me the good-natured warning, "Get ready for some hair-raising experiences." I was sweating when I left his office.

Only days later, my wife and I brought our son home from the hospital. Our neighbor was a Vietnam War veteran. I couldn't understand why a man with a stomach that large had decided that shirts just weren't for him. Perhaps it had something to do with how hot that jungle got back there in 'Nam. Maybe it was because the workers now manufacturing the cheap shirts capable of masking such alarming girth were the sons of the people he had fought in Southeast Asia. Maybe it was because it bugged his wife. We were careful as we took the bassinet out of the car. Our son was home, and we couldn't wait to introduce him to the room we had prepared for his arrival. "Hey there!" bellowed the shirtless one. This was the same man who had rearranged our garage without asking, who had planted trees in our backyard because "we needed 'em," and for reasons known but to God would capture raccoons in homemade traps. He was getting up from his seat on the porch. "Whatcha got there in the basket?" I didn't want this to be my son's first visual of the neighborhood, but there was no clear path to the top of the stairs. Shirtless stood over the basket. He attempted a baby-cooing sound that resonated more like a marine grunt (Slash and burn, boys, slash and burn. Charlie's around here somewhere). "Great baby," he finally muttered and turned to walk back to his yard. I thanked him and moved quickly toward the door. As if to demonstrate that his life, too, offered exciting novelty, he announced that he and his wife were the proud new owners of a jerky machine and we were welcome to some of the homemade teriyaki venison version whenever we wanted it. "You'll be spending a lot more time at home," he chuckled. "Get ready for some hair-raisin' experiences." I was sweating when I went into the house.

Language Acquisition

SACS, or the Southern Association of Colleges and Schools, is the accrediting body for institutions in the Southeast. (No SACS before a fight.) As a brand-new administrator, I had to learn the language of accreditation. The language of SACS, "educationese," is a largely pedantic system of utterances designed to perpetrate a kind of death-by-boredom on academic administrators. Strangely enough, however, it is quite catchy, and I found myself bringing my new language home. I internalized it and, much as if I were eating spinach, felt that I was growing because I was poking it down.

"You should see what Garland did today," my wife said, greeting me at the door with our son's latest accomplishment. "He said some words!" Her face was beaming, but I had just put in a long day at the college. "In fact, he has been saying words all day long." I could see that she was excited, but an administrator always projects a certain level of reserve. "Did you record any of this with the camera?" I inquired with the unmistakable tone of the man in charge. "No, I didn't. I assume he will say more words." That was her reply, and it had an edge. I just couldn't believe it. How many times did I need to go over it? Without the proper documentation, we are unable to say for certain that we have met the goals of any of the matrixes in the Quality Enhancement Plan. It's as though it never happened. I was tempted to ask her if there had been faculty input into today's "miracle." Had she filled out the proper SACS form? I had married a faculty member, and it is soooo like a professor to celebrate the moment without recording it properly. What a rookie. You may as well tell me that one of your students did something great that wasn't required in your syllabus.

Language acquisition is a wonderful process to witness, but even more fascinating is seeing the more complicated facets of communication begin to emerge. Watching my son gain the ability to manipulate the inflection in his voice in order to express himself was exciting. Depending on the intonation, he was irritated, sad, exuberant, or merely passing the time. I found myself mimicking his exaggerated voice modulations, which came in handy when meeting with faculty. So much of academic administration is explaining why a certain program or initiative simply doesn't fit into the current budget. The trick is expressing to creative faculty the need for them to process their thoughts in synchronicity with the budget timeline. Ideas, regardless of how good they may be, just can't be accepted if they occur any time past the general meeting of the board of trustees in April. The budget is set. How an administrator keeps a faculty member fresh and engaged while breaking this news is the trick to a long tenure in the big office. Thus, the utility of mastering the sympathetic tone is essential. "I'm sorry, Dr. Smith, we just don't have it in the budget right now (*raise eyebrow, literally wring hands*), but would you like some tea? I was just about to prepare some for myself."

Garland taught me an even more effective way to use sympathy in administration. It occurred when my son, seven by the time I had become a division dean, decided to ride his bicycle through the neighbor's yard as though he were running the gauntlet of a death-defying obstacle course. The Shirtless One would ponderously bound off the front porch and bark orders at Garland to cease and desist this harassment. "Letting children get away with whatever they want is a form of communism," he would lecture me sternly. (His unruly beard looked like Marx's.) The problem became especially acute around any holiday. The neighbors were celebrators. They loved to put holiday-specific cutouts on the front lawn so that the world might know that they were not merely enduring life but celebrating it in all of its kitschy manifestations. On one particular December day, Garland had taken the turn through the holiday maze at too fast a clip. As he raced between the cutouts of the Baby Jesus and the ice-skating penguin, he lost control and slid into the somber Wise Men and the Santa-suited Grinch. It was a massacre.

I had told Garland a million times to stop racing his bicycle through the postmodern collage of yuletide, and he had simply ignored me. My imme-diate thought was to document the damage in his personnel file and have the neighbor register a negative addendum to Garland's year-end perform-ance review report. The neighbor called me over to his front yard. For the first time in my life, I didn't feel like a civilian. I was the lowliest private in the army as the Shirtless One dressed me down. He seemed reasonably reassured, however, when I promised him that my son's desire to rampage through his "art" was not a sign that I was encouraging the workers of the world to unite. Still crimson-faced from the encounter, I finally tracked down my son. "Do you realize how angry you made the neighbor? This is a man who has killed people. He's killed people, Garland. And he did it for America. I can't tell you how embarrassed I am." Like every other paternal lecture I have ever delivered, my words just seemed to float over Garland. Then, quite by accident, I stumbled on the exact right words and expressed them in the exact right tone. "How do you think this makes me feel?" I meeped out. And that is when the moment changed. "I'm sorry, Dad. I won't do it anymore. I didn't realize how much trouble you would get into." Pure gold. My son had taught me one of the most useful tools of the effec-tive administrator—the power of pitiful. "Good talk, son."

When I arrived at work the next day, still pondering the ramifications of this discovery, I was presented with the latest administrative brush fire. It seems the aging instructor of the death-and-dying class had come to the conclusion that her students just weren't taking their own mortality seriously. She therefore decided to bring the moment home to each of them. Introducing her lecture as "We are all going to be food for worms,"

the professor donned a black dress with a veil. She brought a small coffin
into the room and set it on the table in front of the gawking students. And
then, as if to make the whole scene even more complete, she lined up a
number of dolls from her collection and placed them prone on the table, de-
claring to the class that each of them had passed away. She even hummed
"Amazing Grace" as she laid each of her dolls to rest. In a matter of only
minutes, she had transformed her classroom into a miniature version of the
third day at Gettysburg. There were bodies strewn throughout the room.
The lecture finally built to the climax. She lay down in front of the class
and put her hands over her chest, striking the unmistakable pose of mortal
slumber. Every jaw went slack.

Her innovative pedagogy was the talk of the school. For my money, I sort
of had a respect for her. Yes, it was macabre, but given the fact that most of
the students at the college were bright young conservative evangelicals, God
and sex had an almost unbreakable monopoly on their thoughts. She had
effectively been able to get them to think about something else, no small feat.

It was playing very differently in the Ad building. "I'm getting phone
calls, John," the associate provost told me. He ushered me into his office
and cleared his throat the same way the oncologist does just before he reveals that he has your test results back. "We have to put a stop to this, but
there can't be the impression that we are attempting to interfere with what
faculty are doing in their classroom. You need to sit her down and talk with
her. We've got kids showing up in the nurse's office obsessed with death.
One parent called and said that her daughter cried at the dinner table the
other night. Said everybody there was going to die."

I made my way to the professor's office. The black crepe paper that hung
from the walls was just wonderful. I didn't quite know how to approach
her. At first, I attempted to be stern. She just stared at me. I talked about
her students and how we probably should let them revel in the springtime
of life a bit before we throw the cold water of impending doom on them.
More stares. I looked at the floor and leaned forward in my chair. Staring
deep into her eyes I said, "You know, we are getting lots of phone calls
about your class. Many of them are from irate parents concerned about
their kids." Still no hint in the professor's eyes that she was going to budge.
Then, in a stage whisper, I added, "How do you think that makes me feel?"

Art Is Sacred

I became a provost when Garland was going into the third grade. The time
had come to leave the institution where I had been a faculty member and

midlevel administrator and move into the big leagues. The new college was in the midst of transition. I was to be the fourth person to serve as the chief academic officer in the space of just six years. Like any parent, I was concerned about the transition that my children, and Garland in particular, would have to endure. I talked to him about going into a new school and how scary I knew it was for him. In the back of my mind, I couldn't help but feel the same trepidation as I contemplated the faculty at my new post. They had been quite effective at marginalizing administrators for a long time. They made it very clear that they did not intend to publish, all raises were to be across the board, and sabbaticals were to be automatic every nine years. It would be a tough room. And the question was, Which area of the college would be the most open to conversations about excellence and having standards? In looking for a place to tap into our new surroundings, Garland and I chose the same place—fine arts.

The local community theater welcomed Garland's enthusiastic dream of being an actor. He was cast in a Christmas performance, and he eagerly began learning his lines. Yes, this was an accepting crowd, and I was thrilled that my son had found a community. One of Garland's fellow actors was a young man who felt the need to keep a stuffed frog on his shoulder at all times. Another was a clearly lonely middle-aged gentleman who felt that all he needed was a break to become a Shakespearean actor. Though a native of southern Appalachia, he spoke with the accent of an early modern period Englishman. Yes, this was an accepting crowd. Surely they would be the same at the college. These artistic types are all cut from the same cloth, after all. I decided to draw close to the Fine Arts Division.

My first meeting with one of the division's professors turned into a lecture on academic freedom. "You see," she calmly explained to me, "the theater people, and I like them all very much, tend to get angry when anyone decides to fuck with their art." "Well," I replied, "I think that when you tackle the great issues of the day and force people to think about things that they ordinarily wouldn't consider, you have done your job in the theater department of a liberal arts college." For over a decade, I had taught John Stuart Mill in my political theory classes. I felt as smug as she did about the right to express oneself. "Precisely," she nodded, feeling she had put the horse's bit in the mouth of yet another administrator. Attempting to effect a balanced presentation of myself as a lover of all things high culture who had the church-related institution's welfare in my sights as well, I concluded our meeting by saying, "Let's just make certain that the academic freedom is used for a clear and direct purpose, not simply the need to titillate." I felt good about being supportive without being obsequious. I had also avoided expressing my mild outrage at being spoken down to. Faculty would usually rather their administrators not speak the language of their disciplines, preferring instead to think of them as mindless clerks who would always rather pore over a budgetary spreadsheet than actually read a hard-backed book.

Garland's performance was only a few weeks later. He hobbled out onto the stage, coal dust on his face, limping, with clothes crumpled. He was the perfect Tiny Tim. No other actor in a Dickens play had ever wielded a crutch as effectively as did Garland in that performance. I was enraged at nineteenth-century industrializing England. Dickens, a critic of industrial capitalism, was quite clear in his message. The poor are being screwed and we ought to care. Hear, hear, and Garland was communicating it brilliantly. He even made some impromptu additions to Tiny Tim's role. "Thattaboy," I thought. "Nobody's gonna fuck with your art."

I had been the chief academic officer for less than a year when I became the interim president. As luck would have it, the previous president had decided to align the institution with a strongly conservative coalition of church-related colleges. This had struck a decidedly flat note with the faculty. They had risen en masse, brandishing pitchforks and torches, the look of blood lust in their eyes. Suddenly, I was in the center chair and it was time for our Theater Department's annual spring production. It was a long tradition at the college to present the most controversial productions in the second semester, and this year would be no different. As I prepared to view the first performance of my infant presidency, I couldn't help but recall the conversation I had had with the fine arts professor. Surely the play would be done tastefully and with an eye toward illuminating the more serious issues of the day. As a nation, we are at war, and the play *Lysistrata*, while potentially controversial, was certainly an appropriate performance to stage when we had so many young men and women in harm's way. My son and I were ushered to our seats in the front center of the theater. I was still optimistic right up to the point when the actors piled onstage with their Styrofoam phalluses. "My God, I don't want to go to work tomorrow," I thought as I dreaded the legions of parents, trustees, and alums who would line up to express their displeasure at the performance. What's more, I had to debate whether to shield my son's eyes or just sit there in pained silence waiting for what would surely be a chewing out from his mother when I got him home.

As the play moved to a conclusion, I noticed that my son, always a precocious youngster, was sitting beside me without a care in the world. I asked him what he thought of the performance. "They don't like war" was his response. I breathed a huge sigh of relief. Perhaps others had drawn the same conclusion, that this was the point of the play, though the camouflage artificial penis that one of the actors had sported throughout the bulk of the production was, it seemed to me, designed to distract from any more serious philosophical issue. The house lights came on, and I leaned over to ask Garland if he minded if we stayed for a few minutes. The actors were going to have a talk-back with the audience. I figured that as the chief executive officer of the college—the one who would be fielding the questions from the angry constituencies come the morning—I'd better stay. The first question was technical. "Tell us about the lighting, the sound, the blah, blah, blah." Had others really not noticed that all of the male characters had paraded around with enormous Styrofoam erections for the last two hours? Geez. This college was founded in 1886 by an itinerant Methodist preacher, and, well, this was what we had become.

Garland was restless. "Ask your question, Dad. I'm ready to go home." I tried to put on my professor's face. I wasn't offended. No sir. Although I'm temporarily charged with running the day-to-day affairs of this august institution, I'm an academic. I'm open-minded, inquisitive, and fair. I am the captain of this blue ship cutting through the red waters of this most conservative area. "Ahem," I tapped on the microphone, "nicely done, students. Thanks to your director as well." So academic. "The play hit a number of important themes. To deprive the men of sex until they stopped making war certainly points to the traditional feminist thesis that the personal is political." Who could miss how erudite and insightful I was being? Garland sighed and looked at the plastic watch I had purchased him for his birthday last year. "And of course, with our soldiers in the field, we need to be reminded of the fact that war should always be a last resort." Parents, many of whom had sat in silence for the last two hours, grabbed hold of my comments and looked expectantly toward the stage. There was a palpable pregnant pause in the air. "It just made me horny" were the words that broke the emptiness. A diminutive young woman standing in the back looked at me so sincerely—hell, what part had she even played in the production, little tart? Garland turned his cherubic face to me. "What's horny mean, Daddy?" Shit. Parents started leaving. "Ask your mother." Sweating. "Surely you gleaned other themes from the production," I offered hopefully, almost pleading. I was twisting my program in my hands. The stage party was breaking up, following the cue of the now rapidly exiting audience. "Perhaps the play should be read as a commentary on the folly of humanity's inescapable corporeality," postulated the professor I had spoken with earlier. It's official. I hate her.

I had many questions to answer at home. Garland, ever the talker, spilled the entire narrative to his mother. "And that's when the girl said that the whole thing just made her homey." Innocence was never more obnoxious. "Horny," I said. "The word was 'horny.' The play made an eighteen-year-old freshman horny. A Phillips screwdriver would make a typical eighteen-year-old horny. I hardly think this is the college's fault." My wife of nearly twenty years looked at me the same way the prosecutors had surveyed Hermann Göring at Nuremburg. She was unconvinced that the play had been an appropriate place for our son to be. I reminded her of how proud we had been to join the ACLU a couple of years earlier when we heard about the Patriot Act. "Tell that to the trustees." She wasn't smiling. "And tell it to your son's teachers, who will most assuredly be calling when he runs around the elementary school talking about how horny he is. I'm sure there will be no problems whatsoever in rural Georgia if you just say 'ACLU' real loud."

The next morning, my assistant had never sounded more chirpy when she said, "Board chair wants to speak to you on line one." I took a deep breath. "Patch him through." I instinctively adjusted my tie.

"So, Wells, you think it's OK to have penis plays at the college?"

"Well, it's complicated . . . Yes, sir, that's true, but . . . vulgar is a little strong . . . the context. . . . Yes, but . . . You see, John Stuart Mill, you may have heard of him . . . Yes, sir, right, he was English . . . mmm hmmm, nineteenth century . . . Quite right, you speak and I'll listen for a little while . . . I know what you mean, but academic freedom . . . Well, let me put it this way, sir, the theater folks just don't like it when you fuck with their art."

Too Tired to Goosestep

"Dad, I have a question." It really wasn't the time for a question. There is an unspoken rule in my house. Since I went into senior administration, I get the first hour after I come home to sit in my study reading and listening to Miles Davis. It takes at least that much time to recover my bearings and to become a good Christian again. But Garland seemed to be quite concerned, so, pontiff-like, I waved him into my study and granted him an audience.

"What's a fascist?" Well now, this was a good turn of events. I missed the classroom, and any opportunity to discuss political science, even if perfectly random and transitory, was an opportunity that I was going to take. "You see, son, fascism, as a movement, grew out of a hyper-nationalist rejection of liberal modernism. In its Italian variety, Benito Mussolini sought to forge a link between a modern economy and the traditional symbols of Italian society. . . ." I noticed that his eyes were glazing over, but I didn't much care. I was on a roll, and besides, I had always loved my fascism lecture. I blazed forward and actually began to gesticulate as I made my points. "The far more virulent strain of this dark side of twentieth-century ideology originated in Weimar Germany," and that's when I was interrupted. "Why do you suppose Adrian's father would call you a fascist?" I turned my head quicker than the Panzers had torn through the French countryside. "What? Tell me the context." "She said that her father referred to you as a fascist at the dinner table last night. Said they hung Mussolini upside down at a gas station."

Adrian's father worked at the college as a member of the faculty. He had heard the rumors, no doubt, that the long-term faculty member who had recently announced his retirement had actually been forced out by the administration. One of the great trials of being a college administrator is that the ability of faculty and staff to produce scuttlebutt is far greater than the ability to address each rumor in turn. Otherwise disparate events become linked in elaborate mythological systems that ultimately assign otherwise complex personalities to simplistic roles in a Manichaean struggle between good and evil.

We spent the rest of the evening at the table discussing what it means to be an open-minded person. "Regardless of what people say about you, Garland, you have to have the courage to lead." We talked about the possible origins of Adrian's father's observation. Our conversation ranged far and wide. Other family members, long departed from the table, periodically came back into the room and wondered when we were going to wind up our discussion. We reviewed the list of obscenities that characterized the Third Reich, and we laughed about some of the truly bizarre eccentrics who populate the ranks of higher education.

It occurred to me that talking about the college in this way was actually therapeutic. How delightful to discover that Garland had emerged as such an engaging conversationalist. I had been amazed when my son learned to talk. I marveled when he learned to walk. His sense of humor, so similar to his mother's, brought me endless joy. But that night, I watched as my son developed something far more important than anything before. Perhaps he didn't quite grasp that the isolation of administration sometimes leaves administrators in need of friends to talk to. I am certain that my son saw that for me, a persistent defender of academic freedom and free expression, to be referred to as a fascist drew emotional blood. I tried to hide it. I told myself that this was just part of the job. Time to have a thick skin. My son sat with me that evening and we just talked. He had developed the ability to empathize.

We finally concluded the night by moving into the living room. We were flushed from the laughter and the emotional release of abandoning all professional pretension and openly making fun of some of the professors. As we settled down in the comfort of overstuffed couches, I made the final point that in the interests of a well-functioning democracy, we should avoid inflated rhetoric and view those with whom we disagree as interlocutors and not enemies. By this point, Garland had moved on. Besides, it's boring to camouflage emotional hurt behind high-blown intellectual verbiage. As we scanned the television channels for a good program, we ran across the cable news channel. A perfectly obnoxious commentator was barking at his guest and demanding that he 'fess up as to why he hated America so bad.

Garland gulped his soft drink. I sipped my beer. "My God, what a damned fascist."

Passages

I tried to explain to Garland, now twelve, that moving isn't that bad. He didn't buy it. "I don't want to move. All of my friends are here." I could certainly sympathize. My father had been a Methodist minister, and we moved all the time. "Let me explain it this way, Garland. An academic administrator isn't like faculty. We have to do things in our job that make it difficult to just stay at a place on and on. A provost has about six silver bullets in a gun, and he can't reload. He needs to use those silver bullets to take down the biggest problems he finds at a place, and then he needs to go on to the next place and make it better." I'm not sure he understood it, but he didn't ask many more questions. In fact, he became quite a trooper about moving. The new city we would be moving to is known as a great progressive town, with lots of theater and restaurants. That seemed to have a good effect on Garland's mood.

The farewell events were nice, although I had to admit that had you told me in the heyday of my faculty life that as the departing chief academic officer I would be politely applauded by the faculty but given a long standing ovation from the board of trustees, I don't think I would have believed it. The final weekend before we moved, Garland invited six of his friends to raft down the river with us. We had a grand time. I watched as each of those boys embraced my son at the end of the day and wished him well. That's no small act for an adolescent male. In that sense, I saw my son receive his standing ovation.

As we drove back toward our house, we passed the college. There was the place where I had spent twelve-hour days and many weekends, attended countless meetings, come through tense confrontations, and it was the place where I had known the joy of seeing progress because the tough decisions had been made. My memory flooded with lots of tough days coming home from work that were made better by heading to the movie theater with Garland or simply jumping together on the trampoline in the backyard.

It was time for a new chapter, and the next college was one I had always admired. Garland scarcely seemed to notice as we passed the school. As it faded in the rearview mirror he asked, "Can I have an air soft gun when we move?" He had been asking for one for three years, but I could see him pointing it at his little sister's head. Garland was growing up, though, and sometimes administrators have to learn to say yes for a change. "OK, you've been such a good sport about moving that I think you are mature enough to have one." Garland grinned. And so did I.

A new college and a new air soft gun—time to get ready for some new hair-raising experiences.

A River Runs through It

Queer Theory and Fatherhood

JOSEPH GELFER

"Go on, let him suck your oo-poo."

"No!"

"Why not? Go on, let him try, they're big enough."

"No way, it's too freaky! It crosses the line!"

In our house, oo-poos are breasts—lactating breasts, to be exact. Each of the children has used a different name for them. For Magnus, our third, they are oo-poos. My wife, Amanda, is pretty tired of having hers sucked dry. It's January-in-Australia-hot and I'm shirtless on the couch holding Magnus, and it must be said that without casting a particularly vain pose, my less-than-muscular chest does appear to have oo-poos, albeit rather hairy ones. Magnus looks at my oo-poos, half interested in a flush of youthful optimism, yet well aware that the poor excuse facing him will probably not deliver the milky goods. The thing is, it shouldn't freak me out, but it does. The idea of suckling Magnus just feels, well . . . unnatural, unmanly. For someone who frames a good deal of his research with queer theory, this should not be the case.

So I'm one of the relatively few straight men in the world who uses queer theory. Even with other academics I often have to start off with its potted history: that while born out of lesbian and gay studies, queer theory can be applied to pretty much anything when we understand it to simply be about troubling categories. In my work on masculinities and religion I happily use queer theory all the time: Eve Kosofsky Sedgwick, Judith Butler, Judith Halberstam, I've had them all. Among theological texts I've enjoyed indecent smells with Marcella Althaus-Reid, tumescent penises with Donald Boisvert, and an array of circular group activities with the Radical Faeries. I truly believe in the value of all these things for all men, gay and straight, in the value of troubling what it means to be a man, and not just for the boring sake of subversion. But here I am, freaked out by the prospect of putting my oo-poo to Magnus's mouth. It's probably the first time something has challenged my identity as a man and a father. Having my nipples tweaked by a handsome man in a club? Hey, not a problem. Contemplating three-way dynamics while reading *Michael Tolliver Lives*: Who doesn't? But Magnus on my oo-poo? That's a toughie.

I don't doubt for a minute that most guys have these thoughts, but I'm sure researching masculinities puts an extra spin on the matter. Often as I examine my motivations for my manly and paternal decision-making I frame them by what I know in the literature and contemplate how critical I'd be about my actions if I were analyzing them in someone else. Sometimes I'm happy with my findings, other times I'm not. I'm left to wonder how many of my words are just words that I can easily afford to offer and what—if anything—is genuinely queer about the way I do masculinity and fatherhood. Is it queer to live in a four-bedroom house in Melbourne's western suburbs? Not really. Is it queer to trundle off to work every day on the train while my wife drives the children to school? Not at all. But I do create queer spaces on the page, which I enjoy all the more for the veneer of normativity that my ostensible life provides.

But, you know, creating these queer spaces is a lot of work. It takes many hours at the library, introspective walks, much finger-tapping of the keyboard. Here's the twist with this particular game: Committing to research into masculinities and fatherhood can often require so much time that there is little left to perform your own masculinity and fatherhood. You might find, for example, that you are on the computer writing a creative nonfiction essay about being an academic father rather than being out in the chaos of the family room actually *being* an academic father, despite the fact that the amount of noise out there is making it blindingly obvious that you *should* be out there. . . .

And then you might find yourself playing a little justification game in your head, which claims that despite the fact that you're not doing much of a job in terms of being a *real* father right at this moment, the work being done instead contributes to the greater good of fatherhood. It's not like I'm reading the newspaper in here, folks! Fatherhood as an abstract concept is surely winning here, even if the more immediate environment is not!

And then no doubt in x years' time one of my children will out me in a creative nonfiction essay about being the child of a masculinities researcher. S/he will say how boring it is to have people assume it must be great to have a father who thinks so much about what it is to be a man, but how, in fact, it is just the same as being the child of a clerk at a finance company, except finance company clerks don't shuffle their bits of paper on weekends and public holidays.

But, I will reply in defense, those bits of paper are just so *important*. I've been giving birth to and organizing those bits of paper for almost the same length of time I've known you children. Benedict, our oldest, was three years old when I started my PhD. I was a couple of chapters into the process by the time Ivy, our second, was born. I published the first edition of the journal I founded a few weeks after the birth of Magnus, our youngest. Indeed, those bits of paper are *just like* you children: the endless hours invested, the letting loose into the world, the identity and momentum gathered outside my direct control.

This morning I was correcting the proofs of my new book, which I've been working on across all your lives: a PhD proposal, research notes, various drafts, a submitted dissertation, a book proposal, a manuscript revised and submitted, the copy editor's queries addressed. This modest 635 KB PDF proof, 240 pages of time with me sitting on this side of the door and you on the other. And all the things you did during the evolution of those pages: the scraped knees, hysterical laughter, tyrannical shrieking, unauthorized hair-cutting, precious-object destroying, art production, baking of cakes and cookies, construction of cubby houses. I might not have been as engaged as I could have been, but I *was* listening (let's be honest, with you on the other side of the door it was hard not to). In many ways you informed that work: You provided its soundtrack, kept it grounded, functioned as a bridge between the world and the page.

And perhaps it is to a bridge that the academic work is best likened. On this side of the river I am a regular guy, not thinking too much about masculinity and fatherhood, just doing what appears to come "naturally"; but, just like masculinity and fatherhood, the natural is a social construct subject to all the limitations of its conditioning. On the other side of the river is a different way of doing things: where fatherhood is informed, relationships more equal, and, most importantly, children better served. The academic work is the bridge to get to the other side: The theory and critical thinking provide a path to follow, and the bridge allows me to look down on the river from a suitable height. But, ultimately, I have to get off the bridge to reach the other side, to walk on the far bank where fatherhood is framed by a broader and sunnier horizon.

The door of the computer room has just opened, and Ivy is staring through the three-inch crack.

"Daddy, it's almost time for dinner, so you have to come out now, OK?"

"OK, sweet pea, I'm just going to finish up here."

She's heard that one before and looks unconvinced: "I'll just leave the door open, OK?"

I really had better go.

On Writing and Rearing

DAVID HAVEN BLAKE

We have two computers and three papers due.

My essay on nineteenth-century poetry is already weeks late. My daughter has to write five paragraphs responding to Ferde Grofé's *Grand Canyon Suite*. Her fifth-grade teacher wants to know, from "Sunrise" to "Cloudburst," what each movement makes her feel. My son has seven pages to cover the history of comedy, starting with *Lysistrata* and ending with *Seinfeld*. We have to marshal our time carefully.

Like a general sending battalions into battle, I pace from room to room checking the family's progress. "How many pages have you written?" "What is your argument?" "How many paragraphs since we last talked?" "Do you need to use the same phrase in three consecutive sentences?" On this rainy Sunday afternoon, I harass my children with questions, urging them to finish their work. My wife, whose profession involves unusual patience and listening, wisely escapes to the gym. By 3:00 P.M., the burdens of language, law, and patriarchy have left me very tense.

My own dissatisfactions loom over my children's prose. I have been staring at my notes since Friday, and my progress has been slow. For all the harangues about getting work done, about finishing those essays up, my sentences have been coming out as if they were the last smidgen of toothpaste in a meticulously rolled-up tube. As the rain comes down, I realize how central writing is to the man I have become—this father, professor, hypocrite.

When it comes to fatherhood, I am not a reflective practitioner, and I spend little time thinking about the different roles one can play in a child's life. Fatherhood, to me, is an unqualified commitment and an unexamined fact. It is making sure the lunches are ready, the carpools arranged, the schedules de-conflicted so we can attend the fifth-grade concert. It is keeping track of how long the kids are on the Internet and asking why the browser always closes when a parent walks in the room. It is quizzing my daughter on electrical circuits and stumbling through geometry with my son.

To put it bluntly, fatherhood means little to me in terms of ceremony and myth. I am neither the diminished patriarch searching for his Promise Keepers nor the pious, introspective New Age dad. Being an academic has given me the flexibility to care for sick children, volunteer in classrooms, and prepare snacks after school, but the last parenting guide I picked up was *What to Expect: The Toddler Years*.

To the extent that these blessings have gone unexplored, I also recognize how much my experience of fatherhood has to do with writing, with articulation, with seeking the right words. In my neighborhood, some fathers have massive workshops and teach their children how to handle tools. Others have shrines to the New York Yankees and throw batting practice for hours after work. One neighbor has a music collection that lines his basement walls; he and his children jam on the instruments he has scattered about the room.

For better or worse, my daughter and son associate our relationship with language, with the delights of books, newspapers, magazines, lyrics, the repartee on television shows. My head can be halfway inside the dryer, my arm grasping at some elusive sock, and my son will stand directly behind me and begin to read a favorite passage from a book. How can I find this frustrating when he has seen me do relatively the same thing hundreds of times before?

I come by this mode of parenting naturally. I am an academic father whose father is an academic as well. My grandfather taught eighth-grade Latin and English in a small K–8 school. His sons sent letters home from college, and he promptly sent them back, each blunder carefully marked with an editor's red pencil. Retiring after more than twenty years as headmaster, he wrote a history of his town and a history of his school. He edited the town newsletter with my grandmother's help.

One summer vacation, my grandfather greeted my sisters and me at the New Jersey shore with the promise of a ten-dollar bill for each of us. For the next two weeks, every stylistic error we committed would result in a small fine—say, five cents for answering a question with "Yeah" or "Yup," ten for saying "How come?" rather than "Why?" I left with $5.65. In the envelope containing the depleted cash, my grandmother had lovingly drawn a sinking ship, the targeted errors depicted as cargo falling to the ocean floor.

At the University of Pittsburgh, my father worked in the Cathedral of Learning, a Gothic Revival skyscraper forty-two stories high. With its vaulted archways, hidden alcoves, and cavernous common room, the Cathedral suggested that university life was profoundly old and mysterious, especially when its elaborate nationality rooms—Polish, Hungarian, Greek, Italian, Chinese, Russian among them—were beautifully decorated for the holiday season. The Gothic architecture provided an unusual setting for the burgeoning youth culture of the late 1960s and early 1970s. I remember being nine or ten and marveling at all the long-haired "hippies" who quietly studied amid the settled medieval gloom.

Several years later, my father allowed me to explore Pitt's campus while he taught class. The university catalog often featured photographs of students talking or reading underneath the trees that lined the Cathedral lawn. I especially admired the pictures of students who managed to read while stretched on a branch six feet off the ground. Holding my copy of *The Catcher in the Rye*, I scrambled into tree after tree, but each time I opened the book, I'd lose my balance and fall down. Eventually I wandered to the Soldiers and Sailors Memorial, a less bucolic setting, but one equally picturesque. I straddled one of the cannons that faced Fifth Avenue and several hours later happily finished the book. My reward for completing this rite of passage was that I walked like a cowboy for the next three days.

My most powerful memory of growing up in an academic household comes from the tenth grade. I was showing my dad a social studies paper. It was May, the windows were open, the room smelled like dogwood trees. As we talked in my parents' bedroom, he slowly took his pencil through phrase after phrase, cutting unnecessary words, turning nouns into adjectives, eliminating clichés. I admired the improvements, his explanations even more. Within six months, however, my parents were divorcing; within a year my father was living in another state. I had little motivation to make such revisions myself.

It wasn't until my sophomore year of college that this moment became meaningful. I had turned in an especially clotted history paper, and my professor asked to see me for tutorial work. Sitting in his office, he took his pencil through my sentences and showed me how to tighten phrase after phrase. He watched as I revised a paragraph he had mercifully left unmarked. The scene in the bedroom came rushing back, and I felt terrible shame.

Academia does not have the same mystery for my children as it did for me. My office is in a former dormitory rather than a towering cathedral.

The students who intrigued me in the 1970s helped de-formalize the academic world, opening campuses to children, the elderly, people of differing backgrounds and abilities. Perhaps because my children spend so much time at my college, they have come to regard it as their own. And in the contemporary version of fatherhood, my son and daughter are accustomed to seeing professional life occur inside the home. Work seems less an ancient paternal retreat than the silent activity between household chores. Syllabi, course proposals, student e-mails requesting help, these things are as common in my children's lives as salad spinners and dish soap.

No one in my family has seen me teach, but everyone has seen me grade. Throughout their lives, my kids have observed the peculiar combination of adrenaline and dread with which I greet a stack of papers. I have graded in the hallways outside ballet lessons and in the stands of baseball and softball games. Over the years, I have learned to use my clipboard as a shield, warding off the parents who arrive at four-hour swim meets with nothing to read. I nod, I smile, I wave my clipboard, and in that gesture, I convey both territory and difference. *You've got your BlackBerry. I've got my grading. I am an academic dad.*

Sometimes my son or daughter will take an interest in my markings. They will read over my shoulder on an airplane or ask what all the comments mean. Once I found a master's thesis on the marketing of *Harry Potter* poking from underneath the couch where my daughter had left it. As we talk about my comments, I am struck by how repetitive and yet difficult writing instruction is. Topic sentences, citing evidence, the use of subordinate clauses—my children and their classmates are already familiar with the concepts that they will spend their lives trying to master.

Unlike my grandfather, I don't mark my students' papers with red pencil, let alone the letters my son faxes home from camp. Having retired to the faculty after several generations as dean, my father soldiers on in his belief that he isn't really doing his job if he isn't vigorously amending each error his students make. Only when pressed for time will I write on my children's essays, and even then, my marks tend to be a series of squiggles and question marks that indicate *Take another look*. We much prefer to sit in front of the computer together. I read the sentences out loud and ask how they can be improved. Inevitably the kids will get the phrasing right if they trust the fluency of conversation rather than the formality of the keyboard.

As an academic father, I have to resist the inclination to view my kids' writing as an extension of myself. This detachment is hard enough with students; it can be nearly impossible with my kids. My father and grandfather introduced me to a world in which writing and speaking well signified good character. That lesson—or perhaps it is a kind of faith—probably set me on course to become an English professor. After fifteen years of teaching, however, I have learned that writing doesn't convey character as much as it produces identity. The voice created on the page (or screen) has its own claim to reality, its own role in the writer's developing life. As the printer chirps with fresh new pages about Grofé and Larry David, it is a role that the editor in me must learn to respect.

Parenting, like writing, depends on the slow and iterative process of arranging values, words, and ideas into independent, synchronized beings. Call it the syntax of sons and daughters, the grammar of incipient selves. Writing may be an act of perpetual becoming, but like rambunctious kindergartners, we academic parents struggle to keep our hands to ourselves.

In his achingly perceptive poem "For Julia, in the Deep Water," John N. Morris describes watching his daughter learning how to swim. From the deep end, the parents watch the instructor steadily back away as Julia thrashes toward her. The girl screams for her mother, but the mother remains anxious in the distance, the place where the water is deeper and darker. "She is doing nothing," Morris writes. "She never did anything harder."

Such is the trial, such the blessing of academic fathers.

Doing Things with Words

IRA L. STRAUBER

As an academic, I am trained to do things with words. Indeed, that is an understatement: Perhaps I am an academic because the only work I can do is work with words. My self-identity is shaped by my reactions to my words, and to the words of others. In the dynamic between the two, at the end of each day, I ask myself how my words have performed on my behalf and how I have performed on their behalf. Most days, the self-report is not so good. Nevertheless, because I love the sound of my own words, as much as I let them down, I get an ineffable pleasure in persisting with the only tool I have.

As a parent, I have been trained to do things with words. These last words need some explaining. I am the middle, first male child of a German-Jewish father. That means that I am, as my older sister reported, an only child. My most vivid childhood memories are of a dinner table where the conversations were dominated by exchanges between my father and me: exchanges about school, about sports, about what I was reading, about what I was thinking, about me. Today this memory now makes me sad for my sister and departed younger brother; yet it does nothing to diminish my self-identity as a loved son whose reactions to the world were shaped by the dynamic between my father's words and mine. My father's words performed very well on my behalf, and as a parent it seems that I measure myself by how well my words perform on behalf of my daughter. Here too I get an ineffable pleasure in persisting with the only tool I have, even as my words inevitably let me down.

However, I am confident that my words as a parent have succeeded far better than my words as a "scholar." On either account, I am not being overly modest. I have had my share of academic accolade. But virtually every day, even, when, inevitably, my words as a parent have been less or worse than I would have liked, those words have been an ineffable pleasure.

Indeed, my daughter's very existence depended on words: First the discouraging words of doctors in Iowa and on Long Island about the limited possibility of there ever being a child. Then the words on a prescription bottle, and the words of her mother reporting that crucial time when it was just the right body temperature so that there might be a possibility to counter those discouraging words of doctors. Her birth, then, is owed to words, and her infancy was literally shaped by words.

Despite my sister's "enduring" a childhood when I was an only child, she too learned the lesson of her father's words. Soon after Alison was born (which in September 2009 was thirty years ago) my sister said to me, "Don't ever use baby words with Alison" and "Talk to her all the time." Because I am an academic, and Susan is an academic, we took those words to heart, and from infancy talked to Alison as if she could understand us. We did this not in order to "teach her anything" (that was the goal behind no baby talk) but rather because it was a way of expressing our ineffable gratitude for having a child. Our words were a compliment to physical contact with her.

Of course, "saying cannot always make it so," and, worse, sometimes saying can make it so in the wrong way even when the intentions are ostensibly good. So naturally there have been many injuries, large and small (which escape attention but are no less injurious for that). The larger injuries have served as red flags for the extent to which words have gone wrong or have failed to make it so. When Alison was three she started showing precocious signs of beginning to read, and each night as I read to her I encouraged her to read some by herself. Whether this was more for me than for her is for others to say, and it was said. One day I went to pick Alison up from preschool, and the teacher (whom I had previously admonished for being more concerned with social development than cognitive skills) took me aside to report that whenever I appeared at the school Alison would stutter, and that Alison would only stutter around me. I had noticed that Alison had been stuttering, but had passed it off as just a developmental stage.

My initial reaction, as I recall it, was to think of myself as a failed parent. I don't recall any longer how or why I unreasonably and perhaps unconsciously repressed that thought. But I did repress it, and replaced it with the thought, consistent with the fact that as an academic the only thing I can do is do things with words, that it was my overaggressive attempt to have Alison read that caused the stuttering. I stopped trying to have her do things with the words of her storybooks and returned to reading to her, and, coincidentally or not, the stuttering stopped. By four she started reading on her own, full sentences from books she would pull from the library shelf, but the evening dynamic of my reading to her continued throughout grade school. The words of her teacher, and Alison's stuttering, had taught me my first lesson about words not performing well.

In the third grade (maybe fourth?), I picked Alison up from school and she was upset. A substitute teacher, she reported, had asked all the students to stand up and, in turn, to say what church they went to. I recall thinking such a thing to be altogether bizarre, and that perhaps Alison was mis-reporting what happened. Alison went on to say that when her turn came she did not stand "because I don't go to church" (Alison was good with words and appreciated that a synagogue was not a church). She reported that another student (a Quaker) followed her lead. Alison said that she wrote a note to the teacher explaining why she did not stand, but that the teacher refused to take the note and told Alison she was "disobedient." Alison, good with words, understood that she had been disobedient, but she also thought that those written words of hers had justified her disobedience.

After hearing her story, but not her words, but rather only hearing the words in my German-Jewish tutored head, I told Alison something about the teacher not having intended to do any harm and to just forget about it. In effect, don't draw attention to us as Jews, and the problem will go away. I was satisfied with my words. That night, Alison was unusually quiet, even sullen (actually, she has always been quite good at the sound of sullen silence, something that distresses her mother more than me). The next day, when I picked Alison up from school, one of her teachers met me to report that Alison had refused to speak to anyone all day long and to ask whether something was wrong at home. Of course, there was nothing wrong at home, and there was everything wrong at home: Her father had failed to hear her words and had silenced her as the substitute teacher had silenced her.

As we walked home I thought of myself as a Jew in Germany, having buried my head to the reality around me. That night over dinner, I repeated my words about the teacher not intending to do any harm because I did not want to undermine Alison's confidence in teachers or her sense of security in school. But as we talked, although I don't recall what was said, it was apparent that that confidence and security had been eviscerated. Alison, who loved school, reported that she would not go back. Our response was that the next day we would go to school with her and talk to the principal, and then we would see what to do next. I feared the next day, because in many respects this was still all about me, and about having to say that as a

Jew, my child had not followed the substitute teacher's instruction to report what church she went to.

As I recall it, the principal reported that some other parents had complained about the incident. I do not recall anything else that the principal said, except that she told Alison that she would speak to all of Alison's teachers about the incident. Alison, because she was obedient, agreed to stay in school that day. At the end of the day, one of her teachers met me and reported that all the teachers agreed that Alison could stay silent until she was comfortable speaking again. It was some good number of weeks before that happened: Alison's confidence in teachers and security at school ultimately returned to normal. But the words of the substitute teacher had taught her a lesson about her self-identity—that she was Jewish and different and could be punished for it—that became a permanent part of her identity. And the wrong words of her father had taught her that she could not always depend on me to protect her. When Alison returned from her first summer at Camp Ramah (a Jewish summer camp run under the auspices of the Conservative Jewish movement) she reported that one of the things she liked about it most was that "I don't have to explain who I am."

Yet, of course, we always have to explain who we are, to others and to ourselves. Alison is an adult now. She is writing her doctoral dissertation (in art history, which is her mother's field). Now that she is an adult we are always exchanging words, always trying to explain who we are to each other, who we are to others, who we are to ourselves. We always have words. My dinner table has been replaced by virtually daily exchanges by cell phone, Skype, and e-mail. My desks on campus and at home have framed birthday and Father's Day cards with Alison's words inside them.

There is no gap between who I am as an academic and as a parent. I have selfishly replaced my father's role with myself in a dynamic between my words and my daughter's words. Frankly, her words, both academic and personal, are better than mine. But, as I have told her since she was small, ultimately it is not her accomplishments that make me proud: "I am proud of you because you are you." Perhaps my words have been good enough for her, because despite my words gone wrong, her best words for me are always "I love you."

On Fecundity, Fidelity, and Expectation

Reflections on Philosophy and Fatherhood

J. AARON SIMMONS

On Fecundity

I am thirty-two years old, I have had my PhD for over three years, and, as yet, I don't have a tenure-track job. To complicate things further (as of June 2009), my wife is six months pregnant with our first child—a son that is going to be named John Atticus Simmons (we will call him Atticus). The countdown to D-Day has begun, and I am not sure whether to attempt to avoid the event by ducking and covering or to charge the beachhead in protest.

The two things that I have heard more times than I can count over the past six months are "Congratulations" and "Everything is going to change." Every time I hear either of these comments I just want to reply: "Congratulations? Am I somehow praiseworthy because my biological functions work? Do I deserve laudation simply because I can do what frogs, trees, and viruses can do—namely, reproduce?" Moreover, and this is crucial, I don't want things to change! At least not in this way. I am still working myself to the bone to land that coveted (and, I am beginning to believe, fictitious) stable academic position that allows sufficient time for research while not eliminating the joys of teaching. OK, OK. Stop laughing. I know that I might as well be seeking the gold at the end of the rainbow, but there are really good reasons that I was willing to go ridiculously in debt, spend seven years in graduate school, twice interrupt my wife's career, etc. Simply put, I *love* doing philosophy. I don't want to do anything that will interfere with this. So, to all of my well-meaning family, friends, and colleagues: "Stop telling me what I already know and am overwhelmingly terrified of." For the first four months (until my wife rather vigorously told me to stop) I was responding to the expression of "Congratulations" with "I will pass

59

your congratulations on to my wife. But at the present time, I am only accepting condolences." No one thought that was funny. Sigh.

There are two main reasons that I continue to struggle with the whole idea of being a father—one is ethical and the other is, following the nineteenth-century Danish philosopher Søren Kierkegaard, religious. First, I feel like having a child actually causes me to potentially fail in my responsibility to my own parents (specifically my father). Second, I feel like having a child also might cause me to fail in my duty to God to remain faithful to the philosophical task that defines my life. I will consider each in turn and then try to conclude this essay without causing my wife to leave me if she reads this and my son to have to go to therapy when he is my age.

The Ethical Concern

My father is an art professor. Some of my earliest memories are of sitting in the back of his college classes with my own easel and paint. Surrounded by university students, I would not pay much attention to the particular still life that was placed carefully on the table at the front of the class, but instead would wander into my own world of imaginative fantasy and paint dragons, purple tigers (shouldn't all tigers be purple?), and flying cars. When I was about seven years old, my little sister was diagnosed with cancer, and seemingly simultaneously the Art Department faculty were all cut from the particular university where my father was employed (due to university financial problems). For the next ten years, my father did everything from working construction to delivering newspapers in order that my family would always be provided for. To this day, I find it hard to imagine the psychological and emotional difficulty that my father must have faced in moving from a tenured position in a studio art department to painting the interior walls of a new gas station. Thankfully, after ten years, my father eventually was restored to his tenured position and has for the past decade been able to get back to his passionate engagement with the life of the mind and the eye of beauty. If only I were able to sit in the back of his classes again and spend some time painting purple tigers . . . (*insert appropriate sound of tortured longing here*).

What I continue to find to be so remarkable about my dad is that throughout the years of struggle, I never once heard him complain or curse his state (which stands in frequent contrast to my own comments about the academic job market . . . Arrrggghhhh!). Part of my own resistance to having children is, I think, connected to what I perceive to have been my own father's sacrifices for my well-being (and the well-being of my three siblings). What my dad was willing to do was to put his own happiness on hold in order to provide for his family. I am sure that he never actually enjoyed delivering a newspaper at 3:30 A.M. and then after a couple hours of sleep getting back up at 7:00 A.M. to go paint the new suite being added onto the neurosurgeon's house across town. That is certainly not why he spent so much time in graduate school. That is certainly not why he spent so many hours in the studio perfecting his skill. And yet, when life presented him with obstacles, his own career was something that he was willing to lay aside in order to do whatever was required to eventually open the most doors for whatever careers his children would decide to pursue.

So here is the thing: I know that when Atticus arrives I will also love him so much that I would likewise sacrifice my own status and success in order to maximize whatever opportunities I can for his own status and success. Isn't this precisely what it means to love someone more than yourself? Well, knowing this fact about myself, I feel like I would be somehow letting down my own father if as a result of having a child I were to not achieve what it is that he sacrificed his own career in order to make possible for me. (I should note that after reading an early draft of this essay, my dad wanted me to make clear to anyone else who would eventually read it that his sacrifice was not just for me but also for my children and their children, etc. Rather than seeing this as something that eliminates my feeling of obligation to somehow live up to his sacrifice, however, I actually think that it heightens the duty to take it even more seriously.)

It seems odd, doesn't it, that so many parents spend years scrimping and saving in order that their children are able to go do something great, and then along the way the children get married and have kids and then have to spend years scrimping and saving in order that their children can go to something great, but then the children get married and have kids . . . *and on it goes.* Is there anything wrong with wanting to actually bring my parents' work to fruition? In this case it is not that I am being selfish, but that I am actually taking seriously the seriousness with which my own father took my own life. The problem with having children is that it requires your own future to now be supplanted with a concern for someone else's. My worry is that in this case it actually turns out to be an ethical failure precisely because in caring for my child I fail to respect my father's care for me.

The Religious Concern

My wife says that everything is more complicated because I have a PhD in philosophy. I spend my days (and nights) reading, writing, thinking, and teaching about the nature of obligation, the phenomenon of responsibility, the specifics of moral and political relationships, etc. Though there might be some philosophers who are able to bracket their inquiry from their own existential situations, I cannot. Thinking about having a child is not simply a consideration of financial ability, marital stability, and emotional maturity. It is also something that involves the very nature of one's subjectivity. What is it that I am supposed to do during my time on this earth? Is having a child something that is consistent with this purpose? To make things even more troubling, I specialize in existentialism and phenomenology—both are philosophical trajectories that focus on the lived context in which inquiry occurs. You can't get outside of existence to question existence. Kierkegaard struggled with what it means to be an existent self devoted to the life of the mind and the well-being of others. For Kierkegaard, this meant that he would break off an engagement with the one love of his life (Regine Olsen) in order to singularly pursue what he took to be his life's task—the call to do philosophy (which he understood as a profoundly "religious" task of "bringing Christianity to Christendom"). As he understood it, this call to philosophy was tantamount to God's plan for his life. To do something that distracted him from this calling was to fail to completely follow God's will. Kierkegaard thought that a person could only will one thing with her whole being. As he put it, "Purity of heart is to will one thing." It is kind of like a tennis player who refuses to play racquetball because it would interfere with her tennis game. Being married was, for Kierkegaard, something that necessarily interrupted his singular focus on the call of God. In a very literal way, then, fecundity was a central concern of his thought. For Kierkegaard the birthing process of philosophical inquiry was one that required him to forgo being a parent to an actual flesh-and-blood child (or even to be in a committed relationship with Regine). Yet, as my students often point out— who wants to live a life as isolated and as troubled as Kierkegaard's? A model of a well-rounded life Kierkegaard is not!

The question is how to remain faithful to one's calling while also living a full and fulfilled life. Or, to be more specific, how do I become a devoted father without lessening my devotion to the life of the mind?

On Expectation and Fidelity

When wrestling with the ethical and religious concerns that I have outlined above, I find myself constantly returning to the notion of expectation. While my wife is "expecting" the baby, I am also presently defined by the expectation of what her being "expectant" will yield. I exist now in a constant relationship to the projected due date of October 15. But, one might say, anyone who has read the work of Martin Heidegger knows that to exist is to stand in a complicated relationship to one's future. So, with the above concerns in place, here is the way that I have begun to reconcile my identity as a philosopher with my identity as an expectant father.

To be now is to live toward the not-yet. It is here that I think the possible way forward opens for me. To think that philosophy is something that requires living a certain kind of life is to forget that philosophy is a way of living life itself. To intentionally avoid an event like becoming a father out of fear that one would have to stop being a philosopher (or at least stop being as focused or serious a philosopher) is to fall prey to the temptation to make philosophy what so many of my friends think it is—abstract navel gazing that really doesn't amount to much except anxiety that we would be well to do without. My philosophical career has been devoted to exploring the lived engagement that a self encounters in a world of relationships to others. Wow, perhaps in worrying about becoming a father I actually fail to live up to the demands of my own inquiry! Could that be right?

Being singularly committed to the life of the mind is only something that can conflict with fatherhood if the life of the mind could be detached from the bodily engagement with one's historical, social, and familial space. Since such a detachment is a fictitious holdover from the notion of a modern worldless subject, it is something that should be avoided. To think that being a philosopher interferes with being a father (or mother) or that being a father (or mother) interferes with being a philosopher is to misunderstand philosophy and the context in which it happens. Philosophy is not a static thing; it is a way of being-engaged. This being-engaged is always a lived relationship to one's history and one's future. To be is to be-expectant! In this way, my religious concern with fatherhood is more appropriately recognized as a temptation to make philosophy something that it is not— namely, something that requires detachment from life.

Alain Badiou argues that real ethical life happens in one's commitment to remain faithful to those events that give meaning to one's life. Returning to my ethical concern with fatherhood, what would it mean to "remain faithful" to my own father's devotion to my well-being? It seems clear to me that what my father was willing to sacrifice for was my happiness and not a specific outcome of my professional career. As such, to worry that I somehow fail in my responsibility to him by having a child is to miss the point of his own devotion to me. The "event" to which I must remain faithful is my father's expression of selflessness. I show fidelity to this event by committing myself to my own son while continuing to passionately inhabit the philosophical life. Importantly, my dad did not choose to leave his academic position in order to sacrifice for me. He simply decided that his specific situations, whether positive or negative, would not interfere in his commitment to his children. That is an "event" of charity that deserves my respect and emulation. I hope my own relationship to Atticus will invite such fidelity from him.

Kierkegaard, Meet Atticus

I am not (yet!) tenure-track. Professional success is something that continues to stand as a goal rather than an achieved reality. Yes, I am still concerned about losing sleep and not making publication deadlines. But I am a philosopher and I am going to be a father. I have decided that this need not be seen as a logical contradiction or a professional obstacle. It might even prove to be an opportunity to really live the philosophical truth that I advocate.

Kierkegaard said somewhere that happy people don't write poetry. I guess that depression often makes for good rhetoric. Well, while I certainly don't think that someone should have a child just in order to philosophize about the experience, perhaps philosophy has for too long been written by those who use it as an excuse not to live rather than as an invitation to be fully reflective and intentional about the lives that they do live.

I continue to be frustrated by the idea of being congratulated for expecting a child, and I continue to struggle with the notion of "everything changing," yet I have decided that it is the philosophical task itself that calls me to be the best father that I can be, and vice versa. Of course, I still want to be professionally successful and land that job at the end of the rainbow, but, whether or not that happens, philosophy and fatherhood both demand more than any tenure committee could ever expect. The task of living up to the calling of each (as intimately connected) is what jointly defines my future.

Maybe I will begin sending search committees a picture of Atticus along with my dossier . . . hmmmm.

A Postscript on the Other Side of D-Day

So, we didn't quite make it to October 15. On September 29 at 3:11 P.M. (which is unbelievably cool considering that I had been playing music by the band 311 for Atticus while he was in the womb), Atticus was born. Everyone who read this essay in early draft forms said something on the order of "Oh, Aaron, just you wait until he is born. Your entire perspective will change." Well, with two weeks of fatherhood under my belt, I can assuredly say that they were all wrong. Having only averaged two to three hours of sleep a night for the past two weeks, I was right to worry about the loss of sleep, the piling up of work, and the very real possibility of missed publication deadlines. That said, both of the above concerns I outline are still real issues for me even now. Nonetheless, every time I hold Atticus I realize that my task as a philosopher is not only "intimately connected" with my responsibilities as a father but actually now *includes* my obligation to do whatever I can to maximize his opportunities and happiness. My emphasis prior to Atticus's arrival was on the disjunction of philosophy *or* fatherhood. It has now shifted to the conjunction of philosophy *and* fatherhood. Quite a bit hangs on this shift. Because of this adjustment of emphasis, I have begun to better understand my own father's willingness to do what he did relative to my own future. Well, this understanding and empathetic identification occurs as long as I hold Atticus between 9:00 A.M. and 10:00 P.M. At 2:30 in the morning, not much philosophizing is happening; just a bunch of pleading with God to help him go to sleep.

Sheathing the Sword

GREGORY ORFALEA

That "Jabaly temper." When I was a boy, reference to that overseas distant mountain anger was a source of cold whispers. If someone like my father or his sister Adele blew their stack, or stomped out of the room, we would all think, "Oh boy, that Jabaly temper."

My grandmother Nazera, father's mother, was the Jabaly, from the Arabic word for mountain, *jebal*—she was a mountain woman with all the toughness that phrase implies, from the town of Zahle, on the edge of the Mount Lebanon massif. And although Nazera married one of the mildest men I have ever known—Aref Senior, the handsome, powder-white-faced Syrian who rarely uttered a word—the "Jabaly temper" filtered itself into two of the six Orfalea children, including my father, Aref Junior, who otherwise was a man of generosity, warmth, and love.

I had then and have now nothing but love remembering my father, but on more than one occasion, he scared me. The worst was sparked by an argument over the Vietnam War—which my father ultimately opposed—that escalated sophomorically when I mocked my mother's attitude toward marijuana. My father jumped up at the dinner table. He never let anyone speak callously against Mother—at least anyone other than himself—and the chase was on. I actually lifted a chair to hold him off like a lion tamer. At one point he had me pinned against the breakfast room's green-washed cabinets, his fist raised. But he delivered no punch, and we both went off into our shock, me fleeing the house insisting he was crazy, taking refuge at Aunt Jeannette's home three miles away in the Valley. She helped me settle down, fed me a Coke. After a while, she gently convinced me to return home; I snuck in the back door, went to my room, closed the door, and crawled into the covers, ready to sleep at 8:00 P.M.

Soon there was a quiet knock at the door. He came in and sat down in the coming darkness at the end of the bed, near my foot. For a while, nothing was said. Then he spoke in a raw voice. "Gregory, if I ever do anything like that again, you take your sister and brother and Mom and leave me, because I don't deserve you." I was amazed; I threw my covers off and hugged him.

My mother, Rose—a woman with deep emotions but nevertheless great inner balance—seemed to promise the family she had married into a snuffing of the "Jabaly temper" in my generation. It's probably unfair to place the largest inheritance of familial temper on my poor sister, who suffered over a decade from schizophrenia, but with her violent end and my father's, I imagined the "Jabaly temper" had bloomed into its worst flower in America.

I secretly prayed: Maybe now it is over; that temper born in the mountain in Lebanon 120 years ago has finally petered out.

But then I slapped my eldest son. Three times. For saying "fuck" right to my face when he was ten years old. A word I didn't even know at his age. The third time he didn't say it; my slap was too swift. That "Jabaly temper." Feeling it surge up in myself, I felt ashamed, even horrified.

I stopped, apologized, but wondered what would become of it. My wife thought it too late: The dark genie was out of the bottle in yet another generation.

By most yardsticks, our first son was a hard boy to raise. Archly his own person, Matthew could not be told anything about anything. He once slept out in the neighborhood park in protest over—what? It was never certain. Matthew became our family's rebel-without-a-cause. I remember throwing a chair in frustration over his refusal to do something, and his later throwing a small can of paint, which nicked his chest of drawers. By sophomore year of high school, he just stopped studying, and then chose to go off to a boarding school, a temporary solution to our habit of locking horns. Like me, he had had childhood asthma; he was also somewhat injury-prone. His left leg had a perilously short iliotibial band; it had to be cut and stretched in surgery to relieve chronic pain. In addition to this IT band condition, he suffered for many years from a mysterious necrosis of the kneecap from a football injury that didn't get better until his surgeons used a new treatment—drilling three holes into the dead bone to make it bleed and heal. It worked. The surgeons were so jubilant that they gave a talk at Georgetown University Hospital about the novel treatment. Soon he was captain of his varsity basketball team, jumping to the top of the rim with his five feet nine inches.

Bleeding to heal. It's not so original. In the Levant, it may be as old as time. But it did not remove all of Matthew's quirks. Once during a family vacation along with his two brothers, Matt stayed out all night without saying where he was. By noon the next day, I had called the Ocean City Police Department, and they began to search for him. I had visions of Matt being hit over the head with a beer bottle and out somewhere, unconscious, at best. Suddenly, as we were going door-to-door to bungalows near the boardwalk, up walks Matt, a little dazed in the sunlight. He'd been out all night, socializing. What was all the worry about? he sneered.

The "Jabaly temper" began to rise up in me—at first purely verbal.

"We couldn't sleep last night, Matt. We are still responsible for you. Couldn't you have left a little note at the door? Damn it!"

In the knotty pine room of our cottage along the Atlantic, we got into it again.

"I don't give a fuck, man."

"Don't use the F-word to me."

"Why the fuck not?"

Suddenly, we are clamped together at the shoulders, and I am trying to shake him, saying, "Don't use that word again with me!"

As he raises his shoulders, grabbing me, my hands slip toward his neck, which shocks me as much as him. And then it happens. He flings me—for he is now the stronger of the two, stronger than I from lifting weights—and I hit the knotty pine wall and a towel rack, which breaks and cuts my arm on an exposed nail.

Now is the moment.

There's another surge—I can feel it—in my upper right bicep. A squirt of adrenaline. "Hit him," says an ancient voice. "Hit him," urges the squirt. "He is asking for it. Give him what he wants."

Our two younger sons are watching. Their eyes, I see in an instant, are wide, scared, bracing for the worst.

Then a little miracle passes between us.

I don't hit him. Something holds me back. Something as old as the "Jabaly temper," and maybe older, certainly wiser.

I just stand there, shaken, looking at him looking at me. The fight stops.

I look at the younger boys and realize: I cannot do this. If I escalate, I will lose Matt forever, and maybe the two younger ones, too. It will go on and on and on. My righteous anger will get me and them nowhere, all of us in a tangle of thorns. It will ruin us. Doing what comes naturally will ruin us. And I, I who had a chance to break the deadly rhythm, because I am older and should know more, I will be responsible.

I walk out, dazed, feeling the first bud of grace take root in my soul.

◦§ §◦

This encounter, fraught with possible hell, was the corner my son and I had wanted so desperately to turn after two decades of living together. We later offered each other the bread of apology. From that point on, Matt began to trust me again, perhaps for the first time since he was little. We had both sensed in that extreme moment the lasting consequences of revenge. Not all has been roses since then, but we did turn a definable corner toward love, respect, and forbearance, and have since become very good friends indeed. I like to think the other boys, too, were well served by my self-restraint that day in Ocean City.

Although college classes don't really test your physical patience, for the most part, I felt strengthened to tamp down the arrogant repartee (which is anger) toward the student who flops his or her head in ceremonious sleep while I am reading from a difficult text, or breaks out in a fit of crying over a bad grade, or reacts with his own anger to a simple request to rethink, re-research, rewrite. They are young; they are forming; we must help them, not scar them. Not indulgence, but the quietly firm.

Matthew went on in film studies and graduated from college with distinction. Today he is serving as an assistant editor for a long-running, successful television show in Los Angeles. At night he uses his drawing talents to make animated movies.

As for my own animation. The other day, missing the two oldest boys and wanting to be with them in their newfound home of California, I found myself walking by the old swing set at Lafayette Park in our corner of Washington, D.C. I stopped and looked at a young girl swinging by herself in some contemplation, perhaps, of a boyfriend, or an angry mother or father, or perhaps just wondering in the blur where her life was going. And I saw Matt, the year before our dire encounter in Ocean City, swinging in the swing next to the one this young lady was swinging in, trying to establish the *Guinness Book of Records* record for the longest swing in recorded history.

It was his last summer before college, before leaving home for good, and for whatever reason—saying good-bye to childhood, to us, or just the lark of it—he had sought out the Guinness people in London. They told him that no one had ever even attempted such a thing and therefore twenty-four hours straight of swinging would be sufficient for the record.

I relived, that day he was long gone across the continent in his own life, his farewell to us: the endless swinging, his head wrapped in a pirate's scarf of a washcloth, the gathering crowds, the friends who saw him through the night in the park, the guitars, the chess games, the monitor checking off his duty, handing the log on to the next monitor, the nurse who had to be on-site, the neighborhood leader (a priest) who had to sign off on it all, his pit stop for precious minutes every eight hours to hobble to the closest home for urination, the friends swinging alongside him that morning as he moaned quietly in pain, his legs dangling, the day now the hottest of the summer, ninety-eight degrees and as humid as a rain forest in July, except there's no shade, the swings getting down to a bare back-and-forth, the crowds growing, growing to two hundred by noon, cheering for him, saying good-bye to childhood, all of us, good-bye to what we were, saluting it all, the sun and the hill and the blur, adding an extra hour just to be sure, and coming to a stop at twenty-five hours to great thunder under a clear sky.

Nothing marks that swing set on a hill. Nothing marks that knotty pine room overlooking the Atlantic. Nothing but myself in this quiet moment realizing something at last. The swing, the joy of it, is what I saw that day, that day I held back, all of us breathing hard, as if to add a twenty-sixth hour to his record.

PART TWO

Family Made

THE DIFFERENCE OF ALTERNATIVE OR
DELAYED FATHERHOOD

Weighed but Found Wanting

Ten Years of Being Measured and Divided

ROBERT MAYER

Late Fall 2008

With about ten minutes left to my workday, I've got a minor dilemma. Do I try to take on another major project only to just get started, or do I simply sit there and wait for the clock to reach 7:30? After all, this is one of those rare evenings: There are no essays to grade, no texts to review, no thesis statements to critique. The problem is that as my brain starts to take on that decision, the memory of tonight's weather forecast—a clear night without any light from any phase of the moon—teases me into thinking about the chance to dig out the little old telescope and do some searching in the night sky. It's a chance to feed an addiction I've recently acquired, a chance to look into the heart of the sky in a search for those rewarding minute details.

On the other hand, the day has been long, and I'm not sure if I'll be patient enough. After all, the telescope's tripod is tired and wobbly: Once you find your target, you have to step away for a minute for the scope and the tripod to settle down. Otherwise, you have to watch the image shake itself into focus. Sometimes that image settles rather quickly, and sometimes only a moderate amount of patience is needed for the image to come into focus, but other nights, the ability to pick something out just isn't there. Obviously, some nights the process of finding some unique deep sky object can be easy, while other nights it's exhausting.

My attention, however, is turned away from an image settling into focus to a question from someone standing in the hallway just outside the door of my office. The young man asks me where he needs to go to work on his GED with the College of Southern Idaho. I'll simply tell him to go down to the end of the hall, where the GED complex is. My little corner of the Mini-Cassia Center, a satellite campus of the college, is simply a few stops too soon, so I regularly get this question.

There's a little difference this time. As I think back on the times I've been asked for instructions for the GED office and classroom, the average inquiry comes from someone who has needed a few years to realize he or she needs a general equivalency diploma. I'm usually looking at someone around thirty-five to forty, even forty-five, and that's why this young man surprises me. He doesn't have that wizened look that comes from life beating you around for five or six years after dropping out of high school, let alone ten or fifteen. I've taught English composition and literature full-time for seven years, and part-time for another three, and he has that appearance of the type of student who occupies one-half to one-third of my classes. He's eighteen, no older than nineteen, and for some reason, at that moment, my mind concludes almost immediately that he's not twenty. As I think back now, he stands with a sense of confidence or cockiness, depending on my mood and my reader's mood, and his voice suggests no other issues. If he's going to get his GED, it's not because of some hidden, quiet learning disability a high school couldn't handle, or because he knows he has to speak better English. He looks like the "normal" high school kid.

And as he walks away, I sit there for a moment, looking at the space he's just vacated before I slowly turn back to my computer.

Spring 2007, Late April

A friend of mine is a Boy Scout leader. One of the requirements he's working on with his troop involves teaching them about career options, and he's asked me if he can bring them to my office one evening so I can talk to them about my job. The evening we agree on is a particularly important one for my students; they're starting the English 101 Outcomes Assessment process, which crudely summarized is a one-week exit essay that contributes significantly to whether or not they pass the class. On that evening, I take about an hour to distribute the essay assignment and send the students home early.

That gives me time to meet the Scouts. Three of them show up, and the five of us (including the leader) cram into my office. I say cram because it's less than a hundred square feet in area. The room itself isn't ugly, for I've modestly decorated it with posters and pictures, primarily of the outdoors, but the computer and the bookshelf—a good eight feet tall—dominate the room, along with a couple of piles of folders containing student essays. There's also a whiteboard I've put in one corner to help students who visit, but I don't remember what's on it. This is where I prepare to teach 40 to 60 percent of my classes, forty miles or so away from the main campus but just blocks from my own home.

What I do remember, for some reason, is struggling trying to tell these Scouts what I do. It's not the words with which I struggle, but the sensation that a writing-related job, perhaps a teaching-writing-related job, is so foreign to them that we can't seem to bridge the distance between us. In essence, I'm an alien being to them. Even with the help of the leader, there doesn't seem to be a sense that they can acknowledge that what I do is a possible career for them.

Then again, as I try to think about the three faces, I see why. One is going to go to a four-year college, probably a private, selective school. Another might go to this school of mine, the College of Southern Idaho, although that still might be a bit of stretch for his goals.

The third is my eldest son, Terry, three months away from being seventeen. He has spent most of his life struggling to see what education, hard work, and personal discipline have to do with happiness, and his sources of information give him complex and contradictory answers. One side is his adoptive parents, both with graduate degrees, to whom education is everything. A second side consists of both sets of grandparents, to whom hard work is everything. The third side is his biological heritage. His biological parents had a combined IQ of 120, and his biological mother smoked marijuana heavily during pregnancy. To no surprise, complications have arisen from those facts, complications that cause a conflict with the other two sides in his life. His own overall IQ is 82, but his verbal is much higher than his math; during this time we will learn that he has something called auditory processing disorder, which means what is described to him and what he hears through one side of his head are two different matters. It also hasn't helped that his biological father has tried to force his way back into his life, encouraging him to leave us.

After the Scouts and I have finished our conversations and they've gone, I need a few minutes more to close up my office, and then I head home, where Terry is playing on the PlayStation 2. In passing, I try to jokingly inquire about what he thought about the visit. "Boring, huh?" I ask in a bad attempt at wit.

I don't remember the words of the answer. I just remember it was an affirmative. There was no animosity in the answer, but my own sensitivity gleaned no sense of "going along with the joke" from him.

End of a Semester, Either Fall or Spring, Either 1999 or 2000

The Outcomes Assessment results are in, and this leads to a phone call that puts a bit of fear into an adjunct. (I won't be full-time until 2002.) Two exit essays have been deemed suspicious—they're far too well written for the average student—and I am to bring in the students' entire semester's work, opening day writing samples, and Outcomes Assessment rough drafts to determine if these cases were matters of plagiarism. Fortunately, after a quick review, one case is deemed inconclusive, and the other is accepted as the student's writing—with a suggestion that they are impressed with it. This second student came to my class with skills that initially seemed to be more aligned with visual than written composition. Over the course of the semester, he's transferred his ability to create a visual image with charcoal on a sketch pad to composing a mental image with fingers on a keyboard.

I've always made it a point to conference with my students after Outcomes Assessment is over. Instead of delivering results to them as a group, I deliver them individually. Adjuncts have no office, so these individual conferences are held with teacher sitting across from student in an otherwise empty classroom.

When I explain matters to the one whose work was deemed "impressive," he begins to cry. It's not a sob, but that stereotypical image we have of men trying to hold back tears. A hint of tears comes out, and there's a slight crack in his voice. He tells me what our description of his writing means to him. He tells me he thought he was nothing—a failed marriage, no job, the thought of turning to self-medication of misery—and that when he signed up for my class, he feared he would crash because he thought he was a bad writer. Now, however, this label we gave him means hope. This means he could do something right.

Fall 2008

My second son, Zachary, is sixteen months younger than Terry, his brother. He has a much lower IQ than Terry and is, for the most part, in self-contained special education classes; thus, he must have an individualized education plan, better known as an IEP. IEPs require yearly meetings.

In the teachers' lounge of Burley High sit two counselors, the high school football coach, myself, my wife, my three-year-old son, a man from Vocational Rehabilitation, and Zachary's special education teacher, at a long, light brown rectangular table about twelve to fifteen feet in length. The principal will be here in a few minutes. Zachary sits at the end of the table and has been asked by the special education teacher to lead the meeting. He stiffly and nervously goes through the routine he has probably rehearsed with his teacher, turning the meeting over to others as the agenda dictates. For example, the football coach beams when he talks about how hard Zach works in weightlifting class—considerable praise when one considers how the 5′ 8″ Zach weighs no more than 115 pounds, likely caused by a poor start to life that included not only the same factors as his eldest brother's but also prolonged untreated high fevers related to ear infections.

The principal comes in and also praises Zach. The special ed teacher then calls him a leader in the class but also reminds him he can be better, this Special Olympics State Gold Medal Winner in skiing. For example, they have been working on reading and handwriting.

And then the special ed teacher brings up a special program. My employer is helping sponsor a program that allows students like Zach to attend college. These special needs students would take high school classes in the morning, then in the afternoon either work or audit college classes in programs overseen by local school districts to teach basic life and career skills.

Sometime between 2006 and 2008, Semester Unknown

Of the twelve members of the full-time English faculty of the College of Southern Idaho, six have been in the department longer than I have. In terms of age, I am also in the middle.

A department meeting or an informal lunch doesn't come with the rivalry and animosity I keep hearing about in some departments. Granted, we don't always agree, and we certainly all have our different ideas, but there is a sense that we respect each other. Some relationships I have with my colleagues are more than just collegial; some of them are true friendships where feelings—to a degree—can be shared.

For me, the relationship is one where I can turn to my colleagues for ideas, to get input to try new things. When I started as full-time, I got to teach English 102 for the first time. After three years as an adjunct teaching Developmental (090) and Freshman Composition (101), I was now out of my comfort zone and definitely had to rely on my colleagues for ideas about how to teach the class.

A handful of years later I'm sitting at a lunch table with a couple of my colleagues. When I talk about the feelings of inadequacy I had when I first started full-time, and how I still see most of the department as mentors—with either more knowledge or more experience—I get a surprising response from one. She is one of those professors who has let only a little of her experience wear her down. There's indeed a hint of exhaustion, but there's still that sense of energy. She's definitely one of the people I watch when I need a reason to keep going.

"Really?" she asks semi-rhetorically. "I was thinking I wish I had your confidence."

Spring 2009

Sometimes, other full-time faculty get to come down to the Mini-Cassia Center to teach. One such instructor, another one of those I consider to be a mentor, is teaching English 102 at the center this semester. He is frustrated because some students aren't showing up, some aren't meeting deadlines, and some aren't writing well. I am interested, for it is very likely that some of the students I taught are in his class. We go over the class list, and five of my former students are indeed on it. Two have dropped or disappeared, one is excelling, one is doing B work, and the other is inconsistent.

They all are performing as they did when they were my students.

Fall 2008, the Tuesday before Zach's IEP

Just a few months after Terry's eighteenth birthday, the straw finally broke. We were less than two weeks into the school year, and we were getting reports of him being late or missing class. My wife and I thought long and hard about what to do, for he made it very clear what being eighteen meant to him—the potential "freedom" from the tyranny of school and parents. We wanted him to finish, and knew that pressing him as hard as we had in the past might just cause him to leave. He did have that opportunity now that he was eighteen—he could just walk away.

Then on a Tuesday, September 9, I received a call while I was preparing for a night class on British literature. Terry had been suspended for skipping classes, but we had received no official word that he would not be allowed in class Tuesday. When we dropped him off at the intersection in front of the school that morning, he simply waited for us to drive off, and then left the campus. When my wife went to pick him up after the school day was over, his demeanor made her suspicious, and that eventually led to a confession from him: He had split the day between a grocery store parking lot and the home of his biological grandparents.

My wife was now at her breaking point. Earlier that year we had made the options clear to my son: If he wanted to drop out, he either had to get a job or move out. My wife had already tried one other option, spending some time with military recruiters, including the National Guard, who offered a way for my eldest to get his GED. Terry even showed signs of interest in this chance.

And that Tuesday, the hope of him perhaps using the National Guard option flickered again. When my wife called me, she initially said it was time for him to go. I was just about due for a dinner break, and I said I would come home soon to help. She called back in a matter of minutes to say she was trying the National Guard angle and it seemed positive. But when I came home for dinner, he was angrily packing up and moving out to spend the night with a friend. His anger was so obvious and his choice so shocking that I've tried to force another memory into my mind to replace that one as the last thought I have of him in our home. Now, when asked what I last remember about Terry in our home, I think instead of two days before, when he was helping me show Saturn in a telescope to some of our neighbors in our front yard.

He has since lived in six homes and was even abandoned again by his biological father after following him to Pocatello.

Fall 2009

I'm met in the hall of the Mini-Cassia Center by a student from my English 101 class, a woman in her midthirties. She apologizes for missing class: She was at the hospital with her mother, who had been unable to complete English 101 with me the year before due to health concerns then. Now, the doctors think, the mother may have had a heart attack.

Spring 2009

In late fall 2004, we had a surprise. After ten years of marriage and the adoptions of two sons, we learned my wife was pregnant. In May of 2005, Jacob, our youngest, came into the world, but not without troubles. My wife's blood pressure read 220 over 140 the morning before he was born, and hours later she was flown to a neonatal intensive care unit 130 miles away in Ogden, Utah. Fortunately, Jacob was born with no complications, other than a three-week stay in an isolette because he was premature.

Tonight, I'm taking him to a storybook hour at the Burley City Library. For a town of fewer than ten thousand, and a community more focused on providing a survivable income, this library has impressive potential. Granted, it's not large, but the library staff is trying to reach out to the community. They've asked me to lead a monthly film festival, there's a book club or two, computer stations are available, and grants are applied for. To me, there's a sense of continuity. On the same shelves where I can get more Thomas the Tank Engine books for Jacob, there is an entire set of Tom Swift books. The state of the binding suggests those fantasy books were there when my father was roaming the building.

For story time, there's a medium-sized trifold display on a table about tips for getting children to read, next to it a portable easel for displaying song lyrics, and a rectangular rug on the floor with letters, symbols, shapes, and colors. Jacob, my blond-haired, brown-eyed, gregarious boy, grows excited and proceeds to tell the children's librarian about the letters and their accompanying sounds. His mother made it a point to make sure he knew his alphabet early. He is out to demonstrate to the librarian that he is the expert of this rug of signifiers and signifieds. When she asks him how old he is, I realize he is so excited about the rug that the question bounces off him. "You must be more than four years old," she says. I tell her the truth, that he's still got a couple of months to go, trying to hide my pride.

Later that hour we talk, and I tell her I'm trying to get him to sound out words. She cautions me to understand that there's plenty of time for that. I need not worry.

Spring 2002, 2003, 2004, 2005, 2006, 2007, 2008, 2009

At graduation, I dig out the list of graduating students and underline the names of those I recognize. Some are from my community, perhaps my neighborhood, but more are those I taught.

In the warmer temperature of graduation, it can be difficult to truly focus. However, when students walk across the stage and their names are called, I pay attention. It is not uncommon in those months prior to graduation that when I see a former student in the halls, I ask, "So, how close are you to walking?" Meaning, of course, walking across the graduation stage.

I usually underline six to ten names. Last year, 2008, I thought I saw only three names, but I am proud to report that this year, 2009, the number is back to normal.

End of Summer Semester, 2009

Four days after my last student conference of the summer semester, Zachary is standing behind and to the left of my mother-in-law in the vast expanse of the viewing room of Morrison Funeral Home, just southwest of Rupert, Idaho. On the wall are two video screens playing images that represent the life of my late father-in-law.

Just a week before, we received that phone call an eldest daughter and her husband never want to get at the time they never want to have it. At 3:00 A.M. MDT, we learned that my wife's father, Clair Wardle, sixty-six-year-old resident of Heyburn, Idaho, and father of seven, had suffered a heart attack in western New Mexico during a trip to help his youngest daughter move into her first teaching job and passed away moments later.

For now, Zachary is putting his right hand on my mother-in-law's shoulder, his face calm and his posture straight. His calm demeanor leads me to the thesis that Zachary believes he is there to support Grandma, perhaps as a debt for all that his late grandfather did for him, and when the last person leaves, I sadly get some evidence that might support my thesis. He takes his hand off Grandma's shoulder, steps back to the chair behind him, and collapses into a forward-leaning lump. The face becomes red, the tears flow, and the face contorts into anguish. Over the next five to ten minutes, the flow of the tears will slow, and the young man will slowly work his way out of his less-than-right-angle stature, despite the heavy burden of his father's comforting arm on his back and shoulder, and he will be back to business.

Fall 2009

Sometimes, symbols happen. I'm at the Craters of the Moon National Monument in south-central Idaho, perhaps the most visible reminder in the United States outside of Hawaii of violent forces involved in the building of this planet we live on. The hard black crust of lava, we have to remind ourselves, was once a flowing river of molten red-orange lava that came to the surface via the forces of heat and pressure.

Tonight, there's what's called a star party. Astronomers from around eastern Idaho gather in a trailhead parking lot and set up their telescopes to take advantage of the beautiful skies. I've got the old telescope, while Zach is working an even cheaper and smaller one; we clearly have the smallest, simplest scopes of the crowd, a sign of our inexperience. Still, Zachary has grown to love using the telescope; an evening with the Magic Valley Astronomical Society had a bit to do with that.

After we both land Jupiter in those little telescopes, I go about to find galaxies, nebulae, and star clusters. The Lagoon Nebula is visible even without binoculars, and I think it would be a great chance for Zach to try to find something more complicated than a planet or the moon. However, he declines the invitation and instead calls me over to identify other objects. Now, instead of Jupiter, all that's in his field of view is a spiked, twinkling point of orange-red light: the star Arcturus. Moments later, he calls me over again, and it's another star, the brightest in the summer sky, the bluish-white Vega. Apparently he wants to see stars and the crispness of what's present in one simple image.

One of the goals of star parties is public relations, and as at any star party, the parking lot has become crowded with several visitors wanting to see what we have. To my amazement, a school bus pulls into the parking lot: Several high school students disembark and begin wandering from scope to scope. As I talk to them, work with them, show them the Lagoon, globular cluster M22, and Andromeda and her sister galaxies, it becomes apparent they are enjoying themselves. I listen to them talk to each other, and it also becomes apparent that some of these young men and women might become my students in English 101 next year, or some may take the path of the young man who came to my office asking about the GED. Yet the more I talk to them, the more I realize they love trying to settle their vision to the point that they can make out the double star of Alcor and Mizar with the naked eye.

Sadly, we have to leave early, for there's an appointment tomorrow 120 miles away. We load up the van, and I return to our original viewing spot to make sure nothing has been left behind. After completing the sweep, I head back, only to pass a young man, probably twelve, curled up on the curb of the parking lot. In six years, he could be one of my students. He had been by my telescope several times earlier, always asking what I had in the field of view, always wanting to know what new object I had found. His hair and his face for a moment remind me of Terry, my eldest, and his energy and impatience remind me of what Jacob might grow up to be. I can just make out his countenance—thanks to the combination of night vision and the presence of too many stars—and it's not a happy one. He's frustrated about something. As I walk away, I begin to ascertain what the problem is.

He wants to see more stars. He wants to see another image and make something out of it.

Vespers, Matins, Lauds

The Life of a Liberal Arts College Professor

RALPH JAMES SAVARESE

I work at a highly selective monastery in the Midwest. I took a vow of chastity, relative poverty, and obedience. The six years of my novitiate were brutal, and I falsely imagined that becoming a full-fledged monk would allow for both greater peace of mind and greater autonomy. I was wrong. Whatever I gained was lost to additional obligations: all of that service that only the truly sanctified can per- form. And to think I had, still have, a family on the side—indeed, a secret life— like one of those priests you read about in the paper. My spouse complained that I was never home, and she couldn't understand my godly devotion. Vespers, Matins, Lauds—the Ferris wheel of light and prayer seemed to her an amuse- ment, a joy that I preferred over her and our son.

The fact that our son is autistic and requires more supervision than your typ- ical child made her resent my vocation even more. But to say that she resented my vocation is to be ungenerous, especially when she has been as flexible and for- giving as my abbot has not. My abbot demanded, still demands, unstinting fidel- ity. There was no Mass I could forgo, no fruitcake I didn't have to assemble, no pot I didn't have to scrub. The fact that I published an award-winning memoir about our son—whom we adopted from foster care when he was six and whom we taught how to read and communicate on a computer—is, I admit, a bitter irony. To the world that does not know me as a monk I am the perfect father; to her, much less. I won't even speak of my performance as husband.

I begin with this conceit because the year I came up for tenure I actually dreamt that I was trying to secure a place at Gethsemani, Thomas Merton's monastic home. As a young man, I had been actively recruited by the Trappists of central Kentucky. Though I long ago abandoned my faith, the professor-as-monk analogy seems particularly apt, for institutions such as mine require absurd devotion and a willingness to talk about your activities in almost mystical terms. In addition to excellent teaching and scholarship, to be granted tenure you have to perform all sorts of service—from advising students to sitting on committees to administering programs to conducting searches to attending events to being, as a colleague once put it (drawing out the word's second syllable), available. Part monk, part EMT, you must be ready at a moment's notice to rush to the scene of institutional exigency, whether that be a student's emotional crisis or a recruitment fair put on by the admissions department.

In the dream I kept saying, "I deserve to have a vocation" and "I need to support my family," as if the two assertions were one and the same. Having to support my family allowed me to feel better about insisting on a vocation: work with both purpose and meaning (read: work that devours you). Despite its well-known advantages (such as lots of vacation time and the ability to set one's schedule), my vocation has ensured plenty of conflict in my secret life. During the school year, for example, I sometimes leave at six in the morning and don't return until late at night, especially if there's a reading by a visiting writer, and so I'm gone a lot. Whenever I consider my time away, I think of a woman remarking at the memorial service for her husband, who had died of a heart attack while grading papers in his final semester before retirement: "In August Bill would always tell me, 'See you in June.' And now the June of our togetherness will never come." The woman's two sons, both still in college, wept in the front pew.

Shouldn't I be *called* to my wife and child as well? And what if my vocation at times begins to parody itself? As much as I derive satisfaction from teaching at a liberal arts college, there are moments when I think its demands are not only unreasonable but also counterproductive. To say that we coddle our students would be an understatement. I once described what we do at my college as akin to teaching young people how to become circus performers—in particular, tightrope walkers. Now, we're humane professionals; we don't want anyone to be injured while learning how to balance on a one-inch cord some fifty feet above the ground. A net is necessary. But is encouraging our would-be performers to fall, indeed to luxuriate in that webbed divan, necessary? Will it teach them to be better tightrope walkers? "It's just so comfortable down there. Why not join your peers for tea and therapy?" Another time, in a moment of exasperated exhaustion, with students coming apart all over the place, I suggested that the college set up Huggies diaper stands so that the faculty might rub Desitin on their students' bottoms. (I know, this image both contrasts with, and perversely confirms, the priest motif, and when I made the remark, you can be sure that my dean—my abbot—wasn't very happy.) The point is, our devotion frequently infantilizes.

And it has me wondering who my actual progeny are. In loco parentis can be taken too far, too literally. As I'm spending all of this time with my students, I'm not spending it with my son. Yes, there are summers, and winter and spring vacations, and, yes, during those times I get to be Super Dad, always around, making dinner, jumping on the trampoline. But it's a bit like bulimic parenting: stuffing your heart, only to purge it later and walk around hungry for fatherhood (even as you're more or less professionally satisfied). No second family can make up for the first you are neglecting.

Because my son is autistic, he needs more, not less, attention to thrive. And because my wife and I have insisted on fully including him in a regular classroom with a regular—no, make that an advanced—curriculum, one of us *can't* have a full-time job (or vocation). One of us has to supervise this grand experiment in equal opportunity. Our son is the only fully included, nonspeaking high school student in the state. With each new grade, we've had to show the school system how to do this: how to be sensitive to the profound anxiety and sensory processing disturbances of autism, how to adapt curricula and discussion protocols (our son uses a text-to-voice synthesizer in order to speak). We've insisted on moving beyond the typical "warm body" model of inclusion to something much more satisfying to both the person with a disability and his teachers and peers.

In a recent interview with *CNN*'s Dr. Sanjay Gupta, our son responded to the question "Should autism be treated?" by typing on his computer, "Yes, treated with respect." Dr. Gupta had laid out the typical response of parents to their child being diagnosed with autism—complete despair—and the repeated call to find a cure for this "devastating disorder," and our fifteen-year-old cleverly subverted the good doctor's meaning of the word "treat." The line literally bounced around the globe via the Internet. For any number of autistic self-advocates, it became a kind of rallying cry. But ensuring such respect requires immense amounts of time and energy—indeed an entire infrastructure, which my wife disproportionately provides.

When we first adopted our son, *I* stayed at home and served as the primary caregiver while she pursued her career. Nine years ago, we switched—with the idea that we would switch again at some point in the future. Yet now I make too much money for us to revert to her diminished earning power, and, truth be told, I enjoy having a professional identity. I enjoy being successful. When we were deciding whether or not to adopt our son, I swore to myself that I wouldn't allow my wife to become the stereotypical mother of a child with a disability: someone who literally sacrifices her own happiness for the sake of her child. But that, to one degree or another, has happened. Though she's currently working on her PhD in education (at a rate much slower than average) and though together we're editing a special issue of an academic journal on autism, such activities don't (yet) constitute a career. And she wants a career—something in addition to her motherly vows.

If I've created the impression that I'm not much of a father from September until June, I've misled you. Rather, with immense amounts of parenting to do and a vocation—a job—that won't quit, the ratio of motherly commitment to fatherly commitment in our household is roughly that in a less than progressive one. In effect, our son's needs have allowed us to reproduce a centuries-old sexist arrangement. Hence, in addition to making room for all manner of obligations with my son, I have to make room for guilt and lots of it. (In some ways, this essay can be understood as a spasm of guilt: A drowning man blames the water for his problems, not his inability to swim or the fact that he has waded out too far to make it back to shore safely.)

There is no better example of my guilt, even hypocrisy, than the publication three years ago of my memoir, *Reasonable People*. When I traveled the country to promote it, I received tons of adulation from the mothers of autistic children. So many fathers withdraw or disappear—indeed, the divorce rate in families with an autistic child is said to be as high as 80 percent—but there I was, the epitome of sensitive commitment. The memoir recounts the long struggle to get our son out of foster care, where he was so terribly abused, and, despite the enormous challenges involved in parenting a child with autism, it's one long paean to fatherhood. It's "posautive" about neurological difference, and it's filled with the incredibly touching things that our son typed once we taught him how to read and to use a computer. Things like this note on Father's Day when he was twelve:

Dear Dad,

You are the dad I awesomely try to be loved by. Please don't hear my years of hurt. Until you yearned to be my dad, playing was treated as too hard. Until you loved me, I loved only myself. You taught me how to play. You taught me how to love. I love you.

Your Son, DJ Savarese

When I read such passages, the many mothers of children with autism who showed up at my readings literally gazed at me with longing (and I'm no Brad Pitt). It was as if they wished that I were their husband or, at the very least, the father of their autistic child. Some two or three or eight hundred miles away from home, I'd be basking in the glow of a book tour, a righteous book tour, while my wife no doubt was helping our son with his homework or talking him out of some perseverative cul-de-sac. (Because he was in school, our son could only do the really big events on the tour.) And I haven't even mentioned the long hours locked away in my study writing this book so that I could keep my vocation!

How to have it all? How to have it all without oppressing others? While I acknowledge that the job of being a professor has changed a lot over the last thirty years and that men are now much more involved in raising their children, there's almost no change I can think of, short of a complete revolution in parenting, that would truly help a father of a child with a significant disability, especially one he wished to fully include in society. The flexible schedule of a professor goes a long way in ameliorating ordinary absent father syndrome; I, for example, regularly have lunch with my son at home—he can't stand the noise of the cafeteria. Yet I'm gone several nights a week for my liberal arts college job. Sure, my colleagues know what I mean when I say I can't attend a meeting because I'm caring for my son; they try very hard to schedule around my parenting demands, and they don't consider such demands unreasonable. That, I admit, is a significant cultural shift. And since receiving tenure, I also worry a lot less about missing things.

But there's no way to be an absent liberal arts college professor, and so you're forced at every moment to find an impossible balance. Because so many of us are trying to do so many things well—from teaching to writing to activism to parenting to being a good spouse—we're destined to be dissatisfied. I think trouble is built into the very idea of a vocation, let alone multiple vocations. With the decision to go to graduate school, many of us eschewed the business world for what we believed to be a more noble life of the mind. We thought of teaching and writing as akin to a kind of higher calling, something that makes work more than work. (Of course, only the materially comfortable can afford such a spiritual fantasy.) Whether religious or not, we still, in effect, move through the canonical hours—at home, in the office, on the page. Simply everywhere. And that relationship to what we do guarantees conflict. Picture monks from a hundred different monasteries all yelling at one another.

How White Was My Prairie

MARK MONTGOMERY

At an all-campus forum on race relations, I, a white man, stood up to respond, fairly vigorously, to a charge of (as I saw it) institutional racism, made by an African American colleague. Within seconds a first-year black student started yelling at me from the crowd. "You can't talk to her that way," he shouted, and went on to excoriate me for what he considered my rudeness and my attitude (and for the fact that I was chewing gum). For a small liberal arts college, in an obsessively polite little midwestern town, such a direct confrontation was extremely unusual. Not to mention excruciatingly uncomfortable. I had been publicly, if implicitly, denounced as a bigot, and the word spread across campus like a runaway prairie fire. A couple of days later, my daughter, then a senior at the college, brought up the incident. "Hey, Dad," she said, "I hear you're a racist."

"Well," I told her, "I have to admit, I do sometimes talk harshly to black people." It was true. That very morning I had probably yelled at an African American. "Hurry up, Gibrila," I might well have hollered, "you're going to miss the bus!" It's likely that the night before, to another young black man I had said something like, "Kurt, it's eleven thirty, why aren't you in bed?"

Has my fatherhood of two black sons made me, as a professor, *more* sensitive about racial issues on campus, or *less* sensitive? It's not a simple question.

The Microeconomics of Diversity

My wife, Tinker Powell, and I teach economics at Grinnell College, in the prairie town settled by J. B. Grinnell, to whom Horace Greeley is reputed to have said, "Go west, young man, and grow up with the country." There was nothing here but grass when J. B. arrived (Greeley, obviously, had not been specific enough). Today it is a thriving, if rural, college community with much ethnic diversity provided by the students, and much ethnic homogeneity provided by the residents. We have raised three children here. Our daughter, Mary Montgomery Powell, a "birth child" in the careful terminology of adoption, is twenty-four, and a graduate of the college. Her brother Kurt Powell Montgomery was adopted at birth from San Antonio, in 1991. Gibrila Kamara Montgomery, thirteen, came seven years ago from Sierra Leone, where he was orphaned at age two in the savagery over "blood diamonds," as a recent film referred to them. Everyone calls Gibrila "GB."

If there was some moment when Tinker and I decided that our second child would be adopted rather than born to us, I do not recall when that moment was. We were brought to that decision gradually by a combination of factors. First, I was teaching environmental economics and had entered my neo-Malthusian period; I felt squeamish about expanding the world population. Second, Tinker's pregnancy with Mary was grueling both physically (she threw up for seven months) and mentally (she swears it cost her twenty IQ points). More important, I think (I hope), was a nagging sense of having devoted the first thirty-plus years of our lives entirely to the pursuit of our own happiness. It seemed time to do something about that.

As a colleague of ours once pointed out, adoption has an exquisite economic logic, both as an application of the principle of Comparative Advantage and as a metaphor for the globalization of commerce. Everyone knows that, these days, many jobs are being "outsourced." They tend to be the most tedious, dirty, dangerous aspects of production, as pregnancy arguably is in the process of childrearing. In our case, the outsourcing followed a startlingly familiar pattern. Just like, say, the manufacture of certain auto parts, local production was first moved down near the Mexican border, and eventually to a poor Third World country. The analogy with outsourcing breaks down, however, when you consider that babies produced locally, so to speak, are a lot less expensive than those imported from far away. Financially, this may be true. But, as we discovered, buying locally can have a very high emotional cost.

A primary goal in the adoption was to give some kid a home. We had no interest in children like, for example, the unborn baby in the movie *Juno*, who would have desperate middle-class white couples clamoring to adopt them almost from the moment of conception. We would expand our nest by finding some fledgling who had no nest, killing two stones with one bird, so to speak.

If I expected the search for a child-in-need to make us feel like "special people" who were "making a difference," then what followed was a nasty shock. Instead it made me feel like crap. The first children we looked at were in a group called "Iowa's Waiting Children." These kids had been removed from dysfunctional homes, and the stories in their dossiers were simply heartbreaking. One pair of sisters had only one requirement for an adoptive family: "Someone who won't hurt us." Once you have read that, how can you call yourself a human being unless you put aside your own needs and fears and press those children to your bosom? Reading the dossiers of Iowa's Waiting Children made me feel that the only way I could ever look at myself in the mirror was to buy a big house in the country and adopt every single one of these children. We did not do that, however. We did not bring any of Iowa's Waiting Children into our home. They were too disturbed, too damaged, and they would require not just devoted parenting, but conceivably a change in our entire lifestyle. We wanted another child; we did not want another lifestyle.

International adoption seemed the next logical step. We talked to the Holt Agency, who suggested we consider a little boy in Costa Rica by the name of John Albert, a sweet-faced seven-year-old with thick dark hair. Looking at his video, we fell in love with him immediately. But John Albert had fetal alcohol syndrome (FAS). Like good academics, we started doing research on FAS, reading the literature and consulting Iowa's top experts on what the syndrome can entail. One day, in the office of a specialist in Des Moines, I asked her point-blank, "Is it possible that this child will have to be cared for by us until we die, and after that, cared for by our daughter?"

"Yes," she said, "that is possible."

From a distance of eighteen years, I feel my stomach tighten as I type these words: We decided not to adopt John Albert. No one blamed us for changing our minds. Indeed, most people assured us that it was sensible, it was prudent, it was *morally responsible* not to adopt John Albert—we had Mary's welfare to consider, after all. We went so far as to get help from a psychologist. And adoption experts warn against entering into a situation you'll be unable to handle—a failed adoption is a disaster for all concerned. So maybe turning away from John Albert was a reasonable decision. But after all of this time I still see it as a failure of our courage, and thinking about it makes me ashamed.

As everyone knows, it is much "safer" to adopt a healthy infant than an older child, which is why healthy infants are in short supply. We were surprised, therefore, when Holt told us that there is a little-known loophole in the Law of Demand for Healthy Infants: black babies, especially boys, are not highly prized by white couples. (Why the hell were we surprised?) Why not consider an African American or biracial child, Holt asked? We agreed. And we had a referral almost immediately.

The night before we picked up Kurt, I lay awake in a San Antonio hotel room trying to imagine what this new child of mine would be like. What even would he *look* like? I tried to picture myself in twenty years, standing next to a tall black man, my son, smiling into a camera at some family event. Would I be able to feel for him the same things I felt for Mary? Of course I would. Wouldn't I?

Any adoptive parent will tell you that such fears are normal, and they rarely survive that first moment when you hold your new child in your arms. The night we brought Kurt home, the sky was flashing and shimmering with all sorts of colors. The Aurora Borealis was visible in Iowa for the first time anyone could remember, an event to which I would attach great spiritual meaning if I ever attached spiritual meaning to things. (I don't, but it was still really cool.)

Now we were a family of four: three white and one black. Sooner or later, we knew, Kurt was bound to notice that he was of a different race than his parents and sister, and we began wondering just when that would occur. One day, when he was about three, and had learned the names of the various colors, the fateful moment seemed to arrive. We were loading him into his car seat when suddenly he pointed at his mom. "You're white," he said, big smile on his face, "I'm black!" We looked at each other, wide-eyed.

It's happened, he knows. *Battle stations! This is not a drill!*

Should we explain it to him, right now, right here, out in the front yard? Is it time to tell him that yes, he came from a different place than Mary, that he actually had *another* mommy and daddy, but that we loved him every bit as much as. . . .

We both noticed, at the very same moment, the color of the outfits he and his mother happened to be wearing. Do you mean the shirts, we asked him? He did. *Whew.*

Stand down from General Quarters.

I don't recall any particular moment when Kurt saw himself as racially different. But for GB, who came ten years later at age six, there *was* an exact moment: April 17, 2002, the minute he stepped off the plane at JFK. That was a Wednesday. Monday morning he'd been in an orphanage full of Africans; by Saturday he was taking golf lessons at a country club in which he constituted about 25 percent of the black membership. How did this make him feel? We will return to that question below.

Ethical Treatment of Experimental Subjects?

What is the proper way to raise black kids in such an über-Caucasian part of the country? We don't know, of course. And because of that, some people would say, we shouldn't have adopted our two boys; we are conducting a social experiment on subjects who never volunteered to be studied. How will they form a racial identity in a place with so few people of their race? We have no particular defense against this charge.

How have they fared? My boys differ in the degree to which they are willing to share their feelings: Kurt does so regularly, at high volume, especially if those feelings are unpleasant, whereas with GB it's hard to identify any feelings at all without resorting to a waterboard, which would, of course, contaminate the results. (We assume that rigid control over his emotions developed as a survival skill.) Both boys seem pretty happy in their surroundings. They have many friends, do reasonably well in school, and— being our children but not our descendants—are handsome and athletic. They have some experiences that are very unusual for black male teenagers in America. GB, for example, recently walked into a bank downtown and asked to get money from his account, though he had no checks, no debit card, nor any form of personal identification. Sure, the teller told him, just sign this slip of paper. And they have some experiences that lots of black teenagers have. Instead of DWB (driving while black), GB experienced WWB (walking while black). Coming home from a friend's house one night, he was playing around with a new flashlight and made the mistake of shining it into a parked car. A local cop stopped him, frisked him, and then woke up the elderly couple who owned the car to see if anything was missing from it. Nothing was—he'd just been shining a flashlight.

Get Out of Racism Jail Free Card

And how have *we* fared, as two white professors who parent two black boys in a small, white college town? There are some curious effects. For one, it gives you a greater amount of, shall we say, academic freedom. Race is a highly charged subject on campus, and no sensible person wants to be branded a racist, so the subject is broached with great trepidation. I am allowed to speak on this subject more freely than my colleagues. Most people are unwilling to accuse the parents of two African Americans of being racist, so statements that might otherwise get you branded as, at least, "racially insensitive" are less likely to get you labeled that way. On the night after that the campus forum I mentioned, the student who yelled at me—his name is Steve—e-mailed an apology. He wasn't sorry that he had said something, but he was sorry for how he had said it. What prompted his change of attitude? I suspect he'd been told that I was the father of two black kids, which probably pulled me off his Redneck List.

And here we encounter a sort of paradox. My fatherhood of black children is seen by some as "proof" that I'm not a racist, when in fact I adopted my sons partly because I am . . . well, a bit of a racist. That is, to say, my racism was one motivation for adopting black kids. I take no pride in pronouncing myself a racist, of course. But I was born the year before the *Brown v. Board of Education* decision, and no thinking person raised in the civil rights era had the luxury of leaving his or her racial attitudes unexamined. And if you examine them honestly you are not likely to be pleased with everything you find. We do not exactly *choose* our beliefs, after all. So when we decided to adopt Kurt it occurred to me that my prejudices would now have to be borne personally, meaning that whatever American society did to make a child feel inferior, it would be doing to a child I loved, and therefore, in effect, doing to me as well. I couldn't just will my prejudices away, but maybe I could better understand their impact.

Being a black father (if I can call myself that) has made me less tolerant of racism in its more subtle forms. We academics loudly proclaim our commitment to diversity, and our adoption patterns are indeed diverse: we get kids from China, from Korea, from South America, from Central Asia, from all over the place. But as Tinker and I discovered, it takes a great deal less time and expense to get a healthy black infant from southern Texas than a Caucasian toddler from central Russia. Why is this not a more popular choice? Especially in the academy? I don't know, of course, but I can't help wondering if this stems from some very uncomfortable feelings that I understand only too well. We're professors: we test, we grade, we evaluate, all the time. We spend countless hours differentiating students who are "smart" from students who are "not smart," and it is painful (if we're honest) to imagine our own children in the latter category. What if this unspeakable fear, of racial inferiority, is a hypothesis that we vigorously reject, to ourselves and to others, but not with enough confidence to test it in our own lives?

I teach a course in the economics of education, and I know full well that black boys from poor neighborhoods in San Antonio score well below average on tests of cognitive ability. But my son does not. Kurt is a pretty smart kid. To be absolutely honest, I expected that he *would* be below average— as I said, I'm a racist, I was not being coy about that. I girded my loins to spend a lot of time helping him struggle through school. I knew that it would not make me love him any less, but would probably make me even more protective. It's a cliché, of course, but adopting Kurt has taught me something I could not have learned from a birth child, nor from reading piles of academic literature. More accurately, I might have learned it from academic literature, but I would not have felt it.

Besides my education course I also teach environmental economics, and here Gibrila has expanded my perspective considerably. He has caused me to wonder about the current priorities of the environmental movement. We fret mightily, for example, that burning carbon-based fuels might raise sea levels and change weather patterns. These are real concerns, and should not be ignored, but they will happen gradually, over the course of perhaps a century or more. In contrast, imagine—I borrow the metaphor from Wen Kilama—something sudden and quite awful: a terrorist hijacking a Boeing 747 filled entirely with young children and crashing it deliberately into the ground. What if he did it four times in a single day? What if, indeed, he did it four times every day? Would such a gruesome horror affect our priorities? That neither your children nor mine would be on those planes, only dark-skinned children in faraway places, would not diminish our determination to stop the terrorist, would it? There is such a terrorist. He—or rather she—is the anopheles mosquito. Next year she will kill more than a million children, mostly in Africa, mostly under the age of five, yet Al Gore will probably not make a movie about it. Because of GB I have stronger feelings about my country's environmental priorities—they make me angry.

So here we come back to the original question: has fathering black children made me more sensitive to racial issues—on campus and in general—or less so? Both, I suppose. On the one hand, maybe I was impolite to my African American colleague at the forum on race. (Afterward I kissed her and said I hoped I wasn't rude; she was not at all angry with me.) On the other hand, I have gambled my emotional future on the fate of two young black men who are deeply, deeply embedded in my heart. That can't be bad for race relations, can it?

Meniscus

R O B E R T   G R A Y

I am standing on the pool deck, wet from the shower, shaking, arms crossed as I look out over the screaming children having lessons. I'm trying to find Rowan, my four-year-old son. His two moms signed him up for lessons on Saturdays—mostly to burn the yayas out of him but also because one of his moms, Rory, loves the water and wants him to love it too.

I've never been to this pool before and don't know where Rowan's lesson might be, don't know where his mom is doing her laps, and more seriously don't know where I am supposed to stand or sit, my trunks licked to my legs, shaking in the cold bare light and chaos of the public pool. I am just visiting the moms and our two sons the way I do on average every eight weeks, a schedule necessitated by the fact that they live in a city three provinces from my current academic posting. These intense visits every couple of months mean that I am at a loss when it comes to logistics in swimming pools, Kindermusik classes, or any number of other organized kid functions. I have no idea where Rowan or his mom Rory might be in this cacophony of water and cries. I wonder if the pod of cool lifeguards to my left see me, wonder why I look bewildered and lost and why I keep scanning the tadpole end of the pool. I am not swimming lanes; I am not sitting with the other clothed, bored parents texting or chatting about sleepless nights and schools. I am in the deep end again, but I am also standing on the harsh cold tiles. And this ambivalence seems so in keeping with this whole journey.

But not just the donor journey; for me as a gay man this ambivalence in some way shapes the structure of the closet. One of the dark truths no one tells you the first time you come out of the closet—when you're sitting on a picnic table bench across from your confused parents telling them that the entire script they had for your life will never happen and that you, their oldest son, are gay—is that this is not the last time you will have to come out. At that moment, paralyzed, breathless, ready to faint for fear that the ones who love you unconditionally in their own flawed and lovely ways might not be able to love this new you, it might seem unimaginable that eighteen years later the idea of coming out might bore you, be irritating, like correcting someone's poor syntax, correcting the way someone might assume other narratives about you. One is never fully in or out of that damn closet. It is something that has to be performed over and over, a mantra for each new social context or stranger.

Being "out" in academia and at least ambiguous or coded in the class-room has been an important part of my pedagogy—yes, in a way being queer has become work for me at times. Then, four and a half years ago, Rowan was born and being "out" got a lot more complicated for his moms and me, the donor and sometimes dad. Add to that my general skepticism around the mantle of "dad" and pedagogically, paternally, and queerly, I've made soup.

As a gay professor, I am "out" in many contexts (with family, with fac-ulty, with the campus queer group, with anyone who has ever caught me watching *America's Next Top Model* on my office computer), though each class is a new context, new subject, where I negotiate how much or how little I say: It wasn't imperative that my first-year composition students last year knew how my gay perspective informs my comma usage, but I think that my film theory students this year benefited from knowing why I cried when I screened *Celluloid Closet* for them.

I like to think I have become proficient at these negotiations. I was. Until four and a half years ago when I became a donor dad and I suddenly was handed parenting stories and narratives that queered the hell out of what-ever queerness I was performing at the front of the classroom: Suddenly it seemed to me students were reading me as a dad (thus in their minds heterosexual), and noticing I do not wear a wedding ring (so thus in their minds a divorcé), a sudden and new collection of identities I stumbled over like so many gopher holes. It became simpler to refer to Rowan, our old-est, as my nephew when, for example, I used him as an example of infant development when talking about Jacques Lacan's mirror stage. I invented a whole new closet.

I've never done audience testing on these assumptions. And truly, my students probably aren't that interested in the details of my life. I do, how-ever, think it's important that I, as a queer professor, reflect on what possi-ble readings students might make of me. Here I always try to hold in mind a twenty-year-old me still baffled about what being gay would mean in five years, ten years. A good friend of mine, a sociology professor, once said that he wished someone had told the confused, hind-leg-chewing nineteen-year-old he once was that being gay would mean going to fabulous dinner parties, eating incredible food with lovely men (not to stereotype, but he has had some very fabulous dinner parties, and so have I). So as a professor at the front of the room I believe that in some fashion I need to think about identifying myself as queer. If only to let them know there will be dinner parties.

And, on another level, when I teach theory and when I teach creative writing one of my pedagogical objectives is often to draw their attention to the matrix, or those master narratives that they may not see awry the way those of us who are marginalized in some way or another do. I want them to see that there is a multiplicity of experiences and social realities that should not be subsumed into "They're just like us" decimations.

I was lucky that several academics at the University of Alberta (where I was doing my PhD) got together to discuss this idea of our roles as queer professors. How do we make an effort to identify as queer enough to provide representation for our students seeking community and people to identify with while avoiding possible homophobia (one of the professors who had come out to her class had just had her home vandalized) and without alienating students who need other narratives for learning? We discussed and struggled with the idea of "strategic ambiguity," or, I guess, leaving ourselves open to interpretation.

So I stand in classes of students who may or may not know and negotiate each year, each course, each class, each point I make, asking myself how much they need to know about my life, asking how my sexuality informs my perspective as a writer, filmmaker, teacher, human being. My choice to be "strategically ambiguous" in the classroom was and always has been a work in progress, something that shifts with groups, something I need to revisit at times when I think perhaps it's just become invisibility.

All this was fine and good when I was just a gay man and could refer to my "partner" or talk about people I knew who were queer. As soon as I started referring to my son, all ambiguous signifiers seemed invisible in comparison. "Nephew" was at first a tentative solution, a deflection, yet a lie. I grew increasingly aware that I was trying to resist being boxed up by narratives by prepackaging them myself, by misrepresenting Rowan. Whatever my role, whether dad or uncle, or d-uncle, the one true thing is that he is my son.

As much as "strategic ambiguity" is about a potentially queer pedagogy, turned awry, it reveals how parenthood is in itself a performance. Early on this baffled me: When Rowan was born there were the various "you must be so excited / terrified / ecstatic" responses. There were so many of them, in fact, that when Rowan was eventually placed in my arms the first thing I taught him was how to look into the face of terror. Only later, with his moms off in other rooms doing all the less glamorous work of new parents, did he and I sit in a chair and in the momentary quiet decide just how it was, separate from anyone else's expectations. I am a poor performer, so when I am not just playing with the kids or sprawling after bedtimes with the moms laughing about the day, all the other constructions seem like those old numbered dance step marks on the floor. Step here. Then there. These are the scripted steps that are as far from the bare, blank pool deck as I can get.

And if you aren't clear on how the steps or moves go, I've found people are more than willing to shove you along anyway. At the market, if one of the moms strolls off for organic eggs, suddenly we are a cliché family unit of dad, mom, and the kidlets. More than once a random patriarch has blindsided me in a bookstore or pharmacy, looking right past a mom, and engaged me in some testosterone dad conversation about "How old is the little guy / man?" and I've had to resist bolting for the door or leaping behind a display of protein powder. Maybe I need to go home and practice my father swagger, develop a few ready lines like "Ask the little lady. She keeps track of these things." Here, too, I realize how others are far too ready to let biology explain everything, the way some people have been so excited to meet Rowan's or Isaac's father they've stopped noticing one of his mothers, like it's musical chairs and there are only ever two.

This is a dangerous place, the space between step marks or chairs; it is a place that can define you right out of the definition of parent if you let it. Misstep, and you see how parenthood is an overwrought narrative. For me, the conversation invariably goes something like this:

"You have kids?"

"Yes. They live in another city with their moms."

"How often do you see them?"

There is no right answer to this question, and when I answer I don't look in their faces, don't want to see their math or verdict. Or a family member at a dinner will note that I am "such an active" parent while the moms look on incensed, knowing full well that I have changed less than a handful of diapers. Ever. Once, from the other direction, one of the moms, sleep deprived and lacking filters, in a quiet moment asked me, "Do you miss them? When you're not here, do you miss them?" and in the small space after she asked you could see that even she knew this was an unanswerable question. In among all the expectations and narratives and constructions of what a dad is, I sometimes wonder if there is even enough space, enough to just be whatever the heck it is I am. And in the face of my own not-so-strategic ambiguity, contorted by these questions, how do I perform a useful, productive pedagogy?

This is what I know. Right now I am calling myself a "sometimes" parent. When I am there I cook new and usually tasty meals for the moms and me; I become play toy extraordinaire for Rowan and now his little brother, Isaac; I shop for groceries; I make gin and tonics when it's time. I don't show up and expect it to be about me. It's about the lovely family of which I am a part. Things are at their simplest there, falling somewhere between the extremes of the numbered footprints on the floor that I can't follow and the bare, confusing pool deck.

Last visit Rowan asked me (complaining because I wasn't able to play right that moment) why I cooked so much. So I wonder if I most resemble the classic father archetype more when I am absent and away than when I am actually being there with my family. There is an experience here, perhaps despite all the competing narratives. One of the moms suggested, in a moment when I was particularly frustrated, that perhaps it just is what it is. That seems possible if not only a temporary consolation.

Standing on the pool deck, not in any pool, I finally catch sight of Rowan with two other kids clinging to the pool deck with grins next to their instructor. He doesn't see me there. I feel self-conscious watching him but I can't stop. The instructor is showing them how to do the starfish float, the updated and nicer name for the dead man's float. Rowan is the first to volunteer; excited, he leans back and lets the instructor help him to float. I think I should go sit in the hot tub so I can stave off this cold and stop shaking, but I don't even know where it is. So I watch Rowan a little more, and his glee makes me forget that I am not in any pool, but just right where I am. Even makes me forget I am cold for a little.

Once Was Lost

JOHN BRYANT

In the middle of my life, on a warm but drizzling April afternoon, I found myself in an obscure woods, situated anonymously between suburban Westchester houses and a fenced-in park. This was in 2003, about a year and a half after 9/11 and my mother's death a continent away. Drenched and exhausted, I ran as briskly as I could manage given my fifty years and the tumbledown logs in my way. I would turn and peer into the darkening mists between the barren Beckett trees, and turn and peer again, pausing to catch my breath and call out, "Strawberry." And "Strawberry," again. My lungs burned, my side was pinched, it was muddy and twilight, my voice was cracking, I was cracking up, and calling out, "Strawberry."

My daughter's dog had taken off, out of the house, the yard, the neighborhood, and into the woods. I was on a mission to retrieve the mutt, and Strawberry was on a mission to run away. All around me were neglected trees and tangled vines; no path, only used-up stone fences and the gullies of desultory streams. Occasionally—three times, actually—I would glimpse the red dog with a bushy tail. At a distance, she would turn to look at me over her upturned tail. I would jingle the leash and call her; and after a moment's deliberation, she would make her choice and disappear into the woods. "STRAAAWberrrry." I made the name sound kind and fetching, adding "Here, girl" now and again, but the dog heard my need and split.

Liana, our newest child, was the first to bring my attention to the potential value of dogs. Until then I had myself been dogless and happily so, indeed petless. I should disclose Twitch, my older daughter's rabbit, which we kept, some years ago, in a cage in the basement for a brief period of time. Twitch kept to herself pretty much, giving my two girls little diversion, until one spring day she revealed herself to be a he on my leg. Twitch's chief accomplishment had been the ability to ingest, on a regular basis, a sack of

100

small brown alfalfa pellets and convert them daily into a pile of small brown fecal pellets of precisely the same size. For me, well after my daughters lost interest and well before she or rather he passed on, Twitch was more of an insight than a pet. A pet should offer some consolation for your having caged it; a pet should be something you can pet and be petted in return. Twitch just kept to the cage, mechanically ingesting, mechanically pooping. Perhaps I should have released her into a neglected woods.

Twitch was long gone by the time Liana first arrived. Linda, a friend whom we had known since before graduate school, had adopted one-year-old Liana from China. Linda had just turned fifty, had an extended family of cousins but no longer any mother, father, or siblings; she had wanted a child, but rules did not permit her to adopt in this country. So she found Liana in Nanjing. Liana—we are not so sure. The story is that she had been left, at birth, at a Nanjing orphanage by parents now unknown. Linda found her there in swaddling and brought her to New York, believe it or not, on Christmas Day.

Linda lived upstate in Columbia County in a tidy, quirky converted farmhouse, where she raised Liana among cats. I think we can agree that the less said about cats the better. Linda would have disagreed. Although she was our closest friend, Linda was a magnet for that class of cat you would have to call—and I think I am being kind here—mentally challenged. One was minus a foreleg and used her phantom paw vainly to wash behind her ear. Another had feline dyslexia (the only term I know for this condition) and was not able to negotiate a doorway without hitting the jamb head-on; and a third, the one with a terminal case of cynicism, who eyed us all with utter disdain, passed on from some hideous infection. These were Chloe, Babo, and Sweetpea. As godfather to Liana, I would take her by the hand to visit Sweetpea's grave, over by the hedge.

Although she and Linda did not know it, Liana suffered from chronic sinusitis due, I believe, to the cat dander in their bucolic country home, a perpetual runny nose and nasal voice that cleared up when Liana came to live with us, suddenly, in our catless Westchester apartment. The details of Linda's death are these: Crohn's disease had for decades turned her system against itself. Several surgeries had removed most of her colon, and the condition was in remission when, never having married, she felt free to adopt as a single woman. We and a village of other friends had applauded Linda's plan, helped her fetch the child and tend it, as friends and neighbors will do, but after four years of prednisone, her defenses were too low to withstand the return of her disease. She died September 19, 1998, two months before Liana turned five. We were the godparents, and suddenly Liana was our third daughter.

Cats aside, Liana was mostly fond of Gurghee, a rechristened lion from some Disney movie of another name. In the months to come, as she settled in with us, she slept on Gurghee, chewed on him, pulled him hairless in places, and reduced him to a crumpled shell of his former regal self. Children expect a lot from their dolls. When my mother died a couple years after Liana moved in, and I was sorting through her "estate," I found tucked in one of her drawers my only childhood doll, a bear, which I call Cubbybear. I had long since lost the need of such a bear, chewed and hairless in places, and my mother, too, I suppose. But she had kept it, and now it sits on my dresser.

Liana had had it worse than any of us in our family, though our oldest daughter in college was overcoming anorexia, and our younger daughter in high school was, at the time, beginning to knock on the inside closet door of her sexuality. Come to think of it, everyone has it worse sometime or another. And we did not raise our children so much as we learned to grow as they grew. Liana had some anger issues. When she first came to us, she would burst through the front door, exasperated by godknowswhat, flop down her coat or books, raise her fists not so much at me as in my presence, and growl. After some weeks of this, she and I had a talk, or two. I seated her beside me at our piano. She had every right to be angry what with Mommy Linda's long illness and her having died and all, and what with her having to live with me, an actual male, and Father. And she had every right to express her anger. But the fist and growl would have to stop.

I am not myself too good with anger. I keep it to myself. I believe this stems from my childhood worries that my parents, who argued a lot and vociferously, would split up (which they never did), and that I would be crushed. So I channeled my emotions into reading and writing, found solace in research and libraries, and each word here is a flag of suppression and liberation. My own children, Emma and Eliza, were raised by two parents who put affection and discussion before anger and explosion, as if our home would be a safe haven from the rage against the fear of loss, separation, and the muddy spaces between neglected trees in obscure woods. Emma submerged her anger into depression, which she could not explain in our happy home, and she began to stop eating. Eliza was gay and knew we wouldn't mind, but how do you know, and that anger had to be diverted, too.

In midlife, we remain a happy but healthier family—Ginny, Emma, Eliza, and I—having grown together through so much. And Liana, fist raised and growling, came to us just as we were beginning to move through our desperate times.

Liana, Gurghee, and I found a child psychologist at the Center for Preventive Psychiatry in nearby White Plains. Once a week we would grab the lion doll—whose name, it finally dawned on us, was based on the etymological root for Grrrrr—and let Liana play and sometimes chat for an hour in the presence of an Israeli psychologist who looked (to me) like Linda, and whose name in Hebrew meant "springtime." Once a month, Ginny and I would meet with Aviva to unburden our fears about Liana, death, loneliness, anger. This was all to get to know Liana, of course, a mostly cheerful child who rarely if ever cried—but watch out if she did—who raised her fists and growled.

Because Ginny was a nine-to-five publisher and I had a much looser academic schedule, I was the chauffeur to Liana's weekly meetings with Aviva. We had our routine, which included listening to an eclectic assortment of tapes: The Band, Aaron Neville, *Guys and Dolls*, and Pete Seeger. Liana wanted Pete each evening on the way home, and in particular "Awimoweh." As she sat buckled in the back seat, fading a bit with the lingering taste of Aviva's hot chocolate in her mouth, leaning into Gurghee and picking at the lion's matted and tufted fur, we would listen:

> In the jungle, the mighty jungle
> The lion sleeps tonight
> Near the village, the peaceful village
> The lion sleeps tonight
> Hush, my darling, don't fear, my darling
> The lion sleeps tonight.

And I would watch the road, as winter rain streaked the windshield.

But as fond of Gurghee as we all were, Liana's grand obsession was dogs, specifically any dog.

So after we moved from the apartment to a nearby house with a backyard large enough to accommodate a dog that would be kept strictly outside, we relented, Ginny and I, and arranged to find a dog for Liana. Liana fancied a beagle puppy with a sticker price of over a thousand prewar dollars at a local pet emporium run by thieves. I fancied not. Ginny's requirements were simply that the dog be house-trained, not make noise, not require walking, and not live long: She had been under a bit of stress. Since Liana had come under our care, Ginny had had to push retirement off indefinitely, and raising Liana while coping with a husband had not been part of the script. But the days of fist and growl were behind us, and for her part, Liana, during the year or so it took for us to come to terms with having to buy a dog, maintained what I have to say was, in retrospect, a marvelous balance of diplomacy, patience, and yet constant yearning.

She would coo at the sight of a dog, on TV, on the streets, in a book. She would not beg or whine about the matter. Even so, her whole life was an argument for Dog. Or rather an innocuous insinuation for the purchase of a dog. She read up on dogs and showed us pictures demonstrating their varied features, insidiously forcing us to reflect on our preferences even though No Dog was our secret choice. She would point out dogs and their leashed masters with children walking about the parks we visited, not to sigh heavily at her doglessness, not to advert approvingly to such visions of family perfection—parents child dog—not even to say Daddy Please. She accepted our need to take things one, long, step, at a time.

She would conduct herself with exquisite manners upon first being introduced to an adult friend of ours: "Liana, this is Lee; say hello." "Hi. [beat] Do you have a dog?" was her invariant rejoinder. And what would cut me was that she never put the accent on "you" in her question, as if to say, *Because I don't*, and thereby signal to the world her lonely endurance of her miserable parents. She always put the accent on "dog." As if to say, *Let's talk dogs*, or *Tell me more about yourself, and your dog*. Never would she stress the absence in her life. Always for her there was the presence of dog, out there, somewhere, anywhere. "My dog? I don't have one yet," she seemed to be saying, in her patient hopeful sinuous way. The gods had made man and dog united, the two together, but we thought ourselves happy one day, too happy, so the gods split us from our dogs at birth, to put a hole in us, to give us desire for one another, and so we search for that other self, our special other Us, our dog, so that we may reattach and be whole again. Such was Liana's silent myth.

I cannot finally explain Liana's longing or her grace in waiting for attachment. Eventually, we got the dog named Strawberry.

The only rational approach, I took it upon myself to venture, was that we get a rescue dog, and let Ginny and Liana negotiate the make and model. To date, Ginny was the only person in the family with real-dog experience, as she had had a collie named Sunbeam back in the early colonial days when patroons and their mastiffs strode about Westchester depositing fecal matter with free-market abandon. Memories of Sunbeam had begun to warm her, and she was in jolly spirits as we all set out in the Subaru to Long Island on the Friday before the drizzling April day when I found myself alone in the woods. A friend long ago had told me that he and his partner had found their dog Max (now deceased) at the North Shore Animal League, a large, well-endowed shelter in Port Washington. I had checked out their Web site and had called to get human contact, to find out procedures, secretly hoping that the busy woman I spoke to on the phone would detect in my voice that I am no dog person and that I really should not go through with it and that, like a cowardly lion or dissolving Gurghee, I could be talked out of the whole thing. But the busy woman, sensing my unvoiced anxiety, melted a bit and became infuriatingly reassuring. The league, I learned, took in stray cats and dogs, fixed them, injected them, cured them of any ills, fed them, kept them warm and clean, and did not kill them. The league worked to bring the right dog together with the right family, which meant that the family would have to be scrutinized as much as the dog, in fact more than the dog. Prospective owners had to demonstrate a good track record with pets, and that meant coming with phone numbers of friends (not relatives) who would vouch for your pet-worthiness. Families, we had heard (and would eventually witness), were rejected for want of proper recommendations. The local pet emporium was beginning to sound more attractive. But the league's charge of only fifty dollars was a compelling argument, and I brought our passports just in case.

NSAL's facility is located in a semi-commercial precinct of Port Washington, off the main drag, its back to a field and then a stream beyond. Inside, the atmosphere is astonishingly light, its air astonishingly free of the smells you might expect. The tiled walls are lined with uniform built-in cages, stacked in twos one above the other and on down and around the adjoining walls. The center of the skylit room is a glassed-in area with tiled benches and enough room for prospective dog owners and their future dog to sit and get acquainted.

On the long drive to Long Island, eight-year-old Liana's Asia eyes were about as wide and glistening as I had ever seen them. She sat straight up in the back seat of the car, her nose to the window looking for signs to the North Shore Animal League, grilling me on freeway turn-offs and then, once off the freeway, she grilled me about the number of stoplights left to pass before the final leg of our journey. We had explained to Liana the entire procedure, as best we could imagine it ourselves given my researches. We would have plenty of time to look at all the dogs; we would narrow down the field to five or so dogs; we would spend time with each, carefully weighing pluses and minuses; through Quakerly discernment we would find the dog we all want; we would fill out some papers, pay our fee, and then be on our way.

We entered the shelter, turned left, and Liana chose the first dog she saw.

The shelter is a kind of hospital-slash-museum-slash-orphanage. Here were Long Island's canine renegades and castaways, the lost and abandoned, isolatoes all. Each cage had a label that told the dog's breed or mix, its age, its name, its time spent at NSAL. The place broadcasted life and death in random flashes and, like the hospital where Linda had died, like a hospital my mother would never enter, with attendants busily adjusting things, a bit too cheerfully. Once we had reminded Liana of our plan, we negotiated a slightly more humane version of said plan by simply looking. As we walked the hallway, the building came alive with dogs nuzzling the wire of their cages; though upon closer inspection, some were not so attentive, some were curled in the back, resigned to the cage, waiting to die, indifferent to rescue or reattachment.

Strawberry was tentative at first. A medium-sized "Chow Mix"—that is, a cross between a red Chow Chow and a somethingelse, probably a golden retriever—solidly built, with a willingness to sit and never a bark or growl. In the months before making our trip to the rescue shelter, I had purchased several books on dogs, partly for research purposes—it's what I do—and partly to get Liana, who is not so keen on books, to read. Liana and I had pored over these books on Dogs and had even started up The Dog Book, a kind of scrapbook project of our own with pictures of various dogs and handwritten descriptions in different colored inks. So when we got home with Strawberry, we looked up her breeds. The Chow: an Asian guard-dog, likes her own territory, fiercely protective of family and front door. The golden retriever: a pillow for children, able to endure finger-poking. Strawberry had the coloring, curved-up tail, and short pointy ears of the Chow, but the snout and disposition of the golden. And she never barked. We took photos of Liana and Dog, united in mutual embrace.

And that was all we knew of Strawberry. The following morning, a drizzly Saturday in late April, a friend came to see Liana's new dog. We opened the screen door, and down the hallway, Strawberry saw her chance. She bounded out the door. We had been told to keep Strawberry on a leash and always within sight for a couple of weeks until the dog could lay down her scent and get to know her new neighborhood. We did not anticipate, however, that this rescue dog would so fervently seek escape.

Liana bounded after Strawberry, who was already moving from trot to gallop down our street and between two neighborhood houses, out the other side, over to cross the main road, and disappear into the woods and the afternoon's fading light.

That morning, I had taken Strawberry on her first walk around the block, and felt as she tugged firmly against my hold of the leash that this was going to be the beginning of a great friendship: exercise and companionship. I could hardly believe my ears when I heard Liana yelling and then instantly beginning to cry the cry of a kid, not in pain, but panic and fear. I rolled off the couch, but no longer capable of "bounding," I ran after Strawberry, into the woods, thinking this shall be an adventure, this shall be over soon, this will all work out fine. Moments later I realized that the dog had made choices, the dog had speed, the dog was not coming home, the dog, in fact, did not have a home, or a scent to bring her back to where she had food.

Liana, it needs to be said, does not cry very much. But she was crying when I returned from my futile quest to re-rescue our rescue dog.

Back when Liana was only four, and when we had sat her down to tell her that Linda had died, she did not know then what had happened or what it all meant, and she smiled, got up from the couch, went to the front stoop of a friend's house where others had gathered for comfort, and announced: "Hey everybody, my mom just died!" as if she had won a prize. But she knew.

Later that day when she came to our home with us, and later that week after she began to ask where her mother was and when she was coming back to rescue her from Uncle John and this apartment that was not her farmhouse upstate, after all this while, she broke down. And the crying, then, was like a subterranean lava flow bursting aboveground: deep, sullen, and loud, like an operatic siren. A kind of keening, Ginny later said. Something almost mechanical and from the diaphragm, elemental and primal. And then it stopped, and that was it. We continued to hold her and began to make our family anew.

When I returned wet and fearful from my hours of searching in the woods, I could hear Liana's keening. She was cradled in Ginny's arms crying her deep toneless cry. She had been at it for two hours; she had not left her mother's arms. And all the crying for all mothers lost and things lost that the world had ever heard was in that cry. It filled the room with a sound of emptiness and dread. Eventually, exhausted, she fell asleep that night. With Gurghee. But she woke up at one and cried until three; then slept, and woke up again. No tears, just that keening wail. Liana had got the tune of loss.

The next morning, we sat out on the deck recuperating. Liana made her way to the table, exhausted, in silence, and slumped down in a lawn chair. A neighbor was there to commiserate, and we all made valorous statements about runaways and retrieval. Playing Scarlett O'Hara in a voice I had copied from my mother's southern drawl, I vowed, "As God is my witness, I shall retrieve that dog!" Liana remained silent as we spoke of how Lassies can and will come home. Then she broke her silence, and we all turned to hear her speak, and her words were these—"After I read all those books, *this* is what I get!" Her long night of dread was over.

The next day, while Liana was at school, I began to make calls to animal leagues in the area, discovering that once you announce a lost dog in one part of New York, you automatically alert the entire tristate area. We had the one photo of Liana and Strawberry that we took hours before Strawberry's escape, and we passed it out to the pounds and shelters.

A month went by with no reports back, but Liana and I spoke of Strawberry every day. She went Kübler-Ross on us and passed along those stages which I refuse to remember. I told her that we would give Strawberry a month, and if she did not show up, we would get another dog. We considered whether this was being fair to Strawberry; we allowed we were angry with her; we wondered if we should not be loyal to her and have faith that she would show up; we pondered over why she would leave us and how she was doing and what it was like out in the woods alone. Was she lonely? These were questions we revisited every day.

The final week before our deadline date arrived. We were projecting ahead to another dog and moving on when the phone rang. A red dog matching our description had been sighted in Pelham, fifteen miles south of our village. Strawberry had found her way through the obscure woods beyond our house and down to the freeway nearby. Following the roadway, crossing streams and two other freeways, and heading farther south along the Hutchinson River, she was heading back home to the North Shore Animal League over on Long Island. If she had taken my E-ZPass, she would have made it there over the Throgs Neck Bridge. Instead, she found herself stuck in a small community on this side of Long Island Sound bordered by an impassable, high-pillared freeway. Apparently, she resigned herself to stay there and live off the fat of Westchester County refuse.

Kids in this Pelham neighborhood, and some attentive mothers, would see Strawberry wandering unleashed in their streets, but the dog would not approach them. Valiant boys on bikes made it a point to record sightings of the dog; their mothers left food on doorsteps and in open garages hoping to snare Strawberry. But to no avail. Strawberry was an orphan and run-away; she had no home or reason to trust. Another month went by, and no Strawberry Come Home.

With some good advice from the New Rochelle Animal Shelter, I engaged the services of an Animal Retrieval Associate, or what we used to call a dog-catcher, whose regular job was rescuing herds of abused dogs tied up in abandoned houses. Cricket, for that was her name, was more than happy to capture Strawberry in a humane way. She set a cage with a spring-trap door and a can of tuna fish. Another week passed to no avail. I suggested moving the trap closer to a more recent sighting; again no go. Then in the following week, Cricket suggested that we escalate, and we replaced the canned tuna with fresh filet of beef. This is, after all, Westchester County.

The next day, we got the call. Strawberry was back in our arms. She has a new name now. We call her Molly.

I am a scholar of nineteenth-century American literature, with a lifelong focus on Herman Melville. I research into Melville's life, re-read his works with increasing pleasure, and write about him and them. I bring Melville into my classes as a way to bring students deeper into themselves. And I believe that my reading, writing, researching, and teaching are all one thing, and one thing tending toward one end: Let me fill this void, my longing, my loss; let me love.

Shared Attention

Hearing Cameron's Voice

MARK OSTEEN

My son, Cameron, who is autistic and nearly nonverbal, slides a card through his Language Master machine.

"Daddy's office," the recorded voice says.

He runs the card through the machine once more: "Daddy's office!"

"Oppice, yes," Cam affirms, looking up at me.

He's telling me he wants to visit my office at school. But if the thoughts are his, the recorded voice is mine: I dictate his array of choices, I speak for him. I am his language master.

I made the card in order to introduce Cam to my workplace. But this effort to integrate my dual lives as professor and parent wasn't too successful. I'd finish a couple of errands, drop off papers, and before trying to answer e-mail I'd hunt for a snack or drink to keep Cam occupied in the departmental lounge, a characterless space furnished with the potted plants, dull carpet, and bland chairs typical of such places. Perhaps that's why Cam tried to "improve" it. On one visit he urinated all over a chair, leaving a permanent stain commemorating his presence. Often he'd pour his soft drink onto the rug. More often he'd pull a branch or stem from an aspidistra or pothos plant, then deftly run his hand along its length, stripping off all the leaves. Voilà: a pruned plant. But he didn't stop at pruning; if permitted, he'd completely denude every plant in sight. It never occurred to me that these "behaviors" might have been designed to draw my attention away from my errands and back to him.

Instead, to prevent Cam's botanical operations, I'd give him a white athletic shoestring. Those strings are the medium for his favorite "stim" (i.e., self-stimulatory behavior). Each one is a miniature puzzle: With his brows furrowed in concentration, Cam pulls the shoelace apart thread by thread, then wraps each filament around his fingers and snaps it—twang!—like a tiny ukulele. Small puffballs of gossamer thread soon collect around his seat. He picks up each fiber, blows it into the air, and studies its gradual descent. When all the fibers have been extracted, he stashes the cloud of lace beneath a couch.

Though Cam's activities may seem strange, they are not entirely different from what ordinarily transpires on these couches, habitually occupied by anxious students cramming for an exam, perusing a reading assignment, or waiting to inquire about a grade. My son's concentration is as deep as theirs, and those plants and strings are, like those students' essays and exams, the fruits of hard labor. More than that, they are his signatures. The objects speak for him: CAM WAS HERE.

But if the strings saved the plants and focused Cam's attention, they didn't bridge the gap between my parental and professional lives. The truth is, I didn't really want the lives to merge, and made an effort to keep my work sacrosanct. The resulting conflict between work and family was especially clear during the summer, when I was on dad duty for most of each day. Those months defined the phrase "divided attention."

As I tried to write or do research in my basement office, upstairs Cam was busy with his Applied Behavior Analysis training (i.e., one- to two-hour sessions of discrete-trial learning)—learning to imitate gestures, working on puzzles, matching pictures. It was hard to concentrate while keeping an ear cocked for warning sounds. Several times a week I'd hear shuffling or squeals, then dash upstairs to detach Cam's fingers from a therapist's hair or shirt. I'd assess the situation. Is he hungry? Just delaying? Does he need a break? Often I could bring him back to earth with a rapid-fire imitation drill that forced him to look at and listen to me closely. Seldom did I scuttle his work session altogether, because doing so would end mine as well.

I often fretted that a mellower father, a father less focused on his career or less determined that his child succeed, would have halted the sessions when they hit rough patches. That father would have sacrificed his job for his kid. But work was my refuge from the world of autism, where rigid routine battled for dominion with perpetual chaos. Without work, autism would consume my entire life instead of just most of it. Reading, writing, and preparing for classes let me carve out a small space where order and sanity prevailed.

I complained mightily about Cam's interruptions. Yet sometimes I welcomed them. Suspending work to deal with my son actually cleared my head and let me collect my thoughts. His sessions shaped my day; our rhythms and moods mirrored each other's. Intentionally or not, he inserted his learning into mine, interjected his voice into my inner world. Against my will, we were sharing attention.

On Wednesdays, when his school let out early, I took Cam to his gymnastics lesson. Through the waiting room's large windows I'd watch his coach patiently coax him to climb the vaulting horse, dive into a foam-rubber-filled pit, or stand on his head. He'd comply reluctantly, and only for the promised reward: a few minutes of bouncing on the gym's large trampoline, placed at floor level and surrounded with pads for maximum safety.

My efforts at grading papers or reading during these sessions were generally fruitless. I wanted to watch Cam perform, but I also had to be vigilant, for frequently he'd dash away from the coach to pilfer someone else's soft drink, or simply burrow down into the foam pit, utterly unconcerned that no other student could use it while he lay there. More troubling were the episodes when, disturbed by a loud noise, impatient to jump on the tramp, or just not in the mood for gymnastics, my son would pull his coach's hair, slap her, or kneel and refuse to rise, while emitting loud, wordless roars.

Tossing aside my book or papers, I'd thrust open the gym door and try to salvage the situation without losing my temper or causing a scene.

But there were also rare but glorious moments when Cam would spring onto the trampoline and leap, totally fearless and untrammeled, high, higher, highest—nearly to the ceiling. His face, so often creased with worry and frustration, would open into a wide smile of purest joy.

At these moments he had my undivided attention.

In 2001 a profound change came upon us. After several difficult years of medication trials, stalled educational progress, and rampant aggression from Cam, we made the agonizing decision to place him in a residential school for "special needs" children. His first day at the new school coincided with the opening of my fall semester. For the first and only time in my career, I skipped the first day of classes. It was not a difficult choice: My son needed me.

As my wife and I wandered around my son's campus, feeling lost and bereft, I was suddenly pushed from my comfortable role as professor and cast into that of a college freshman's parent. Hadn't the parents of the students I was (not) teaching experienced the same mixture of excitement and dread just days earlier? More upsetting was the realization that my son—then only twelve years old and far less capable of understanding his situation than those freshmen—was doubtless being assailed by the same anxieties: Where do I go? Who are my teachers? Who am I? Our new lives were starting, but none of us were certain we wanted them to start.

Again that uncanny reflection: My son's life not only paralleled my professional life, but mirrored and illuminated it.

Sending Cam away to school ripped a hole in my heart that even now, nearly nine years later, hasn't fully healed. Strangely, however, only when he was no longer a daily presence was I able to integrate him into my professional life. The physical distance eventually created an emotional distance that enabled me to see what I couldn't see when Cam lived with us full-time: that he could be the subject of my work.

I began writing a book about our life with autism. Now instead of interrupting my writing, Cam became its focal point. As I worked through the book, the memories—many of them fraught with guilt, recrimination, and a pervasive sense of failure—gradually became "material." Paradoxically, the more I revisited them, the more I committed them to words, the more distant the events and accompanying emotions seemed. The process of incorporating and transforming these experiences allowed me to think of them as something other than problems, puzzles, or pains.

Writing the memoir also showed me that living with Cam, far from interfering with my professional skills, had actually sharpened them. For example, despite the scantiness of his oral language, my son has always been a noisy, histrionic child. He speaks most volubly with his body, and over the years we've learned to interpret his language: those gleeful scissors-kicking jumps; that contented or angry rocking; the myriad variations on his wordless shouts; the fine gradations in a face that to the uninitiated seems blank; an entire lexicon of claps.

Cam's claps are his personal Morse code. A single clap after he has sung a line or done something he finds remarkable serves as an exclamation point: "How about that?!" A series of claps in front of his open mouth creates a booming effect that means "I'm getting mad" or "I wish I could tell you what I mean." Several loud claps and a grimace means "I'm anxious" or "I don't like what you told me" (e.g., "Stop splashing water outside of the tub"). And let's not forget those declarative, rhythmic claps he favors in public places: "Here I am!"

Sometimes, too, he gives forth a long stream of syllables that sound like gibberish but really aren't. My wife and I have had to become detectives, deducing our son's emotions, desires, and thoughts from these facial expressions, gestures, and syllables: to know that a loud "Coke!" doesn't always mean he wants a drink, that "loo-ee" isn't a name but a way of expressing contentment. In capturing Cam's languages in the book, I came to understand how I had learned to "read" him, which in turn helped me listen to him more attentively.

Learning to read my son, hear him, see him, not only refined and deepened my sensitivity to language; it also trained me to attend more closely to the nonverbal languages of film and music (I'm a jazz musician as well as a film professor). Listening to Cam even helped me listen more closely to my students—especially to hear what they were *not* saying. In short, I understood that my nonverbal child had made me a better scholar and teacher.

Living with Cam and writing the book about him also transformed my thinking about the nature and value of consciousness and intelligence. Like many other academics I had long believed that intelligence is the most genuine measure of human value and that verbal fluency is the true currency of intelligence. An inarticulate person couldn't be smart; an intellectually disabled person, in turn, must be a lesser person. Cam showed me that these values—premises on which I had based my intellectual life and sense of self-worth—were specious, prejudiced, benighted. Like a brilliant professor, he had taught me what I hadn't even known I hadn't known.

Most of all, perhaps, writing about our life with autism allowed me to become Cam's medium—to let him speak through me in a deeper and more effective way than the Language Master machine would ever permit.

This aim of speaking with and for my son has in fact become the anchoring principle of my research on autism and the humanities—an approach I call "empathetic scholarship." By "empathy" I don't mean pity, for empathy recognizes that all humans share needs, emotions, and flaws but does not condescend. It preserves what the philosopher Martha Nussbaum calls a "twofold attention," which "both imagines what it is like to be" in another's place *and* retains "the awareness that one is not."[1] Empathy is not divided attention but *shared* attention: a conversation with and through another person.

The writing in the essay collection on autism that I edited, as well as my own scholarship on autism, issues from this empathy, which ideally enables us to combine the experiential knowledge we've gained as the loved ones of autistic people with our own professional training. Empathy lets us integrate our dual lives.

Through this twofold attention I have also come to recognize and celebrate a kind of radiance—a peculiar electricity that pervades and intensifies everyday life with autism. Capturing this radiance requires that I appreciate my son, whether he's physically with me or not.

But alas, most of the time he is not. And the void his leaving created couldn't be filled by writing a memoir, nor by any scholarship, no matter how well conceived. Perhaps that's why five years passed—one year of dazed relief, two years of depression and paralyzing guilt, two more years of battling Cam's new medical problems—before I could extract empathy from the churning mass of my tangled emotions. When at last I came to terms with our decision—accepted that we had no choice, that we had to save our son and family by sacrificing our selfish desires—I was able to purge most of my guilt and self-loathing. But can academic research replace those missing claps, hoots, and squeals, or substitute for the pungent aromas of Cam's favorite foods—Cheez-Its stacked with green olives, white rice drenched in soy sauce? Can it make up for the sight of him curled up in bed beside his stuffed St. Bernard, or supplant the rough touch of his long fingers, callused by years of shoestring play? Research engages the mind, and may even touch the emotions, but it can't fill your senses, make your heart race or your eyes brim with joy.

Even when Cam is at home, he no longer uses the Language Master. Though he remains largely nonverbal, he has moved on to other, more sophisticated communication devices. Sometimes their voices are mechanically produced; sometimes they are those of a teacher or aide. But I still make it a point to record my voice to name his favorite places: Burger King, the ice cream shop, and, yes, Daddy's "oppice." Nowadays, however, he rarely chooses this destination; he prefers to hang out with his helper, a young man close to his own age. That's as it should be; my son no longer needs my attention or voice so much as he once did.

Although it remains a poor substitute for Cam's actual presence, writing about him has not only ended the era of divided attention; it has also let me hear his voice more clearly when he *is* with me. Writing about Cam has both enabled him to speak through me and helped me to speak through him. It seems he has become my language master.

Note

1. Martha Nussbaum, *Upheavals of Thought: The Intelligence of Emotions* (Cambridge: Cambridge University Press, 2001), 328.

Accidental Academic, Deliberate Dad

KEVIN G. BARNHURST

In seventh-grade "Career Planning" class, I had to take one of those psychology tests that ask the same few questions a dozen ways each, as if you could forget your answers every few minutes. But as the unpopular oddball, I was clear about schools. Learning was fun, but school was not. Every time the test asked about more education, my answer was none. Tech school? Nope. Master's degree? No, thanks. PhD? What for?

But in high school I changed my mind about education: A sheepskin might be my ticket out of the lumpen middle class. But how? The only thing I was ever any good at was homework. Most subjects were hopeless for someone unable to remember rules. Sports couldn't help someone unable to recall how to move his body the same way twice. But a bad memory mattered less in academics—teachers mistook it for creativity.

I sat through the entrance exam and got junk mail from one engineering school in the South, plus Dartmouth College, a brochure that got me dreaming. When I finished the application form, my parents just laughed. Who in his right mind would send fifty dollars to a rich East Coast school? I ended up at Brigham Young University, the only place fool enough to foot the bill. My stepfather considered college a waste of time: "Why don't you get a job and do something useful?" he asked, but he did drive me fifty miles south to the campus and dropped me off, suitcase in hand.

The place I rented in the international house had seventeen students cooking strange-smelling foods, but I stayed in my room doing homework. My major, Latin American studies, went fast, with classes like Latin dance. Two years plus one semester later, the BA got me two internships apprenticing with bureaucrats—first in the USDA writing trade policy papers and then for the UN analyzing tariffs for imports like "edible offal"—but no job.

I went back for a master's degree, starting out in economics at Maryland, but dropped out because of health problems. I moved back to BYU part time and finished coursework in communications before getting kicked out. Seeing a draft of my project, the advisor said I didn't understand "the nature of graduate work" and swore he'd never allow me to get the degree. But when he went abroad on sabbatical, another professor alerted me so I could finish. Instead of a job, I ended up with freelance gigs in editing and design, based on two grad school courses I'd taken.

Becoming a dad was different. My own family was a put-together mob of thirteen kids, a real yours-mine-ours plus, in my case, theirs. I longed for what I never had: a dad. I liked the din of home life, but wanted a small family, I told my wife-to-be, "Maybe just five." She had other ideas: a big family with three kids. When the first arrived, I was a stay-at-home dad and soon discovered this rule: Put an adult and a child together, and one of them gets bored. So I changed my mind—one was enough, a dream fulfilled.

Instead we had two more, quick. Friends asked if we knew "where babies come from," but we knew. Each came from a birth control method that failed: diaphragm, condom, and the pill (these would make swell nicknames, I joked). I wanted to call my first son Chance (we had also used spermicidal foam on our honeymoon). Instead we named him Joel Sky, the first for something serious, the second for something fun, a flyer for Sky's Christmas Tree Lot.

A few weeks later, my wife conceived a second, disproving the old saw that nursing prevents impregnation (and neither did the spermicidal gel). We named him Andrew West, the first name a serious form for what we preferred (and good thing, too, after Drew Barrymore got famous) and the second to mark our move from the East.

The pill worked best, blocking sperm for a year. Then the third came along, and we named him Matthew Penn, the first name sticking with the biblical theme and the second in honor of my first published essay. (I can't explain the double t's and n's.) After having three in four years, another dream fulfilled, my wife wanted her tubes tied on the delivery table.

Teaching began as a stopgap during the recession that followed the oil crisis of the late 1970s. Our income, pieced together part time, began falling off. But a friend told me Westminster College wanted to create a noncredit workshop on editing and design, an odd combination back when designers went to art school and editors studied English. I got the work and called the course "Getting Graphic," clueless about academics.

But with three kids, I needed more than part-time work. Another friend told me an ad in *Editor & Publisher* described me to a T: teaching graphics for an English department in Keene, New Hampshire, not far from my Dartmouth fantasies.

In late June I sent (on green paper) a one-page résumé and a cover letter with the sentence "I'm drying out here in the desert—please take me back east to revive." After the July Fourth weekend, a dean called to ask me for an interview. I flew in and spent the first day puzzled by all the one-on-ones with art and English faculty. The second day, the dean hailed me from a second floor balcony, on his way out of town. I'd be getting an offer, he said. He wanted only to be sure I wasn't "swinging from trees."

A few weeks later we were driving back east, with a car full of boys in diapers and a U-Haul full of stuff. August found me teaching four sections, two each of freshman composition and news writing. It was my first real job, but I'd never taught a full semester of anything or written news beyond the school paper. It turned our progressive marriage into breadwinner-housewife roles.

The first term I designed a program in graphic arts, and the next I began teaching the main course. But I ran through all my lecture notes from Getting Graphic in the first three-hour evening class. When we met years later, one former student said, "There was one great lecture, but after that it was the worst course I ever took."

My years at Keene are a blur of planning (including a continuing ed program), prepping, grading, and coping with colleagues and bureaucracy. We bought a house, replaced our car, and settled in, but I hardly remember my sons except for all the washing (of cloth diapers). Our marriage deteriorated. One stock argument involved summer. Wasn't I supposed to be off, to give her a break from childcare? No, summer was my only chance to write.

By the fourth year I had managed to go to a few small conferences and publish two essays. My wife had managed to lose her patience. We began a trial separation, the boys splitting each week between her home and my new apartment.

Then my dean got a call from his chum Jim Carey, a dean at Urbana (who had read my essay in the *American Scholar*), asking permission to talk to me about a job. Soon the head of journalism called, but I put him off, asking him to send "some literature" that I never found time to read.

He called again. Would I go for an interview? I said no—that I liked my job (but not that the Midwest held no appeal or that I was going through a divorce). He pressed, asking, Why not just take a look—no expectations at all? And by the end of the call I caved.

My Urbana visit involved every possible blunder. I criticized the predecessor in the job. I'd done no homework: "What does the word *ill-ee-nee* mean?" I asked. "It's on all the signs around here" (to demonstrate my powers of observation). "Oh, the *ill-eye-nigh*?" he said. "Our mascot." That night I found the venerable Jumer's Castle Lodge a muddle of Americana in mismatched paisley—and said so the next morning. They offered me the job anyhow. Driving to the airport, the head proposed a salary, and a professor begged me to consider. I said I'd look at whatever they sent, thinking to put them off.

They took me as a hard bargainer. Within days, a better offer arrived: more money, graduate assistance, and less teaching. I said no again, but they came back with double my salary, one course per semester, new teaching facilities, and more grad assistants.

Faced with that breathtaking offer, I rationalized: The job sounded easy, and with that kind of money I could visit my sons and fly them to Urbana for holidays and summers. I said yes.

And I regretted the decision. After the move, my only time to talk to the boys was at 6:00 A.M., Central Time. Ever try talking to a child long distance? The conversation survives two sentences. It was a struggle for them, dragged out of bed on a school day. Once a week I would make small talk with each one in turn, saving up my stories and peppering them with questions about school, play, and, when all else failed, the weather. We were talking more (or I was talking to them more) than ever before, but I wanted them on my lap, not sleepy voices in the dark.

Another option was gifts. One evening I wandered through the boys' department at Target, looking for something to send them to cheer me up. When it dawned on me that I didn't even know their sizes, I fled the store in tears. By the holidays I had loaded the house with presents, aiming for quantity and size but mindless of what brands or styles they preferred.

Wanting company, I took them out of school early and sent them back late, demanding a full week for Thanksgiving or two over winter break. But what to do with them after the turkey or gifts?

Summers were worse. The first year my ex-wife and I each drove five hundred miles for the hand-off, but I'd brought only small travel games to fill the nine-hour return. My rental apartment had room only for sleeping bags on foldout beach lounges.

We tried camping once, but I forgot to check the weather, and we had to pack up in pouring rain to return home in the dark. At the apartment complex, we would walk to the pool and I would read on the deck, leaving the boys to splash and dive by themselves. By luck we ended up at the hospital just once, after Matthew banged his head on the concrete edge and bled profusely.

We tried day camp, and only later did the tales of hazing leak out. Too young for his brothers' program, Matthew chose something called Douglas Fun Camp because it had "fun" in the title. After the last day, I asked what he thought. "It was OK," he said, "but why was I the only vanilla and everyone else was chocolate?" At four he had no concept of race, and at thirty-four I had no idea how much race mattered.

At work I remember a big empty office—no books on the shelves except what textbook publishers had sent. There I sat, wondering what to do. I had figured out how to stretch lecture topics over a semester (before reading Paul Feyerabend's autobiography) but had little teaching to do.

A New York agent wrote to suggest I expand my first essay into a book, but I replied that I'd written all I had to say, and, anyway, I didn't know how to write a book. I started another essay, this time about newspapers, but it would take five years to see print.

Then a campus office asked me to review an internal grant application. Instead of the single, sustained essay like the one I knew how to write, the applicant churned out papers going over the same ground, each citing his previous work and adding a small, incremental idea. Journals had published every one. It looked like what I had to do to keep my job.

Around that time, Dean Carey gave me forms for a Lilly Foundation fellowship, but the topic, academic leadership, seemed dull, and I had no project to propose. That hint was all the academic advice I would ever get from him. I applied instead for a Fulbright to teach (I now knew how) and for a safe bet chose a place nobody wanted to go: Peru. Carey signed the application, but when the award came through, the department refused to let me go. No one else knew how to teach the one required course I taught. Finally the Fulbright Commission suggested I go in the summer. I decided to defy the department, go on my own time, and take my sons. Friends exclaimed, "You're crazy! There are terrorists down there." But I said, "Well, people *do* live there."

The boys were too young to travel alone, and so their mother came along to Cuzco and Machu Picchu, not that far from Shining Path guerrillas. After she left, we returned to Lima, where I worked, and the hired help watched my sons in our Miraflores apartment. They hardly left the fifth floor. We went on one outing to a nearby beach, where they swam in the winter surf while I fended off thieves. The country faced shortages, and when we found rice in one store, limit one kilo per customer, each boy bought a bag to share with my colleagues.

The bombed electrical towers outside Lima left us without power except for an hour a day, when we rushed to cook, clean, bathe the boys, and fill up containers with water. The timing was unpredictable, and so sometimes we just waited. After one sprint while the pump was working, I jumped in the shower and soaped myself up, but the power went out and the water stopped.

Another time I walked home exultant after discovering two hard-to-find luxuries in a small bodega: sugar and chocolate. The boys were excited, too, after all day with no television. To fill the time, they had begun inventing fantasy games that scared the daughter of our Peruvian cook.

A year later, my colleague wrote to say he'd been in Miraflores and turned down our street, Calle Tarata. But all that remained of our apartment was some concrete dangling from iron rebars. A bomb had destroyed the building along with a bank on the corner.

Back in Urbana, work relations had soured, and my efforts to socialize flopped. Watching the World Series with the journalism faculty was a bad idea for someone ignorant of baseball. I could comment only on the color of the grass, a point I never lived down. Once I offered to get a block of seats at an Illini basketball game, only to learn that everyone else had season tickets.

Colleagues over in the Institute of Communications Research sensed the problem and offered to team up, coauthor papers, and get at least something into print. But then the journalism profs considered me a turncoat for fraternizing with "academics."

Meanwhile, Joel was becoming a rebellious preteen, and his mom asked if he could move in with me. I canceled a conference talk and withdrew from a news industry event, angering colleagues and my dean, but I stayed home with Joel that summer. When he started school, I went back, working overtime to save my job.

He became an academic latchkey child, but instead of going to our apartment, he would visit neighbors. On the first floor, the Owl Lady would give him snacks and get him counting owls. He never found all her collection: ceramics, wood carvings, framed oils and prints, soft goods, and novelties. But other neighbors were grad students who started gossip about my late arrivals home.

At his mostly black school, Joel got in trouble for mouthing off at teachers and, after relentless teasing, for clobbering a girl half again his size. On a field trip to a local history museum, he got a sliver under his fingernail from an aging handrail. He wouldn't calm down, and the teacher apologized when she called: "It's only a sliver." I drove him to the ER, where the doctor thought the same—that is, until a local anesthetic made it possible to extract the wood fragment reaching to Joel's knuckle: tough kid.

But also a softie. He wanted to see *The Marriage of Figaro,* and my way of resisting was to turn it into a big project. He had to get recordings from the library, compare them, and pick a favorite. He had to follow the Italian libretto with a translation on facing pages. Then we went, armed with books and sheet music, but I had goofed. The performance was in English.

At work, the mid-probationary review hit me by surprise. In three years I had published nothing. A fundamentalist graduate assistant wrote a complaint about me, her depraved supervisor. After discovering I was gay, I blithely came out to everyone. My sons took it in stride, and my ex-wife's dry comment was "Well, that explains a lot." The tenure committee chair now wanted documentation to disprove the student's allegations that I was an unfit professor.

To buy time, colleagues in the Institute encouraged me to apply for a fellowship at Columbia. When it came through, the department head once again said no. That was it. The dean at Syracuse had courted me for a job earlier, but I'd said no. Now I asked, Would he hire me and then let me spend the first year at Columbia? He was delighted for me to fly "the Syracuse banner."

Joel and I packed up and left Illinois, but he didn't want to live in the big city. After summer, he stayed in New Hampshire. I thought of him as a stay-at-home type, but of course got that wrong.

The fellowship was to write a book, and by coincidence an editor from St. Martin's Press had walked into my office to announce, "I want you as my author." When she asked what book I'd like to write, I said I could try expanding my essay on newspapers, and she produced a contract.

Andrew, then eleven, decided to come along to New York. We rented an apartment on 116th Street, and I enrolled him in a magnet school for aspiring writers (following my dream, not his). It was near campus, and so I went with him the first day, then left him to his own devices for the twice-a-day, ten-block walk along Broadway. I worked (and dated, to meet the right man).

With his freedom, Andrew ran into trouble by skipping school and making mischief at home. Our university flat was a sabbatical rental with parking and a cleaning lady, and I quickly learned New Yorkers would not hear complaints about too much space. It also had hallways long enough for Rollerblading, and Andrew discovered he could make dramatic crash landings in the living room. I had to clean each scratch and use a tiny paintbrush to fill the grooves with varnish.

Then came a phone bill he ran up, calling 900 numbers to show off for a friend after school. I got the charges reversed, and the phone company blocked all sex-chat lines. But after we moved out, the landlord returned from sabbatical and called to object to dozens of charges that came on the next bill.

I didn't meet my man, but we enjoyed the city. On weekends we Rollerbladed along Riverside Park or explored Manhattan by train. We went for Indian tandoori Sunday afternoons. Some nights we ordered in. When we called up a dim sum place to order a "No. 51, Chicken Buns," the delivery arrived with fifty-one containers. I couldn't throw food away and so froze them for later, but Andrew soon lost his appetite for buns. I also tried to cook, frying up, for example, the homemade pesto left in the freezer by our landlady. How would I know to serve pesto fresh?

I finished a draft of the book, and the publisher accepted it as-is, leaving one chapter a raw literature review. On the long drive for a talk I gave in Washington, D.C., Andrew began what became our habit of philosophical debates. He was a positivist, the default product of capitalist America, and I was reading critical theory by then. I thought of him as a humanities-word guy, but of course got that wrong, too.

That summer in New Hampshire, I started dating my "gay lover," Richard, an environmentalist who won me over by playing video games with my sons. He offered to teach them tie-dye, and I invited him to dinner, but their mother had planned a week with them in Maine. We met for dinner anyway.

The next year, when I arrived at Syracuse, the book came out and got me tenure at the Newhouse School, despite objections that my personal-essay style wasn't "scholarship." "Have you read it?" one tenure committee member asked the dean, who said yes, and that was it.

All three sons soon joined me in Syracuse, where I bought a big American foursquare on Greenwood Place, near campus and their schools. They would get home before me, search the cupboards, and snack over cartoons. I would arrive cranky about their unfinished homework.

The boys took a turn each week making dinner, with rounds of pasta, tacos, and a casserole Joel called glop. Thursday was take-out pizza night, and I cooked on weekends, as well as shopping and doing laundry. I made a pie chart of chores and a cardboard spin-wheel to rotate their names. They each cleaned a room to pass inspection, and I paid allowances to match their work. They then disappeared with their new Syracuse buddies.

Each night I called Richard to drone on about my day of single parenting. Not much for the phone, he finally said, "So much happens to you!" His days were just the opposite, but he gave up his staff job at Boston University to become Uncle Charley to my three sons, our own sitcom: the only family my sons knew who ate dinner together every night at six, making polite conversation.

Tenure was no road to popularity. Where I grew up, folks said just what they thought, talked openly about money, and repeated what others said no matter who could hear. Not these rude habits but my lack of a doctorate is what Newhouse colleagues used to keep me out of the way.

After working there, a colleague took a chair at Amsterdam and then, to get my colleagues off my back, invited me to write a dissertation in Holland. First I had to document my entire academic life, a dossier the council of deans considered the week of September 24. That day I had a massive heart attack, but the efficient Dutch, while approving my candidacy, also discussed whether to award the degree posthumously.

I had too much to do before I died: sons to rear and places to go. They had complained they were too young to appreciate Peru, and I still remembered illustrations of Spain from a sixth-grade textbook. So I began applying for grants and leave, hoping to write the dissertation there.

My fall sabbatical got approved, and for spring the semester abroad program assigned me to teach at the Madrid Center. The two-semester deal surprised my dean, but I went anyway. For the sabbatical, instead of the important Complutense in Madrid or the up-and-coming Navarra in Pamplona, I accepted the invitation of an unknown university, La Laguna, in the Canary Islands.

That fall in Tenerife our apartment overhung the Atlantic Ocean. Andrew complained that he wanted the crashing surf "to just shut up" at night so he could sleep. He attended *instituto,* a high school where he made friends, passed most of his courses, and excelled in calculus, despite having studied only French. I hadn't believed it when he said he'd just "pick up" Spanish, but he did.

Richard lost sleep because of my computer keyboard clicking and printer churning out chapters late in the night. He'd also taken French in high school, but squeezed in two semesters of night school Spanish before we arrived. For help with the language, I invented errands: To mail a letter he would look up the words, memorize some sentences, venture to the post office, and ask his prepared question. The Spanish clerk would reply too fast, but Richard used signs and a word list to get by. He developed a big vocabulary for food just by grocery shopping.

Matthew understood a lot of what he heard but could hardly open his mouth to speak, despite years of Spanish in school, clear pronunciation, and a non-gringo accent. He was older and bigger than most of his classmates at the elementary school, and he soon stopped taking the bus with them, either preferring to walk kilometers to town or instead not going at all.

For his birthday in November, I wanted to cheer him up. The local open-air market had fresh shrimp, a luxury we never saw when I was young. I bought it, oblivious to his dislikes. At dinner I pressured him to take a taste, but after swallowing one shrimp, he began to cough and wheeze, then excused himself and went to bed. Even the cake could hardly lure him back.

After one term, he left Spain. His classmates, in fun, had pestered him with memorized English phrases, ogled his fair hair and eyes, and chanted for him to count to ten in Spanish. But I was busy doing research. Back in New Hampshire, he had another reaction to seafood and started carrying an EpiPen. I thought he was vulnerable, shy, and a bit lazy, but here, too, I was dead wrong.

In January we moved to Barrio Salamanca in Madrid, and I began teaching two courses while revising the dissertation. Andrew bumped along in the *instituto* near Ventas bullring and started drinking wine. Richard kept house, and Joel came only for a nine-day visit. In New Hampshire he had found a job and met a girlfriend. I wanted him to stay longer in Spain, but he said, "Dad, I have a *life*."

In May we flew to Amsterdam for the public defense. The committee from Spain, England, the United States, and Holland wore academic robes and marched into the seventeenth-century Aula at the Spui, behind a sexton who pounded a large staff to call the audience to attention. I stood at a podium, flanked by two paranymphs, grad students who had read my dissertation (and translated an extended abstract into Dutch), ready in case I lost my cool.

The next year I was on the market, PhD in hand, and got two offers. A verbal one from Rutgers vanished between December, when the dean called with the good news, and February, when he hired someone else. Meanwhile I returned to teach in Spain, but my family was worn out. Only Richard managed to get an "adventure leave" from his new job for two months.

Chicago seemed like a cow town when I flew from Madrid for an interview. The offer from UIC came after weeks of waiting for the first choice to turn it down. But I was used to playing second fiddle. All my academic jobs (I heard later) came after searches lost other candidates. No matter. UIC hired me.

I moved to Chicago alone. The boys were in college: Joel at Keene, Andrew at Earlham, and Matthew at Carleton. Even Richard stayed behind to do a master's degree at Antioch New England. But I was dogged with my weekly phone calls. When Richard, Andrew, and Matt finally moved to Chicago, the calls turned into Sunday dinners, until I dragged Richard off again. On yet another fellowship, this time in Italy, I went to the corner pay phone and placed calling-card calls to my sons.

Maybe academic life puts distance between fathers and sons. Professors mete out judgment, harsh about error and doubtful of quality. Dads serve up wholehearted appreciation, or at least so it seemed to me. My stepfather finally got a real son of his own and was nothing but a fan. But teaching taught me something about myself: I used to start out semesters unsure about the students. Now I know I'll be fond of them before the term ends, so I start with that in mind.

It took me years to realize how much I admire my sons and respect their choices. Instead of being a stay-at-home type, Joel moved to the U.K. to pursue a career in the arts, landing his dream job in high school technical theater. It was fun to visit him on another sabbatical and see him grown to manhood, respected by coworkers, and settled with his wife and her family.

Instead of a humanities-word type, Andrew majored in math, took a master's degree (through real travail) at Loyola in Chicago, and found jobs doing data analysis. But we still have philosophical discussions. Matthew started out studying (of all things) first marine biology and then performance studies, but ended up working an intense physical job in clinical massage therapy—no shy-slacker type. Woodsy Richard decided to enter the family business, doing a doctorate.

UIC promoted me, made me department head, and gave me a Big Ten fellowship. It was for academic leadership, but by then Jim Carey had left Illinois. He was less a mentor than a surrogate parent in my adoptive bourgeois family. His most memorable words, looking me up and down as we both left an international conference in Washington, D.C., were something like "When are you going to grow up and start dressing the part?"

Academic success came despite my wearing jeans, T-shirt, and a baseball cap, despite my spotty training and bad memory, despite my checkered past. Fatherhood is not so easy. I'm a talker about emotions, sex, and experience, embarrassing my sons. They make talk from gaming and pop culture references—things that leave me blank. I like nothing more than having my sons around, but when they come home I seem distracted with too much to do. It's a bad habit that covers the fact that, after all these years, I still have no idea how to be a dad.

Late Fatherhood
among the Baptists

ANDREW HAZUCHA

I never told my father this, but there was a time in my life—in my late
teens, to be precise—when I resented him for waiting until he was forty to
have me. And even though my mother was thirty-seven when I was born,
just three years younger than my father, it was my now late-fiftyish father
and not my mid-fiftyish mother whose age was a slight embarrassment to
me as I moved into my senior year of high school and saw many of my
friends' fathers, like mine, attending their sons' baseball and basketball
games. How virile, how hip those forty-something fathers appeared in the
stands! How young they looked next to mine.

During my undergraduate years and then the decade I spent in graduate school, my relationship with my father deepened, grew richer, and as
I moved through early adulthood I came to revere many of the qualities
in my father that I hoped I would possess when it came time for my own
fatherhood: an innate compassion, a restless intellectual curiosity, and a
healthy skepticism toward religion. While weighing my first job offers in
academia and trying to decide whether to accept a teaching position at a
state university in Minnesota or a religiously affiliated liberal arts college
in the South, I naturally called my father and asked him what he would do
if he were in my shoes. Would he accept a job at a school run by Southern
Baptists, I asked him? "Not with what I know now," he replied. "But when
I was your age, I probably would have taken it." I accepted the offer to teach
at Carson-Newman College in Tennessee, then, with some foreknowledge
of the tribalism and strange culture wars I would soon be entering. I had
my father's blessing. I was thirty-three years old. And, although I didn't
know it then, it would be another fifteen years before I had my first child.

For those who have never taught at a Baptist college in the South, the
culture may seem alien to the point of otherworldly. Many of my students
were entirely comfortable during class discussions confessing their faith,

articulating their personal relationships with Jesus, describing how God was directing all the events in their lives. In my very first semester at Carson-Newman one of my first-year male students told me in my office that Satan was trying to make him have premarital sex with his girlfriend; another eighteen-year-old student, a female with a perfect attendance record, missed class with no warning one Friday and apologized to me on Monday for her absence, saying that she had gotten married over the weekend. Their stories collectively communicated to me that it was necessary to marry young and follow the biblical imperative to go forth and multiply as soon as feasible, even if it meant curtailing their college careers, so that they could have sex without fear of God's wrath. Some students avoided the dilemma of choosing between abstinence or marrying in college by using the logic made famous by Bill Clinton (defining oral sex and anal sex as something other than sex, and therefore acceptable to God). The intellectual ruses they were willing to deploy to accommodate their problematic sexual urges made it clear to me that an unmarried and childless male in his early thirties, as I was when I began my teaching career, was simply bizarre to them. Why hadn't I begun multiplying? Either I was gay or had given up on ever finding a mate and raising a family. To them, it would seem, late parenthood at best was symptomatic of bad judgment or bad luck; at worst it was the sin of having squandered one's best years.

When teaching such texts as Philip Larkin's "Church Going" or Kate Chopin's *The Awakening*—which I did frequently in literature classes in an attempt to offer my most deeply indoctrinated students a counternarrative to their evangelical upbringing and inflexible family values—I was often met with puzzlement or glances of deep concern, as students stated that they would pray for the souls of these wayward writers. Occasionally I would challenge them in a more direct and personal way, telling them, for instance, that one night I had a long conversation with an ethereal being who listened with loving concern to my innermost secrets and invited me to relinquish to him all control over my life. "The personal relationship I've developed with my Space Moose," I concluded with a look of gravity on my face, "has consoled me and given me an opportunity to live according to his will." Some of my students, I learned later, added me to their prayer lists.

I left Carson-Newman College after eleven years of teaching there not only because of the oppressive religious atmosphere but because the chances of finding a soul mate in east Tennessee were not promising. Laboring under a 4/4 teaching load with forty to fifty freshman composition students each semester, I had little opportunity of socializing outside my decidedly small circle of progressive faculty friends. And all of them were married or had partners. So when I hit the job market again after a decade of teaching at a religiously affiliated school, I was looking to move to a secular institution with a lighter teaching load, even if it meant increased administrative duties.

As fate would have it (and for reasons too complicated to enumerate in this essay) I landed in Kansas at Ottawa University, a small liberal arts institution affiliated with the American Baptist Church, a denomination that I had been assured was much more open, tolerant, and ecumenical than its Southern counterpart. In another strange irony, shortly after accepting the job at Ottawa University I began dating my partner, Emily, and after our being together only three months, she made the decision to move to Kansas with me. From the very earliest stages of our relationship we had discussed having a child together, but she wanted to wait until she had gained some experience as a nurse-midwife in Kansas, and that would necessarily take a couple of years. Our plan was to have the birth at home without the intervention of a medical establishment that viewed midwifery with the same skepticism that I reserved for expressions of religious faith.

Fast-forward four years. I was going for a walk with Emily one February morning when she delivered me the news. "I took a blood test yesterday that showed elevated levels of a hormone called beta hCG," she said slowly, with great seriousness. "There are only two possibilities. Either I have a brain tumor, or I'm pregnant." Then she smiled. At the age of forty-eight I was going to be a first-time father.

What does it mean to be a father in one's late forties? Men who have fathered children in their late sixties (let me wait until I'm Strom Thurmond's age to have a child, I jokingly told Emily one day while anxiously contemplating the thought of starting a family now, and the ways it might affect the trajectory of my academic career) would no doubt laugh at the implied anxiety behind this question, but I could not forget my teen years, nor could I throw off my profoundest reading experiences. I had written my dissertation on the eighteenth-century novel *Tristram Shandy*, which begins with the moment of the narrator's conception disrupted by *coitus interruptus*. Narrating this inauspicious event from his mother's womb, the protagonist-fetus Tristram asserts that his father, Walter Shandy, could not possibly get the job done while inseminating his mother, and hence, as Walter himself avers, "My Tristram's misfortunes began nine months before he ever came into the world!" The overarching joke of the first four volumes of this nine-volume novel is that Walter Shandy has managed against all odds to sire a son in his old age, and because he is a worn-out man whose best years are behind him, his exhausted "animal spirits" are transferred to his son at the moment of Tristram's conception. Misfortune follows misfortune, as the intended Trismegistus is misnamed Tristram at birth, his nose is crushed by forceps as he moves through the birth canal, and he is accidentally circumcised by a window sash while still an infant. All of these minor tragedies are attributable indirectly to Walter Shandy's fatherly infirmity and hands-off parenting style.

As an academician advancing through middle age, I harbored fears that I was a version of Walter Shandy. Sheltered in the ivory tower, living a life of the mind rather than of action, I was akin to the highly theoretical Walter Shandy who could not dwell comfortably in the real world. But my child, I knew, would force me into that world with a vengeance, the world of cloth diapers, early morning hours in the rocking chair, and inconsolable hungers for things I could not provide. Moreover, I was soon to be an unmarried professor of English and department chair with an out-of-wedlock child at a Baptist college. Would the moral opprobrium of the institution come down on me like a Jonathan Edwards sermon? Or worse yet, would I become a kind of Shakespearean pantaloon, a figure of ridicule?

Somewhere in the depths of my consciousness I could not forget those surreal experiences at my first teaching job, nor the reasons I had given up a tenured associate professorship and a coterie of good friends there and moved back to the Midwest. Just as I had resisted joining a church while teaching at Carson-Newman (one of the ostensible requirements for tenure, but which, inexplicably, never came up in my tenure reviews or my final tenure meeting with the provost), I had an aversion to family, because family in that particular corner of East Tennessee meant traditional heterosexual marriage, conservative patriarchal expectations for womanly—or rather "wifely"—behavior, and an intolerance of other sorts of conjugal arrangements. Gay and lesbian faculty members were permanently in the closet, while an unmarried female associate professor who cohabited with a member of the opposite sex was forced to marry in order to receive tenure. One recently retired male professor, divorced for over twenty years and living with another woman for nearly a decade, was told by the new provost that if he wished to receive a contract and pursue his plan of teaching at the college part-time as an emeritus he would need to marry his girlfriend.

This was the rule-bound environment I had rejected when leaving Carson-Newman and making my way to another college, which, although a Baptist institution, had all the appearances of a less severe, more kindly place to work. Ottawa University thus far had proven itself to be different

in kind and not just degree; run by a visionary academic dean and provost
who shared the aspiration of making Ottawa a socially progressive institution with a core commitment to social justice issues, it was the kind of
school where I would not face the same hang-ups about marital or premarital behavior. My previous resistance to fatherhood at a Baptist college was
no longer fueled by rules for prescribed behavior. And yet my skepticism
about Baptist schools of any kind had not entirely left me, which is to say
that I still needed convincing that unmarried late fatherhood could work
for me in Kansas. Emily's news would put our circumstances to the test.

The birth of Benjamin was the beginning of the end of my fears. As
any first-time father knows, the birth process necessarily involves a certain
letting go, although when it happens au naturel, at home, sans doctors, the
father may be even more jittery about this perceived lack of control. In reality, though, a homebirth empowers both mother and father and gives them
enormous control over the birth process. This was the case with Benjamin:
surrounded by a midwife, a nurse, and a dear friend of Emily's who was
taking photos of the natural birth, I had complete faith that these women
would monitor and encourage Emily as she labored through the night.
More importantly for me, they made sure that I was integral to the process,
instructing me how to apply counterpressure to her back as she labored,
asking me to provide her with food and drink when she needed it, and
keeping me focused on my task of staying by her side with words of encour-
agement. Emily wanted me to remind her while she was laboring that she
had climbed both Mount Snowdon and Scafell Pike—the highest peaks
in Wales and England respectively—while she was five and a half months
pregnant, and I did so when she was resting between contractions. Finally,
after seven and a half hours of Emily's pushing, Benjamin's head cleared
her perineum and I caught him in my hands as the midwife and I jointly
guided him into the world.

Just as the natural birthing process gave Emily and me the gift of
ownership over Benjamin's birth and validated our decision to eschew a
more medically intrusive procedure, the Ottawa University administration's
response to our news bore out our decision to go to Kansas. The new academic dean, whose own two sons had been delivered by a midwife and
who had encouraged me to stay home during the three days prior to Benjamin's birth as Emily began her contractions, wrote a university-wide e-mail
announcing the news and congratulating the new parents. Over the next
forty-eight hours notes of congratulations came over my school e-mail
account in droves, including a most gracious one from Ottawa's president

in which he reflected upon his own fatherhood and wished me all the joys that my new state might supply. "I can tell you that my sons are the best part of my life," he wrote. "I wish the same for you and Emily." Two weeks after Benjamin's birth, I walked over to the human resources department at Ottawa University and had him added to my school insurance policy—a family insurance plan that already covered Emily as my domestic partner.

Lest this account be misconstrued as some sort of utopian narrative in which a long-suffering single professor meets the woman—and teaching position!—of his dreams, I would refer the reader back to *Tristram Shandy* and emphasize that it's the absurdity of my journey that ought most impress you. The truth of the matter is that I still work for Baptists, who rarely reach any consensus on doctrinal issues and thus engage in frivolous internecine warfare nearly all the time. If it is true that all religious wars are fought over who has the best imaginary friend, then religiously affiliated academic institutions—even the most enlightened of their kind—fight viciously and continually over how best to merge open intellectual inquiry with a commitment to the imaginary transcendent. I still labor under a heavy 4/3 teaching load, despite my dual role as English Department chair and chair of the Arts and Humanities Division. When Benjamin was born I immediately gave up the annual summer study abroad trip to Ireland that I have been running for over a decade, knowing that to abandon Emily and him for three weeks would be to abdicate my fatherly commitment to co-parenting. And when asked to serve as interim academic dean when the aforementioned new (but now among the ranks of the old) academic dean announced his resignation earlier this year, I turned down this rare chance to move from the faculty ranks into administration, wishing ultimately to be more of a presence in my son's life than a man who would be working a nine-to-five job on a twelve-month contract.

In a sense, then, this homebirth was a kind of secular miracle in that it clarified my ethical and practical commitments to the heretofore distant values of home and family. My respect for Emily, from the first profound, went off the charts. I marveled at her inner reserves of strength and her calm determination throughout, and watched with amazement as her midwife brain kicked in during labor and she repeatedly checked her own cervix to plot her progress. While I worried about the plethora of possible birth defects whose likelihood increased with increases in paternal age, Emily, who declined to have a routine ultrasound during her pregnancy and didn't want to know in advance the gender of our child, remained confident that all would go well. Benjamin's tranquility as he came through the birth

canal was therefore eerie and calming at the same time; I was expecting
a wailing lump of needs protesting his entrance into "this scurvy world,"
as Tristram Shandy would say. Instead he stared at me with watery eyes
and an ancient wisdom, refusing for a moment to take his first breath. I
wondered if he was healthy. And then he cried. As I laid him on Emily's
chest and cut the umbilical cord, my emotions ran riot. I couldn't wait to
call my father to tell him that we would use his name, Rudolph, for our
son's middle name. Looking at Benjamin as he latched onto Emily's breast
and began to nurse, I contemplated this moment and all that it signified.
Oh Benjamin, I thought, child of my right hand, I give you this gift: I forgive
you already, in advance, for resenting your gray-haired, late-sixtyish father
as he sits in the stands or audience and roots for your success, wishing
you Godspeed as you make the inevitably painful journey from boyhood
to manhood.

Being a Dad, Studying Fathers

A Personal Reflection

WILLIAM MARSIGLIO

Phoenix, my youngest son, was born when I was forty-nine years old. His birth energized my fascination with the daily labor of fathering, something I had largely ignored as an ignorant, working-class teenage father thirty-one years before. True to his mythological name, Phoenix offered me new life to be an engaged father. He also inspired me to practice what I "preach" as a profeminist family and gender scholar.

At eighteen, on the verge of entering college in a few months, I signed my name to a marriage certificate and, five months later, paternity papers. I drifted blindly into my new life as husband, co-parent, and father to my firstborn son, Scott. Looking back, I'm ashamed to say that as a relatively naïve and traditional young man, I skirted many of the labor-intensive activities of infant care. Granted, once Scott grew into an active toddler, my commitment to fatherhood strengthened, my love deepened, and I devoted much more time to playing with him. I even dabbled in some of his daily care. A special bond had taken hold.

But, in the nearly four years we lived together, I was not the "New Age" father I now extol. Back then I had a very different view of time and gender equity. I had no real sense of urgency, nor did I recognize what I might be missing, either in terms of a father-son relationship, a co-parental partnership, or my own personal development.

Unskilled in caring for babies, consumed by other responsibilities—initially as an athlete and always as a wide-eyed college student—I automatically projected my child's mother as his competent, primary caretaker. Later, during my fourteen years as a nonresident father to a minor child who lived far away, I stepped up and became a more attentive dad when Scott visited. Unfortunately, our extensive time apart discouraged Scott from seeing me as a nurturing, engaged father. The magical bond from the early years waned as time, space, our separate life rhythms, and his adolescent quest for independence bred a more superficial father-son bond. During those nonresident years, our blood tie and distant memories of a more intensely shared history anchored whatever sense of "we-ness" we shared. Sadly, that connection lacked the rich intimacy, familiarity, trust, and depth that flow from sharing everyday rituals, every day.

Now, decades later, I am both a middle-age father to a young boy and an academic social scientist devoted to studying men's relations with kids, mostly as fathers. Blessed to have a second chance to cultivate the early years of fathering a vibrant, impressionable child, I am also uniquely situated: Each fathering moment is ripe with prospects for personal growth as well as professional development. From planning a second child, to conception, to pregnancy, to childbirth, and to the ultimate challenges of fathering a new life, my most recent journey bears little resemblance to my first. I see the contrast in my self-image and my desire for others' respect. When I was a young father, I sometimes wished that others in public would not see me as a dad. In my selfish mind, others' perceptions left me feeling trapped and unavailable as a romantic man. And in private, family space, I sometimes deflected the responsibilities of parenting to others. I was not averse to donning a passive, ill-informed persona when basic child-care needs arose. Changing diapers was outside my comfort zone; I had no clue that embracing this "chore" could foster my bond with my son.

Today, after decades of personal growth and academic experience, I cherish more fully my intimacy needs and opportunities. My mission is to create memorable rituals with Phoenix through play and nurturance that will grow our emotional attachment. I am also a much more astute observer of the social gaze. Ever since I went public with news of Phoenix's conception, I scrutinize how family, friends, and strangers react to my style of striving to be an engaged, nurturing father. No longer do I hide or downplay that I am a dad; I am honored. I love to take him grocery shopping and ride him around in his "big green machine." As a profeminist, I realize that I do not deserve, nor do I seek, special praise for what I do—most mothers, and many fathers, do it as a matter of course. Yet I am quick to feel the insult when someone questions my motives or right to be a doting dad.

My fathering story, though novel on the whole, has pieces that resonate with other fathers. As a qualitative sociologist, I know this well because I regularly ask men from diverse backgrounds to describe in detail how they perceive and interact with their own and others' kids. My firsthand fathering with my sons helps me refine and focus my interview questions. In technical terms, my fathering gives me "sensitizing" concepts. These

insights open my eyes to facets of the social and identity processes I sub-
sequently explore when I talk with fathers. I also personally benefit from
doing research when I hear men speak passionately about their time with
kids. Those messages fortify my own commitment to fathering well.

In turn, because my work is distinctly theoretical, I often reflect throughout the day on how men think, feel, and act as fathers over their life course.
I consider how their fathering is shaped by family structure, social class,
physical sites, perceptions of what it means to be a man, and other circumstances. Not surprisingly, then, my scholarly insights seep into how I frame
my own approach to fathering. In particular, my scholarship has led me
to consider issues related to men's involvement in the pregnancy and childbirth process as well as how men construct their father identities, manage co-parenting relationships, and interact with their children in myriad
ways. One of my conceptual models accounts for a man's self-awareness
as someone capable of creating and caring for human life. A man's sense
of readiness to become a father is a key concept; it guided much of my thinking when I contemplated having a second child. Without question, my
professional expertise on these and related issues focuses my vision while
coloring my interpretations of what being a father and co-parent means.

Concepts bring our social worlds to life. They shape the contours of
what we experience; they allow us to "see" realities that we might otherwise
miss. The nomenclature of my subfields, some of which I have generated
myself, provides me with a set of conceptual tools to anticipate and define
the processes that matter to me as a father and co-parent. For instance, I
recently took a small step toward supporting gender equity in childcare,
inside and outside my own home. On the heels of publishing a book, *Men
on a Mission: Valuing Youth Work in Our Communities*, that examined paid
and volunteer male youth workers' involvement with kids in the community, I hired Alex, a twenty-year-old male "nanny." Alex was the boyfriend
of Rosie, Phoenix's first and very special full-time caretaker, who left the
state for a year to take a job. By hiring Alex, I sought to build "social capital"
for Phoenix. As I talk about it here, social capital involves meaningful exchanges, sometimes culminating in an alliance, between a parent and other
adults who are invested in nurturing a child's well-being and development.
In many ways, Rosie was an invaluable asset for Phoenix's development,
and I wanted to increase the odds that she would remain an active member of Phoenix's life long after she returned from her temporary job. I
thought getting Alex directly involved with Phoenix might help to keep her
in the "family." Hiring Alex also enabled me to expose Phoenix to a male

caretaker to reaffirm for him that men can be loving, gentle, and responsive to his emotional and physical needs. Finally, aside from his delightful ways with my son, Alex is musically gifted. I anticipated that if I were to forge a long-term friendship with Alex good things would follow. Most importantly, he could nurture my desire to learn how to play the guitar and we could collectively foster a love for music in my son—something that I missed out on as a child. Beyond sports, I hoped to craft another avenue of affinity with Phoenix. Of course, parents outside the academy and unfamiliar with my research specialties can and do make similar choices. However, I suspect my nuanced understanding of the many dimensions to how social capital is expressed, built, negotiated, and becomes consequential prompts me to think more systematically about my fathering and act more deliberatively.

For me, telling my son bedtime stories, or putting him to sleep by singing the special song—"Baby Rock"—I wrote for him, or being there to pick him up when his eyes open and the whimpering begins, or giving him his nightly bath, or helping him to soothe his "booboos" inspires me to think more rigorously from a sociological perspective about what gives these rituals meaning and how they matter—for each of us. Moments of intimacy and bonding can appear spontaneously. But some are neatly tailored into the routines and places that texture daily living. In my "free time," as a sociologist and father, I ponder the blessings of being a more attentive, resident dad who is eager and able to comfort my son as he transitions into and out of his vulnerable sleep state or tries to manage his fear of discomfort from a fall or a cold. I recognize too how Phoenix's mother gives me the space and time to bond with him in my own ways. I take none of this for granted and I think about it often.

As a preoccupied teenage father and then a nonresident young father I missed out on most of these precious occasions. I definitely spent little time thinking about my fathering experience. Stuff happened and I reacted, or I let someone else respond. As a more focused, experienced, reflective, and responsive resident dad I can freely soak up the bonding that goes with my child's shining moments—as well as his tantrums. Having both a flexible schedule and a family-friendly department chair gives me added freedom to be with Phoenix during every phase of his daily cycle. My favorable set of circumstances raises the odds that I will witness unforgettable child-rearing gems—like having my eighteen-month-old son fix his eyes on me while sitting in a bubble bath before uttering his very first sentence, "Dada, read book."

Regrettably my commitment to excel in college and then pursue a career that required many more years of training led me to skimp on my time with my first son. Ironically, though, Phoenix and I now reap the long-term dividends of those choices. I realize, of course, that because I was a senior scholar when Phoenix arrived on the scene, I had more autonomy to be an engaged father. The balance between the external and personal pressure to produce publications had shifted, and I felt freer to pull back. Having already produced my share of books and articles, I was at ease with publishing a bit less—at least for the foreseeable future. If, on the other hand, Phoenix had come into my life when I was an assistant professor committed to achieving tenure and establishing an international reputation, I would have felt much more anxious.

As it stands now, I have the luxury of turning down writing, reviewing, supervisory, and traveling requests with only minimal concern that I am compromising myself professionally. Yes, I could, presumably, enhance my reputation even more, but at the end of the day—or more accurately, at the end of my life—what will matter to me? The answer lies in the decisions I've made in recent years. I am not shy about telling my colleagues that I'm unavailable for projects because I want to balance my work and family life sensibly—in a manner that keeps me busy, yet not too busy to create my precious moments with Phoenix each and every day. In the first two years of his life I chose not to attend any conferences that would require an overnight stay, save one that I had committed to prior to Phoenix's conception. I even declined an invitation for a sponsored trip to Denmark to give a keynote address on fathering and intimacy. The thought of leaving my eighteen-month-old son at the time for an extended trip was too unpleasant. Before Phoenix, I would have accepted and gone without a second thought.

In our gendered world, being male helps my cause. I have more latitude than my female colleagues in saying no without prejudice. In some wings of the academy, like sociology, being an engaged father can actually engender warm sentiments from colleagues and staff. That has been my personal experience.

Perhaps the best way to capture the intersection between my lives as father and sociology professor is to convey how joyful I felt writing this essay at home the past several June days. On numerous occasions I heard Phoenix's innocent voice echo down the hall as he flexed his newfound language skills with Alex. He ran down the hall saying "dada" and into my study several times each day, demanding his privileged spot next to my chair. Because Phoenix is foremost in my mind as I manage my career commitments and work pace, I seldom face hard deadlines that prevent me from celebrating, at least for a while, his every request for "dada time." Seeing his long curly locks, baby-toothed smile, and unbridled exuberance is the most refreshing writing break I can imagine. His presence snaps me out of—yet back into—the passionate mindset that goes with writing this revealing autoethnographic essay about being a father and scholar.

Lest I paint a distorted portrait of myself as a professor who has effortlessly swapped his zest for doing scholarship for his love of fathering, I will share the fleeting conundrum I encountered yesterday afternoon while writing this essay. My son was napping in another room under my video monitor surveillance. I was consumed by the druglike sensation of being in a "writing zone." Fresh ideas were flowing faster than I could type— and I type quickly. A subtext of pride gripped me as I imagined the final, polished product in hand, others' accolades sounding in my ears. It was then that my son's stirring in his crib caught my attention. Fifteen seconds or so passed as I darted my eyes back and forth from the computer screen to the baby monitor, hoping all the while that I would have just a few more minutes to compose my thoughts into coherent sentences. Then, with frenetic speed, I tried to get my thoughts down in any form possible before Phoenix had a chance to stand or start to cry. I was reminded that despite my "devoted dad" identity, the seduction of the prestige that accompanies published writing remains strong, even addictive, to me. But, alas, the joy of a child's love is pretty damn potent too. I saved my work and happily rushed to my privileged spot next to Phoenix's crib, calling his name aloud along the way.

I am content that my academic post afforded me yesterday, and many other days, the choice to work at home, accessible to my son. Had I been writing in my university office instead, I would have avoided the immediate work-father tension, but one more precious moment would have gone undiscovered. Serendipitously, as I composed these final words, joy came to me again. I turned in the nick of time to see my son, playing with Alex outside my study window, hit a baseball solidly off of a tee after weeks of mishaps. I ran out to congratulate him and he hugged me.

Single Dad in Academia

Fatherhood and the Redemption of Scholarship

ERIC H. DU PLESSIS

I have been a single father for the past ten years, raising a boy and a girl two and a half years apart. From rugrats to rock singer wannabes, my children are an integral part of every hour and every day of my academic life. To most of my colleagues, my fate looks like a catastrophe visited upon a helpless college professor; but raising my kids while teaching at a midsize university in Virginia has become a most rewarding and challenging experience. I was the typically harried educator with a twelve-hour teaching load, a retinue of departmental responsibilities, a study abroad program, and additional duties as assistant editor for a scholarly journal. Like most of my colleagues, I was used to hectic schedules and deadlines, so I reckoned that the harmonization of academia and single fatherhood would prove no more daunting than my other obligations.

I was blissfully unaware of broken-down school buses, of an entire county closing at noon because of the threat of inclement weather, urgent conferences with principals, or the unpredictable social life of preteens. It became axiomatic that my office hours would never synchronize with the pediatrician's. Professional conferences, student papers, publisher's deadlines, committee meetings, syllabi, and galley proofs began to compete with tae kwon do tournaments, guitar lessons, birthday parties, rotavirus, appendicitis, and Cub Scout meetings. Even the rigors of medieval French boarding schools or the schedule of a graduate student hadn't prepared me for the daily responsibilities of a single dad.

In time I discovered the true meaning of sleep deprivation. We all awoke at six thirty in the morning, the common lot of most families, but an awakening made more challenging by the lingering impact of the previous night's activities. My son had ADHD, and the medication he took to control focus and hyperactivity precluded his going to sleep before midnight, and then only to foster dramatically elaborated dreams. Rousing him from his truncated slumbers the next morning required the patience of a child psychologist and the tenacity of a drill sergeant. My daughter didn't share his disability, but the vividness of her dreams and a creative imagination populated her bedroom with nightmarish creatures, sending her running down the hall at 3:00 A.M. for immediate rescue. I was ill-equipped in the middle of the night to do battle against demonic beasts or to prevent a boy's imaginary spacecraft from crashing into the surface of Neptune.

I'd had my share of sleepless nights as a student, but never knew until I became a single dad that I could actually function on so little sleep. Teaching wasn't much of a problem, as long as I kept moving about, engaging students, and establishing productive dialogue during lectures and seminars. Committee meetings were more treacherous. Soft and inviting furniture, controlled room temperature, and the natural tendency of most academics to drone and pontificate created numerous temptations to fall asleep. I became addicted to potent cups of tea, dark as ink to guarantee I would be back home on time as the school bus pulled in front of our house with inexorable punctuality. Single parents are sorely sleep deprived. Most are in dire need of a nap around three o'clock in the afternoon, and to them is imparted the revelation that aspirin isn't a substitute for five hours of uninterrupted sleep. My morning routines became strategies refined to a science. Getting the kids up, bathed, dressed, medicated, and fed followed like choreographed chaos, leaving me time to warm up the car in the garage and load the trunk with school bags and packed lunches. We would then squeal out of our driveway in a daily attempt to beat the school buses already backing up traffic for a quarter mile. My children didn't mind riding the bus on their way back in the afternoon, spending an hour with a sitter until I got home, but the three of us insisted that I drop them off to school every morning,

My classes had been tailored to a three-days-a-week schedule, with all my courses and meetings arranged between 9:00 A.M. and 2:30 P.M. The rest of the week, I was available for parent-teacher conferences, dental checkups, and pediatric appointments. Tuesdays and Thursdays, once reserved for writing projects in the library, became dedicated to errands, grocery shopping, oil changes, laundry, housekeeping, and yard work. But no matter how many ways I could devise to stretch my schedule, there were still only twenty-four hours in a day. It became obvious that I had to initiate significant changes to accommodate the remaining fragments of my professional life. As a college professor, my obligations were divided into three distinct areas: teaching, administrative duties, and scholarly research. My teaching schedule was the easiest part to reconcile with family obligations. Indeed, once my children were both in school, the county's instructional calendar fitted quite nicely with the university schedule. Thanks to the understanding of my department chair, and the kind indulgence of colleagues, I taught all my courses when my children sat in their own classrooms. A convenient scheme, but also a problematic challenge since it meant that any emergency involving them would by default interfere with my teaching. Fortunately, this arrangement proved to be a practical solution. Despite the number of incidents and illnesses over the years, my absences from the university actually turned out to be fewer than those of my colleagues.

And yet, while my children were safely in school, their presence lingered as an integral part of my academic obligations. It seemed as if all the imponderables in the life of preteens—and my own kids' propensity for extracurricular mischief—shadowed me into every class and conference room. Discipline problems and health-related incidents became the usual reason behind phone calls from assistant principals or school nurses. I decided to inform my students as succinctly as possible about my being a single dad with two young kids in public school. My cell phone would be the only one allowed to ring during class. They all cooperated, feeling sorry for this fortyish academic, and commiserating with a fate still alien to their daily lives. Once or twice a week, an emergency call would interfere with my lecture. Students who had already taken a class with me awaited these interruptions as an entertaining part of the syllabus. I would apologize for the disruption and take the call, preferring the witness of my students to the clamorous chaos of the hallways outside. And the entire class would pause, enjoying the psychodrama unfolding behind the exchange. When the call didn't originate from Mrs. Blaylock, the dreaded head nurse, I was left negotiating with the disciplinarian on duty about the immediate fate of my turbulent son, already sitting in my interlocutor's office, a defiant frown on his angelic face. I played for time, reminding the assistant principal of my son's ADHD, pleading for an hour's reprieve so that I could finish my lecture and come pick him up to begin his two-day suspension.

Most of the time, my entreaties worked. I would reshuffle a meeting, tack a note on my office door, and run to my car for a fifteen-minute drive to bail out my son. He and his sister gradually became regular fixtures during office hours, doing homework on an adjoining desk. At times, however, the phone conversations took on a more embarrassing turn, as when my daughter's preschool insisted that I should come at once to help defuse a temper tantrum. The director's near-hysterical voice could be heard ten feet away, informing me that my three-year-old represented "an immediate and present danger to the safety of the entire staff." The young felon was expelled that very day. She ended up spending two hours in the back row of my literary seminar, coloring books and eating M&M's passed on to her by sympathizing students.

I encouraged my children's interactions with academia, trying to involve them in campus activities more meaningful than their passion for skateboarding over the crosswalks. I had hoped they would be intrigued by the botanical gardens, the science labs or the resources of the library, but their interactions with academic life turned out to be quite unpredictable. My son participated in a few educational opportunities, but his visits to the university did not always work out in the manner I had anticipated. When he was seven, I decided to introduce him to the wonders of college life by taking him to the grand opening of the new planetarium. He had developed an interest in astronomy after trying out one of the state's most powerful optical telescopes. The evening festivities featured an astrophysicist's presentation on new advances in planetary studies, with special emphasis on the fate of Pluto, recently demoted from the ranks of planets within our solar system. From a scientific point of view, the evening's topic was somewhat controversial, and I found myself a little disappointed that both students and faculty had deferred to the speaker's opinion without criticism or dissent. Toward the end, I stepped outside into the hallway for a brief discussion with a colleague, leaving my enraptured son to the delights of constellations gracing the spherical ceiling of the planetarium. The conversation took a bit longer than I thought, and when I walked back inside, the light show had given way to an open forum between the speaker and the audience. And there was my seven-year-old standing with a microphone, in a heated exchange with the evening's distinguished guest. "You can't just demote Pluto from its planetary status, it's an affront to Clyde Tombaugh," pleaded the distraught little boy. "Well, I'm very sorry, young man," the miffed academic replied rather curtly, "but the International Astronomical Union has already ruled on the matter—" "I totally disagree with their decision," my son continued, unimpressed by this appeal to authority, "Pluto fulfills two of the standard planetary requirements: It has a thin atmosphere and is orbited by at least three moons that we know of!" Accustomed to the hushed civility of such proceedings, neither the audience nor the moderator knew what to do with the diminutive protester. I gently took him by the hand, and we walked out of the room past rows of grinning students.

The second challenge I needed to address pertained to administrative duties, and while my teaching benefited from the solicitude of other faculty members, I couldn't expect such preferential treatment when it came to committee meetings. I would occasionally arrive late because of unscheduled pediatrician appointments or a surprise teacher conference, and if at first I felt self-conscious and uneasy about my lack of punctuality, I gradually determined that beyond expected apologies, I would no longer feel embarrassed by the creative interruptions my children imposed upon the schedule. As when I was in class, my cell phone became the only one not silenced during meetings. I learned to be as unobtrusive as possible, setting it to vibrate and sitting next to the door, so I could excuse myself and take the calls with a minimum of distraction to my colleagues. And whenever I had to leave early to meet the afternoon school bus at my house, I would notify the meeting's chair at the outset and exit discreetly, catching an occasional exasperated glance from around the conference table. To some extent, in this society still inclined to discriminate against women in the workplace, I almost benefited from a reverse form of stereotyping. A middle-age single dad with two young children tends to elicit more sympathy than single mothers facing similar circumstances. The majority of university administrators in academia is still male, and it is telling how many of these men looked upon my situation as if it were a most unfortunate predicament, while not necessarily extending the same courtesy to the single women teaching on our campus.

Another particular adjustment in my academic schedule had to do with the conferences I used to attend, either as an officer or a participant. I could no longer take part in international meetings, given the time and distances involved. I scaled down my participation and limited myself to regional meetings I could reach and return from within a day. I also resolved to keep an occasional out-of-state conference, but only if it extended into one of the weekends my children would spend with their mother. Besides, as time passed, I realized that I no longer enjoyed out-of-town trips. My kids missed me, and I felt as if I were shortchanging them. I relished my role as a single father and was eventually tagged as a Jewish mom by most of my colleagues—a label I accepted as a genuine compliment. Only my work as the assistant editor of a scholarly journal remained unaffected by my circumstances. In fact, the evaluation of manuscripts was remarkably well suited to late-night reading, once the house was quiet and the children finally asleep. Few writers ever imagined their learned submissions resting against my daughter's monitor as I read, the rhythmic sound of her breathing weaving a peaceful counterpoint into the rustle of turning pages.

Of all three areas in my academic life that required an adaptation to single-parenthood, scholarly research proved the most problematic. I need absolute silence and isolation to function as a writer, and liberal amounts of time, free of constraints, impositions, or deadlines. Of course, these requirements are not compatible with the life of a single father. I tried to change my neurotic work habits and lower my expectations. Book projects no longer appeared reasonable, so I began to focus on articles, by nature more manageable. I decided to do the critical reading and the spade work of bibliographical research in the time I had left between classes, working in bursts of two to three hours throughout the week. The actual writing I kept for those Tuesdays and Thursday mornings that were free of household chores or other obligations. And then, with guiltless abandon, I sequestered myself in a silent study room on the fifth floor of the library. There were, however, new obstacles I should have surmised. While my cell phone functioned as an electronic umbilical cord, I found out that microwaves did not reach inside a soundproof room shielded by thick walls and thousands of books. I began mapping out the quietest areas in the library that would still allow phone signals to get through.

I survived as a scholar, doing research and publishing articles in refereed journals. For a couple of years I settled in an academic routine that paralleled my teaching and, most importantly, that I could integrate within my life as a single father. In time, however, I longed to work on a book manuscript, missing the depth and scope of a long-term academic project. A solution readily presented itself. I'd always had a predilection for literary translation, because of the complexity of linguistic, artistic, and cultural challenges it represents. For quite a while, I relegated it as secondary to the tasks of literary history or textual criticism, even though my first attempt had been a successful book of Gothic short stories for a university press. Now under contract from an academic publisher, I agreed to pen the first English translation of an early novel from a prominent nineteenth-century French novelist. The four-hundred-page saga, with a hundred elucidating footnotes, would become a project in which to immerse myself for a couple of years without the dread of interruptions. The process of translation makes it possible to take oneself in and out of the task, without losing the continuity or internal coherence required of a book manuscript. Ten years earlier, my interest in literary translation had been sidelined by professional considerations rather specific to my field, and today, quite unwittingly, my children were allowing me to reverse this decision.

In most colleges and universities, faculty members devote the bulk of their energy to teaching and advising, while their academic progress is often measured by the quality of their published research. In leading institutions, a weak record of publications constitutes an insurmountable obstacle to the granting of tenure. In my own field, there were other, more subtle considerations as well. Literary translations, like textbooks, are a time-honored tradition, yet they are often regarded as somewhat pedestrian. Both are considered "technical" in orientation and less indicative of one's brilliance in terms of intellectual achievement. Though the translation of literary texts into another language requires considerable skill, it is traditionally devalued within the academic community. A translator, no matter how gifted, is still considered a craftsman rather than a thinker, a copyist instead of an original creator. But in trying to accommodate my fondness for book projects with the schedule of a single father, I had unexpectedly rehabilitated my earlier passion for translation. Caught in the academic shell game, it is easy to lose one's sense of identity and to blur the line between political correctness and artistic integrity. It also seems expedient to convince ourselves that the parameters of success to which we readily submit are legitimate, while in fact having little or no relevance outside of academia. We are never encouraged to question the fact that scholarly pursuits might inherently possess less validity than they have. To do so would challenge established principles, and lead us to dispute one of the most significant goals of the academic profession.

I had embraced the life of a college professor wholeheartedly, even altering the choice of my original career by beginning graduate studies after a brief stint in medical school. Indeed, the standards of professional success in higher education seemed worthwhile and legitimate, especially as they related to research and writing. But it was the intrinsic value attached to these goals that I had overestimated, and now they stood exposed, seemingly less relevant when placed in the larger perspective of family life. It took the full-time, unexpected responsibility for two young children to make me reevaluate the significance of these professional achievements. A rather traditional education in Europe had drilled the following precept into me: "You can only criticize objectively something in which you've already excelled"— criticism from those not making the grade being generally interpreted as expressions of envy or bitterness. Reexamining some of the intrinsic values of academia, especially in the way they competed with other priorities in life, made me appreciate that it happened after reaching some of the established goalposts of my profession. I became a single dad several years after being tenured and promoted to full professor, and this allowed me to maintain a balanced perspective as I critically evaluated my academic life, without resentment or regrets. It also relieved me of the guilt I might have felt by ascribing to my parental obligations the possible failure to achieve success in academia. I had always planned to continue with writing and publications as a matter of personal satisfaction. Like many of my colleagues, I truly began to enjoy the challenge of scholarship, and the ability to keep it in a balanced perspective, when I no longer had any obligation to do so.

When night came and the children were all tucked in, I sat alone at the dinner table and graded papers, savoring the fragile and temporary silence permeating the house. The responsibilities and full schedule I faced each day were no worse or more demanding than the traditional obligations of any other single parent. In fact, even if I had to make several adjustments in my academic life, both in matters of time and space, I discovered that the most significant transformations were taking place on a personal level. Priorities concerning my private life had long been rescinded to make room for the needs of my kids. And though I wondered at first about the sort of impact it would have on my work, I came to realize that being a college professor was remarkably suited to raising one's children. Had I become a physician, an attorney, or a corporate executive, I could never have integrated family life and professional requirements so seamlessly. No medical practice, courtroom, or corporate office would have accommodated my dual allegiance.

I came to realize that these adjustments were actually a welcome necessity. There would be obvious changes in work habits and professional orientations, but these could be implemented without sacrificing academic excellence. Teaching evaluations from students, and their anonymous comments over the years, told me that I essentially remained a dedicated and effective professor. As far as scholarly research was concerned, two of my later academic books became well-received literary translations, while my publications in reputable journals continued at a slightly slower pace into the twenty-first century. My administrative duties didn't seem to suffer. If anything, my colleagues remarked that I seemed to grow more content, almost serene, as a result of this challenge. I still can't tell whether they were seeing the beginning of wisdom or the nonchalant gaze that comes with sleep deprivation.

My children succeeded in bringing about a personal reevaluation of my profession, which I wouldn't have initiated without becoming a single father. Their presence compelled me to take a step back and adopt a wider perspective. And in turn that process revealed my own propensity to overestimate the intrinsic value of idols in university life. Whether one chooses to ply a trade or to answer a calling, there is still more to this existence than the adulation of a career. Because of their innate vulnerability, children have a privileged ability to draw us out of existential attitudes and narcissistic tendencies, their immediate needs effecting a salutary and maturing transformation. Working as a single father in academia magnified my professional life by humanizing and balancing its priorities. And today, still years away from retirement and having journeyed from kindergarten to high school, I am awed by and grateful for the way academia has supported me in raising my kids, as no other career would have allowed. More than ever, I remain dedicated to my students and to the perennial value of scholarship. But as an academic and a single father looking upon my children as they move on into life, I know that they stand as the best work I have ever done.

Superheroes

STANFORD W. CARPENTER

An Admonition

During his 2008 election campaign, Barack Obama was vocal about African American men being more involved with their children. The sentiment is easy to agree with, though it is infused with class, ethnic, gender, and racial assumptions. Being more involved sounds simple, but it is not a purely individual choice. It is a choice that, even under ideal circumstances, involves negotiation and management. In the context of the disintegration of a family, it is mediated if not determined by the state. When I first heard Obama's plea, it hit close to home. I am an African American male. I have a daughter. But my circumstances do not fit many of the assumptions about African American fathers. I grew up in an intact middle-class African American family, and I am a professor at the School of the Art Institute of Chicago. The idea of being an uninvolved father is completely anathema to me.

Utter Fear in the Face of the State

On Friday, September 26, 2008, the state became a part of the already complicated negotiations that constitute parenting. The night before, my wife announced that she was leaving. She intended to take our then two-and-a-half-year-old daughter with her. She handed me paperwork for a custody hearing the next morning. I did not have time to get an attorney. So I went to court knowing that, even with an attorney, African American men fare poorly in the legal system. I couldn't believe that I was becoming what I swore I'd never be: the African American father of a child from a broken home. As I waited to go before the judge, all I could think of was the day my daughter asked me who my favorite superhero was. "You," I responded. "Can I be your sidekick?"

After some back-and-forth that included questions about my job, the judge continued the case until I could get an attorney. She also determined that my wife and I would have temporary shared custody with equal time until a permanent arrangement could be established. Shared custody with equal time is an atypical outcome given the circumstances. I am almost certain that my occupation contributed to the judge's atypical decision. As of this writing, no "permanent" agreement has been reached and the "temporary" parenting arrangement has persisted for over a year.

Recalling Past Lives

My father is a corporate executive. For him being involved meant creating space within a demanding, highly structured work life. In spite of a two- to three-day a week travel schedule, my father coached Little League, attended my school activities, and even flew across state lines to watch me run college track. He was in the delivery room when I was born. And also when my daughter was born. As I held her for the first time, he looked at me and said, "It's your turn," meaning my turn to be involved, to be present. This was his admonition.

I brought my daughter and wife home from the hospital the day before I had to start teaching my spring semester class. The Mellon postdoctoral fellowship that I had been awarded at Johns Hopkins University did not come with paternity leave. But the 1/1 teaching load gave me the option to do a lot of my work from home. This flexibility and control over my time makes being an academic a real privilege. Indeed, the profession ranks third, according to *Money* magazine's 2009 "Best Jobs in America" for precisely these reasons.

Toward the end of the semester, I was offered a tenure-track job at the School of the Art Institute of Chicago. The dean let me defer for a year so that I could finish out the second year of my postdoc. My wife's maternity leave ended as the spring semester came to a close, and we needed to make parenting arrangements for the summer. We hired a part-time babysitter who lived across the street so that I could have a couple of days a week to tend to my professional obligations, but I would be the primary caregiver. The summer was an adventure. My daughter and I explored museums, met with colleagues, ran errands, and visited friends. It was wonderful, though at times startlingly so. On several occasions I was stopped by mostly older African American women and praised for being an involved African American father. I was polite. But it was disconcerting to be praised for doing what my father did for me, for doing what I was raised to do, for meeting my own expectations. It saddened me to think that my daughter's experience of an involved father was, in the eyes of so many people, anomalous.

And I felt a tinge of guilt for having the privilege of being involved without having to sacrifice my career.

The summer ended, and we enrolled our daughter in daycare. I resumed my 1/1 teaching load at JHU. My classes had been conveniently scheduled on the same day so I could commute between Chicago and Baltimore. I would be away for either two days and one night or three days and two nights. If my flight got in early, my wife would pick me up on her way back from work with our daughter in the car. We would play monster on the bed. If my flight got in late, I would sneak into her room, pick her up, and rock her back and forth. More often than not she would wake up and we would end up playing for a little while. I had the luxury of sleeping in the next day. On the weekends, I took my daughter to swim or Gymboree classes.

Whenever I was tired, I thought about how much easier it was for me to manage work-related travel than it was for my father. He did not have the option of sleeping in the day after a business trip or of working from home. He could not easily shift his work hours around my schedule. But somehow, he managed to be involved. Now it was my turn.

State-Mediated Parenting

When I returned from court, my wife had already begun the process of packing and moving. I had to figure out which of my daughter's things I needed to replace immediately and which could wait. I had to find an attorney. I had to . . . well, let's just say the "had to" list was long. I was teaching three classes. I canceled them with a single mass e-mail to my students. Very few jobs, whether they are work-from-home or office-based, allow their employees to literally disappear for what amounted to, in my case, eleven days.

So there I was. Alone. My first instinct was to create some emotional distance by treating this calamity like a research project. I wrote my daughter's name on a piece of paper. My hands shook. I turned the page. Gradually my eyes started to focus on the impression left behind by the letters I had put on the previous page. Impressions. Traces. Memories. A flash of conflicting thoughts gave way to a single coherent statement: I am going to be a single parent. Whether it would be 50 percent of the time, less than 50 percent, or more than 50 percent, I was going to be a single parent. I stared at the paper with my daughter's name pressed like a watermark in the background.

I remembered a conversation with a mentor, years before my daughter was born, about how she had managed being a single parent. "There are things that just don't get done," she said. "There are things that you just don't do." It was shocking to hear. She is a well-published, tenured law professor at an Ivy League school and a MacArthur Fellow. "You see what I do, not what I don't do." She went on to explain that it was not about missed opportunities. It was about understanding the academy, what can and cannot be negotiated, what has to get done and what can be put off. And most importantly, it was about understanding consequences, because there are times when "things just don't get done." While this is good advice for everyone, the part about things not getting done speaks directly to the dilemmas that single parents face. A child's needs are nonnegotiable. My mentor had a way of putting it much more diplomatically than I ever could. But the message was clear: Put your child first. Accept the consequences. Move forward. Don't look back.

I decided that my first priority would be to contact academics who could give me practical advice. So I made a list of administrators and faculty from a variety of institutions who were children of divorce, divorced, single parents, or witnesses to similar circumstances. I kept the list short. I limited it to friends, mentors, and role models that I had a good enough rapport with to be able to call them at home. I made a lot of calls. I made lists of actions, concerns, consequences, and priorities. I started rethinking my to-do lists in terms of what I could get done and what would have to be put off.

Establishing a New Normal

When the fall 2008 semester came to a close, I started the long process of taking stock. By summer 2009, I had broken up my life into a series of constraints and complications. I wanted to minimize the intrusion of my work life into the time that I had with my daughter, and so I needed to leave more room for the unexpected. For example, when my daughter's mother fell ill, I had to pick up parenting duties on several hours' notice. In theory I could have said no, it's my day off. But the reality would have been that both my daughter and I were more likely to get sick. So I'd lose work time regardless. The only issue would be the quality of the lost work time. I had to pay closer attention to my own health. I had to rethink my travel decisions. I decided to make sure that I had a backup plan, just in case my daughter needed to be cared for when I was scheduled to be elsewhere. All of this is possible, though it did require some adjustments.

I reexamined my workload, not so much with an eye toward reducing it as rethinking how to manage it. Academics tend to measure time in terms of quarters, semesters, years, and tenure clocks. Our most demanding deadlines tend to be self-imposed, literally written into our syllabi. So I started including a new category entitled "expectations." I return papers with ample comments to students not in a week but in two weeks. Under previous circumstances I would respond to e-mails, text, and voice messages relatively quickly. Now my syllabi indicate more forgiving response times for each mode of communication. They also include an escape clause. If I do not respond in the allotted time, the student can expect some sort of accommodation proportional to the length of time it does take me to respond. It's not just about managing student expectations. It's about managing my own personal stress.

I take a similar approach to many of my other professional obligations. I try to be explicit about the easiest and fastest ways to reach me. I do my best to negotiate deadlines that give me wiggle room. I do this in part because multitasking in my professional life leaves me distracted in my personal life. By doing one thing at a time, I have fewer to-do items hanging over my head. This does not guarantee that everything will run smoothly, but it localizes the professional stressors.

My daughter knows that I work. She also knows that work is something that I do primarily when she is asleep or at daycare or with her mother. She is aware that I work longer hours to make up for lost time when she is away. Getting less sleep over two days is manageable. But cutting back on sleep for eight days is not safe. Yes, it is possible to have a babysitter or relative on standby. But ultimately, my daughter wants my attention when she is with me; she wants me to be sitting on the bench while she is on a play-date; she wants me to cook her food.

Our New Normal

On paper it looks easy. But in reality it can be . . . complicated. Most people at my institution know that I have a daughter. Most of them do not know that my wife left a year ago or that I am engaged in an ongoing custody dispute. My daughter and I have built a new life together. We spent a morning not too long ago spreading out pieces of colored paper and various toys to select new colors for her bathroom, her bedroom, and my wife's former office, which we decided to transform into a recreation room. Over the next three days while my daughter was with her mom, I precut, predrilled, primed, and purchased supplies. When my daughter returned, we painted and put the pieces of her recreation room together. It took me a day to pull all of the original art out of storage and about the same amount of time to hang everything. But it took us a week and a half to decide where everything would go. Obviously, my flexible schedule made all of this possible.

When we're together, we do everything together. Recently, we attended a party at the dean of faculty's house. Since it was on a weekend and would likely have few children her age, I decided to approach the party as an adventure. My daughter decided that we should both wear "lightning bolt" T-shirts—a gold-leaf silk-screened lightning bolt Shazam T-shirt for her and a black with glow-in-the-dark Flash lightning bolt for me. She gave me permission to add a sport coat. At the party, it was obvious that we were dressed to match, and my daughter quickly announced that she had selected our outfits. At one point she told the dean of faculty that her daddy knows "everything there is to know about superheroes." She then proceeded to let the dean in on other facets of the Carpenter household.

I've even taken my daughter to a dissertation defense in Maryland. I thought travel would be the most difficult thing to manage, but I was wrong. I used a frequent flyer ticket to cover my daughter's airfare. Instead of staying in a hotel, we stayed with some good friends of mine who worked in the academy and had children around my daughter's age. The dissertation committee chair arranged for one of the department assistants to watch my daughter in the room directly adjacent to the conference room that the defense was being held in. My daughter remained in the conference room for all but an hour and forty-five minutes of the two-and-a-half-hour defense. The rest of the long weekend was chock-full of playtime with children she had not seen since we had relocated to Chicago and various kid-friendly excursions.

Being Involved

What began as a private matter has become a public concern. "It's your turn," my father said. The baton was passed . . . a promise from one generation to the next. To be present, to provide, and to sacrifice. Obama's admonition to be involved was an appeal, a political gesture meant to raise expectations. The admonition does not, however, take into account that having access, a prerequisite for involvement, can be a struggle in and of itself. However fortunate I may be as an African American assistant professor, I am at the mercy of a judge. When I stood in court on Friday, September 26, 2008, my involvement with my child was not a choice. It was a request to be granted or denied by a representative of the State. Her decision was temporary. We, my daughter and I, are still waiting for a final resolution.

PART THREE

Forging New Fatherhoods

AMBITIONS ALTERED AND TRANSFORMED

Maybe It Is Just Math

Fatherhood and Disease in Academia

JASON THOMPSON

Everyone wants the good news, so here it is: I was the doomed kid born poor and raised in violence who worked his way through school, earned his PhD, and got a good job. In the history of my family, I was the first and only. I read consistently; I read a lot. We moved a lot; I had few friends. We were dirt poor; I had a library card.

I never dated, never went to a dance. I spent a lot of time with my dog, Prince.

The local private college sponsored a bridge program for high school students; in one year I was accepted to the school on scholarship. In five more years I had a classics degree and a Fulbright. Two more years and an MFA. Several more years and a PhD. Now I'm an assistant professor and new father. It's supposed to be easy now, because I *made it.*

Summer 1990

The Summer Scholars program was about to be officially over, and in three short weeks I discovered that I was a poet, having fallen in love with a girl from Egypt. Of course I had to go back to high school, to junior year, but I had some college credit under my belt. To celebrate, my first professor, Dennis, had me and the TA, Rob, over to his house. We drank beers and talked. I timed it at four and a half hours: my longest adult conversation. I looked around the tidy four-bedroom, the wall art, bookshelves, and real furniture, and I knew: I wanted to become a professor. I didn't think about my home life then, the seven people living in the three-bedroom house in Hilltop, Tacoma, my miserable clothes. I only saw a future with this present sheen, where smart people read books, ate well, and talked deliriously. At seventeen I saw what I wanted. It was not my mom's two roommates and two returned adult children sleeping on couches; it was not the laundry room I was living in, with my thrift-store bookshelves and cold bus mornings at the corner of Twelfth and K, where that year two tourists were gunned down for asking directions. Now I was in Parkland, off the college campus, in a professor's home.

Gerald Michael

Gerald Michael was the name of my father, a maintenance man whose parents both died of colon cancer when he was a child, an orphan who was raised for a time by either a relative or friend of the family named Ms. Ruby, and then sent to a work farm. I know he had brothers and sisters, and that all but one of them died of colon cancer. My parents divorced in 1974; I was one. My father, a lifetime smoker, died of heart disease, though probably the cancer that resulted in a partial colonectomy would have gotten him, or diabetes. He did not finish high school, he did not go to college, and often in his life he would admit that he had only ever read one book all the way through, *Robinson Crusoe*.

My father and I met in 1980, when I was seven. He didn't have time to do it on the water, and so in the front of our tiny house on an abbreviated lawn he tied an empty beer can to the end of his fishing pole and taught me to cast. Back and throw.

I am reaching into the past. I am the sound of success that day: the can going out to the gutter, to the broken street in front of 11 California, to myself at seven, and to my father, who was the age I am now, thirty-five. He dies in 2007.

What weighs us down enough so that we may properly fly? What castoffs do our eyes settle on, and why, and how do we know what will carry? Why do we settle for some grass when the ocean waits exactly ten miles west? What is it that makes a father the ache you burn to touch, the hook through the lip, the slip not the step backward, the fall?

Bad Dad

I've never been to Santa Barbara; I once spent the night with my mom and her boyfriend Jim in his broken-down car outside of a closed Chevron in San Bernardino. Mom opened a knife and said good night. That killed all san appeal: san, sans, Saint, Santa.

Whenever I find myself doing something even slightly negligent with or for or to Isabelle—when I dose her with Children's Motrin if I suspect that her low-grade fever threatens to keep her home all day from childcare ($666.00 [monthly tuition] ÷ 21.67 [average workdays per month] = $30.73 lost per day and the 16 combined hours of teaching, research, and service that Nicole and I will get done)—I see myself on the cover of *Bad Dad Magazine*. It's supposed to be a monthly, but the overwhelming numbers force it into a weekly. Past covers include Michael Jackson dangling Prince Michael II over that crowd. Mostly, though, it's me in a posture of unlikely misdeed.

Preliminary Web searches of "Worst Fathers" reveal predictables like Lot and Bing Crosby (also from Tacoma, Washington), but for me the worst was Dioscorus, the pagan father of Saint Barbara, whom I found once reading martyrologies in New York. Dioscorus locked his disobedient daughter up in a tower, and when he returned from his business discovered that she had been converted to Christianity. When she would not give up her beliefs he took her to a prefect who had her tortured, and when that did not work, they passed a death sentence on her. Her father beheaded Saint Barbara himself, and right afterward he was struck by lightning and killed. Santa Barbara, the patron saint of artillery.

At thirteen I flew for the first time, to Georgia, to stay with my aunt, and I found myself spending a few days with my dad, who was building a house—our second meeting. We slept in a tent inside the complete foundation; I swooned to be with him under the sheet lightning. Before it was over we framed and raised the north wall. That time stretches into months in my memory, though it couldn't have been a week. Later I learned that Jim and Mom were fighting and nearly broke up: Jim was talking crazy and loading and unloading his gun, I forget the name he gave it. He had a son out there too somewhere, I think, with a white ex, and he wanted to kill her or kill himself. I found all this out later; at the time I thought things were good.

I will not be Jim, or Gerald, or Art; I won't be Michael Jackson, Lot, Crosby, or Dioscorus. I cannot be any of the fathers I have known.

Lunch with the Dean and His Wife

Another Friday, another week down, but not off the hook from work—we're to have lunch at a Cajun restaurant with the dean and his wife. It's lots of Cokes and fried fish baskets. The conversations lulls, and his eyes focus on me. "Jason. Yes. Didn't you have trouble getting a loan for your house?" The lemon in my tea curls into a smirk.

Back in July, a few days before our move, we were about to close—Nicole was still writing her dissertation and recovering from an MS attack (these may leave permanent or temporary damage in almost any area: vision, motor skills, balance, ambulation, cognition, etc.). Our jobs as assistant professors were to begin in August. Out of nowhere the mortgage lady tells me that the underwriter won't sign off on our loan: "You need more income or less debt," she explained slowly over the phone, as if I had simply not thought of that, as if our problems were no bigger than math.

We had wanted to rent, but the rates were too high. I can only think to ask my new chair to write a letter promising extra classes, and after some frantic e-mails and faxes, it's all finished, and of course I'm humiliated but at least I still have my house.

And then the bad news: The chair's letter won't fly. The only fix is to put up my truck, which I do. In the end, I did close, I did put up my truck, and now we are paying $416 every month for a truck we already paid for with student loan money. My old truck was failing, and we needed something reliable with AC: Nicole could no longer walk in the Arizona heat to and from school.

"Yes," I nod and smile, "there was a tiny glitch. But it all worked out in the end." I laugh, and he nods, and the wind picks up some garbage outside. Across town Isabelle won't sleep at daycare, and back in Seattle my brother sits in the basement. Nicole changes the subject to something we can all safely discuss; I forget what it was.

Art

Art was the name of my maternal grandfather, whose father was an alcoholic and probably beat him. He was the youngest of seven brothers, all cruel. He retired from McNeil Prison and had a handful of healthy years before heart attack, then stroke, then diabetes, then Alzheimer's finally killed him. He had dropped out of high school, like my grandmother, because of World War II: Art enlisted; Marjie went to work at the shipyards. My grandfather landed on D-Day in a storm of artillery shells and never talked about it once.

A sportsman, a fisherman who only had daughters, three in a row, his life's disappointment. These children would eventually produce fourteen others, but only four boys, and of these, he would be separated by chance from two. To my confusion and fright, this left me and my brother, Michael. He preferred Michael.

Once he promised me five dollars (glorious sum) if I could catch a butterfly with an empty saccharine bottle. Of course I spent the afternoon jumping around the yard like an idiot until my mom found out and called it off. She explained that my grandfather was making fun; I was eight, and began to dislike the old man in the chair.

Of course I loved him, too. Sometime after his first stroke he took me to the golf course to teach me the game. I was perhaps ten, and when I asked him the difference between a 7 iron and a 9, he barked out, "About twenty yards." No one laughed, so I didn't understand that a joke had occurred. It was a hot day, and we drank Cokes and I watched as he swung mightily and nearly fell down each time, and with every step after. The front nine stretched out for hours. Later my grandmother explained that he had actually done a brave thing.

The timing of the two men—of their being in my life—meant that at the time I was acquiring my first memories, my father was living in Georgia with his common-law wife, and my grandfather was enjoying that handful of healthy years—bourbon and pinochle—before his long decline. I experienced my father as an absence; my grandfather, as a cold disappointment.

And my mother, who since '74 had been a single mother of three, of course had boyfriends: Jim, Dan, James. These were all broken men, they were all heavy-duty mechanics with muscle, or they were all alcoholic ex-helicopter gunners in Vietnam, or they were all athletic and comfortable but with stomas and angry stepsons. My childhood is peopled with a confusion of boyfriends. They ignored me, mostly. I infuriated them, sometimes. On the whole we all agreed to not like each other, like my sister's boyfriends later.

Weekend Dad

It's another Saturday, and I'm roaming the aisles of Bart's, the only flea market in Laramie, Wyoming. So that Nicole can get the extra sleep she needs, I have to get Isabelle out of the house from about eight, when she wakes up, to about twelve or one. Trouble is, because Nicole and I put ourselves through school, we're in a terrible financial mess: student loan debt + credit card debt for medical expenses + the job market + groceries, sometimes. I can't spend a dime. So I talk to Ms. Iz as we slowly walk the floor. I point out items that I'd like to buy one day; she asks for crackers. Together we observe thousands of castoffs that still have value. Raisins are eaten.

On our way out, one of the three women pattering behind the counter pauses to ask, "Are you a weekend dad?" I darken, confused, and she rushes on with great sympathy, "Do you only get her on the weekends? We notice that you come about every other weekend."

"No," I want to say, "I'm a weeklong dad whose wife has a chronic, debilitating, and incurable autoimmune disease that every day attacks her brain. I've got this daughter—see here?—and this position at the university, where

I should be doing more research and writing more essays, but I've got to take care of this little girl and her momma. Did I mention that she's an assistant professor, too? If my family weren't a thousand miles away; if I had one friend in this town; if we didn't have a mountain of unforgivable debt; if I weren't teaching an overload; if we could unpack our house after living here for a semester; if the wind would let up; and if small-town folks like yourselves could just hold off on figuring out the newcomer in ways that break my fucking heart, then maybe I could just be a dad, and this could just be a weekend."

"No," I manage, "I'm just a dad," and I wrench a clenched jaw into an angry smile that stays behind as we clang through the door. Next weekend someplace free and anonymous, like the highway. Cheyenne would eat up two hours; Rawlins, four.

Nicole and Isabelle

I meet Nicole in 1998, outside of Babcock, a dorm converted to GA office space. She is beautiful, a stunner who has undergrads and senior faculty alike tracking her down for a coffee, a chat, anything, anything. I walk directly into a signpost—I mean straight into it with my head—and we somehow become friends; she writes fiction and I write poetry. I date her friend and she dates mine, and we stay like that for a few years before graduating to big cities, Chicago and New York.

It's 2003, and I'm reading the welcome e-mail to the new rhetoric and composition class. Nicole's name is on the list—we separately chose to come back and get PhDs, and we end up together in Tucson a second time. When I see her again my heart breaks.

It's my thirty-fifth birthday, June 11, and I'm asleep after a long day on our house-hunting trip to Laramie. Our jobs begin in two months. Nicole wakes me up: She's vomiting uncontrollably. I fight through sleep and lie with her on a bathroom floor, hoping that this MS attack is not real, but soon we struggle to the car: Nicole can't walk, so she leans against me and we nearly make it to the elevator. It's vertigo, constant, unyielding. My heart splits between wanting to speed her to the hospital and wanting to run back to the room, where I've left Izzy alone. The doors open, and I yell at the night shift worker to help Nicole into the car while I race upstairs, pack a bag and the baby up, a chorus of failure in my ear.

I'm twenty-nine, no job, living off the good graces of cousin Adam in Newnan, Georgia. He is an EMT who built his own home and has two gorgeous daughters. I spend six weeks reading novels and writing poems, wanting a wife, hoping for a girlfriend, and getting nowhere. At night we bring snacks and a blanket out to the yard, and on our backs the girls tell me stories about the constellations. One afternoon I start *Portrait of a Lady* and remember Nicole, whom I once called Ms. Archer. She was the one.

Christmas 2008

It's four in the morning, and Michael takes the turn a little wild for Mom's '83 Land Cruiser. Isabelle sits strapped asleep to the middle seat, taking my seat belt, and there's no heat. It's about ten degrees outside. Yesterday my flight from Sea-Tac was delayed five full days, leaving Nicole stranded in Laramie and alone for Christmas. Michael, my bipolar brother, volunteered to drive us the eleven hundred miles home: His mania allowed for it.

We make it in twenty-seven hours of straight driving and his talking through every bit of mountain pass: the Cascades, then the Blue Mountain range, then the Rockies: Washington, Oregon, Idaho, Utah, Wyoming. Dad, the government's conspiracy to suppress the truth about UFOs, how Barack is just as bad as Bush, just you wait and see. Michael details every shadow of his paranoia as we shake through five states, and somehow Isabelle sleeps in her wet diaper. Between I-90 and our exit (313 off 80-E) not a patch of clear road; it's all snow, ice, or both. No music. The truck has one wiper. By some miracle we make it to Laramie safely, exhausted, wired. Michael and I inhale pizza and chug water before passing out. Tomorrow I'll hand him enough cash to make it back and I'll pack up my family. He'll take 80 west and I'll hit it east: By Christmas day he'll be safely back in Washington and I'll have driven another eleven hundred miles to Nicole's parents in Michigan. Then after three days I'll drive back. School ended ten days ago, and not a day to relax or work. We bought presents for the baby, but none for each other.

Baby Photo

Nicole's wanted an official photo of Izzy for a long time now, and she's already a toddler; we figure time is running out, and I capitulate to a "consultation" at Beethoven, the only photography studio in town.

One enters a large room full of antique photography equipment, cast iron, and oiled wood. Museum-like displays stand squat under picturesque samples of prior Beethoven triumph: a naked child in black and white, a family in matching clothes. We wait for twenty minutes and eat cookies while Isabelle takes it all in. Finally the owner ushers in mugs of coffee and apologies: She is pregnant and the water wouldn't boil. I push down a bad joke and sip like this means something to me. The fourth generation of Beethoven proprietors starts talking, and I drift, mostly out. She asks what the photograph should mean, "and not just to you, Mom, but to you as well, *Dad*."

Right there. I get up and take the now fussy Isabelle into the studio proper, and in ten minutes Nicole comes in with Ms. Ludvig, who seems to be losing her sale. She pointedly lets me know that "the typical young family invests between three hundred and five hundred dollars." She assures me that for only $180 for her creation fee she can create an atmosphere; $165 more would gain two actual 5 × 7s, "because, you see, I'm not a cookie-cutter photographer," she assures us, "like some others."

She'll take the $180 today, right now in fact, and we can schedule our experience on Wednesday—have we considered a sofa-sized portrait? Isabelle is fussing more than ever, Nicole has followed her up some stairs, and suddenly we're in a high-pressure sale. We suggest that we go and talk it over, and the photographer's puffy face darkens.

"What exactly is your resistance?" She pauses long enough to answer: "I'll tell you: Most young families aren't used to making this kind of investment." A string of veiled insults and mild accusations follows as Mama Beethoven grows desperate: Isabelle's infant beauty is, after all, fading; the promised photography will "melt our hearts"; any objections to the investment should obviously be overruled by her money-back (verbal) guarantee. We lunge for the door while the now disgusted Beethoven shakes her head with scorn: "I am saddened that I wasn't able to reach an agreement with you today," she offers, feigning meek, tears at the ready, and we're trying for the door, trying for air, trying to get out of the experience sure to melt our very hearts.

Endings

It's the new year, and Nicole, Iz, and I have been handing various colds to each other. In our bodies they morph into other things: an upset stomach in me evolves into a vomiting for Iz and skips Nicole; Isabelle's ear infections in me become an upper respiratory infection and make Nicole's MS fatigue flare up, but not enough to take her out. There are more medications in this house than memories.

It's the new year, and even working together as two assistant professors Nicole and I can't pay our bills, not between the truck loan, the student loan debt, the credit debt, the childcare, and, as ever, the expense of Nicole's MS. Her first MRI here ended up costing $450—that's after meeting our deductible. I remember our struggles in Tucson, with idiot doctors in substandard clinics open to the poorest of people, like us, and I remember telling her, "Don't worry, honey. When we take our jobs, we'll have *real* health care." Back then, I would smuggle her prescriptions in from Mexico. The truth is that Nicole was on state health care and we never paid a dime for any of her MRIs. I'll call the hospital and make some kind of installment plan, like my mom's Christmas layaway schemes when we were kids, like my crippling truck loan, like an election promise.

It's the new year, and it's also the old year, which is to say that there is little hope that our finances or health will improve, which is to say that we still live as graduate students, the way we did in Tucson for five years. Colleagues invite us to dinners, to functions, to excursions, and we forever can't make it, and we can never explain it. Though it's clear enough: too much work and too little money. Maybe it is just math. I am a father, I am an academic, Nicole is a mother, and she is an academic with MS, and our baby needs us. It's exactly the life I have chosen. Eighteen years ago I stood in Dennis's living room in awe of an English professor's life; I don't know why, but though I have now joined the professorate I am still on the outside of that life peering in.

It's the new year, and Michael is back in the basement with Mom. Art's ashes were mixed with Marjie's and planted by their youngest daughter in the shade of a tree. My father's common-law wife lives alone in the house that he built for them, failing. I imagine her sometimes looking through the window I framed, touching the jamb with her curled index finger, Georgia lightning above. Isabelle is crying; I have to stop this.

Dreaming of Direction

Reconciling Fatherhood and Ambition

MIKE AUGSPURGER

Two weeks after the birth of my third child, I had a dream. This wasn't just any dream. It was one of those long, cinematic dreams that seems to mean something. I remember only one comparable dream in my adult life, and, at least in my private narrative of my life, that other dream has always signaled for me the beginning of a fairly important love affair. Ignore for a moment that that affair ended badly: My point is that this felt important. I woke my wife up.

I won't bore you with the details (this is what a spouse is for, after all), but I'll give you a sketch. After a long set of preliminaries, I found myself climbing up the outside of a bedraggled but stately old building. I crawled through a window into a dark hallway, dismantled part of the ceiling, and, now accompanied by an old friend, pulled myself into the attic. There we discovered a workshop full of clay sculpture and handmade jewelry. My friend pointed out a pendant and claimed that I had made it. I argued with him, insisting I had never seen it, but upon inspecting the room, I came to realize I that had made all of these pieces: This was, indeed, my workshop. As I looked through the sculptures, trying to understand when I had made them, I woke up.

A little background: I received my PhD in American studies nearly eight years ago, and since then, I've been wandering the dark hallways of a series of bedraggled but stately old buildings, seeking a home in academia. In seven of those eight years, my job title has been preceded by that odd descriptor "Visiting" ("But I live here!" I mutter. "I work here! I'm here all the time!"). In the meantime, the chance that I will eventually find a permanent home on a faculty has become more and more remote. Now I need to interject, defensively, that my auxiliary status is not easily explained by my own failures ("Of course it's not, you poor fellow," you think): Indeed, I have proven myself to be a good, if unspectacular, teacher, and I

have published more work than many of my tenure-track friends and colleagues. The most important impediment to finding a, you know, real job
has been my circumstance as the trailing member of an academic couple.

In these eight years, not surprisingly, I have thought of alternative careers
pretty near constantly. I have searched the Web for geographically viable
options to train myself as a lawyer or a mechanical engineer, and I have
fantasized about earning a living as a writer, a woodworker, or a restaurant
owner. One late night, roused by our middle child and unable to return
to sleep, my addled brain conceived a plan to create a home heating business, to be called Dr. Steam or the Boiler Professor or some such thing, that
would specialize in repairing old steam heating systems (my imagination,
if not my genuine talent, ranges widely). None of these options, as yet, has
felt genuinely desirable and/or feasible. But my failure to pursue any of
them has worried me: Have I been too tentative in my pursuit of an alternative career?

Predictably, then, my first interpretive response to my dream was to
think of it as my unconscious urging me to shake off the quotidian, leave
academics behind, and embrace some new career, some new art. I only had
to discover what that career was (again, I am not too demanding of my orac-
ular dreams). My wife, though, offered a different reading. (Jane's dreams,
incidentally, tend to offer little room for interpretation: A month before
the kids returned to daycare after this third child, a many-windowed space-
ship, which looked suspiciously like a university building, came to pick
her up; she reassured the children that she would be back soon.) She had
read that pregnant women commonly dream of discovering a new room in
their home—she had had just such a dream in the months surrounding the
birth of our first two children. Perhaps, she suggested, this was my fatherly
equivalent.

Unfortunately, the two readings were both viable, and they simply repro-
duced the dilemma that had dogged me for years. There was no guidance
here. Was the new room I needed to explore representative of my life as a
father or of some undeveloped ambition? Less metaphorically: Was I comfortable sacrificing career, ambition, and vocation in order to put parenthood at the center of my identity, or did I need to embrace a new career and
new ambitions? For women in academia and professional life, obviously,
this is not a particularly new or startling question (although for many it
remains a powerful and painful one). But as an ambitious male graduate
student, it was not a question that I anticipated I would need to address.
Much of my career since graduate school, then, has seen me slowly coming

to terms with this question, and trying to give an honest answer to myself and my family.

Since my teenage years, I have struggled to reconcile two competing visions of my life. On the one hand, I had every reason in my youth to cultivate career ambition. I went to an excellent public high school, was supported by encouraging and well-off parents, and excelled at schoolwork. Like many other talented students at upper-middle-class schools, I built my identity around the list of activities and awards I accumulated: marching band, theater, newspaper editor, assistant to the vice president of Latin Club, etc. . . . I even lettered in a sport (well, sort of: golf). My self-absorption and confidence, in retrospect, are laughable. Perhaps the most embarrassing sign of this self-absorption was my high school obsession with Ayn Rand: Rand offered me a vision of my own superiority, and I simply assumed that my friends and I would one day be a part of the talented cadre of doers and makers who ran her fictional world. I assumed—and my parents and teachers did, too—that ultimately I would do something important.

Another part of me, though, rejected the careerism so central to our high school environment. This may be shocking to some of you, but as a teenage American male, I felt the need to identify myself as a rebel against the false and compromising world around me. At seventeen, my friends knew—or at least I imagined they knew—that they wanted to be doctors, lawyers, and engineers; I saw choosing a career as a kind of sellout, as a failure to recognize that learning should be valued for itself. My fellow high achievers aimed at Yale and Harvard and Duke: In my valedictorian speech, I poked fun at this Ivy League ambition (did I mention my self-absorption and confidence?), and I decided to go small and south, to a liberal arts school in Memphis. As much as I had taken part in the résumé-building arms race, I worked (and you can imagine, it took some work) to see myself as apart from that world.

Ultimately, a career in academia provided a perfect solution to this inner conflict. In college, I drifted toward my softer, more idealistic values. A career in teaching—teaching something as useless as literature, by God!—satisfied my desire to separate myself from the tawdry world out there. It also offered a vision of a peaceful adult existence: Rather than working seventy hours a week like my lawyer and doctor friends, I'd be sauntering around campus in my tweed jacket, holding forth on Nietzsche and Hemingway and Stallone (I was heading into American studies, after all).

However, becoming a professor was hardly a rejection of ambition: the status of the PhD, the sense of joining a community of elite thinkers, and the allure of expertise all compensated for any shortfalls in money or power. When I found out in graduate school that there was such a thing as an academic star, you can imagine my excitement. By the time I was working on my thesis, I was still talking about teaching, but, like many of my colleagues, I had been inculcated—even as I actively resented it—into the graduate school culture of research, research, research.

Then trouble arrived. She was five foot four. She had sparkling blue eyes, legs that never stopped, and a focus on nineteenth-century women's domestic history and the American West. We married the year before we both graduated, and agreed to follow whoever got the first decent job. In a direct test of the goodwill of our relationship, we even interviewed for the same interdisciplinary job at an honors college in Arkansas. Indeed, we were sitting together at the same table. We tried to convince the interviewers that they needed both of us, but they weren't buying it. And as fate would have it (I'm sure it had nothing to do with talent, accomplishments, or composure, right?), they hired her and not me. And before we knew it, we were Arkansans: she with her impressive "Jane Simonsen, PhD" nameplate on her door, me with my "Dr. Mike" scrawled with a Sharpie on a scrap of paper, taped to the edge of my adjunct cubbyhole.

Initially, my ambitions weren't discouraged. This was just paying my dues, I figured, and something would come along. The next year my manuscript was accepted by—say it with meaning!—an Ivy League press, and I received a Fulbright that allowed me to teach for a year in lovely Regensburg, Germany. I came back to Arkansas as a visiting assistant professor rather than an adjunct. (One of my visiting colleagues campaigned for black leather jackets with "V.A.P." printed on the back. The chair turned down the request.) I had not yet grabbed the golden ring of a tenure-track position, but my fingers were getting closer.

Then trouble arrived. Again. This time, though, her legs were shorter and chubbier. I won't claim that I was gung ho to start a new research project—the prospect of catching a couple of six-inch bluegills and pumpkinseeds was usually enough to draw me away from my writing desk—but our daughter did tend to eliminate what free time I had. Jane had a more work-intensive job, so I took on a significant portion of the caregiving. I read a lot of nursery rhymes, but not many monographs.

Meanwhile, I was getting a little embittered with academia. A little. The first year after my book came out, reviews were good and I got a nice royalty check: The book sold five hundred copies in only three months. Maybe, I thought, someone would read the thing! Given a full year, maybe it'd sell even more, right? Guess how many it sold the next year? Go on, guess. GUESS, DAMMIT! All right, I'll tell you. It sold -112 copies. That's negative 112. No, I don't know what that means. No, I did not ask. And thankfully, no, the press did not knock on my door (yet, anyway) to ask me to return the royalties from the first check (it sold three copies this year, if you care to know). Meanwhile, my department held a search for a tenure-track twentieth-century Americanist. Here, finally, was the golden ring. But they did not hire me. In fact, they did not interview me. Stars in their eyes, they hired some—say it with meaning!—Ivy League PhD, and explained to me that they did not want an American studies graduate in their English Department.

Now, you know as well as I do that this was simply the academic equivalent to "Let's be friends": If they had really cared for me, they could have overlooked my interdisciplinary warts. And like any good jilted lover, I swore off love: "I'm done with you, academy!" I exclaimed. While I might not have the panache to get roaring drunk while giving a year-end talk on Merrie Olde England, as the protagonist of Kingsley Amis's *Lucky Jim* does, I could still be Lucky Mike: fortunate to escape, forever glad not to have been roped into a tenure-track job at Piddling State University. So I started to look around: I took the LSAT (oh, how I had missed standardized testing, the great confirmer of my existence) and applied to law school; I fantasized about architecture; I discussed the possibility of running a hot dog stand with a friend from St. Louis. I was finally able to gain enough distance from teaching to acknowledge that this job might not be the best use of my skills: I'm a private and somewhat unsympathetic man, a math and philosophy geek, who has been pretending to be a warm, engaging humanist for fifteen years now. When is it, I began to ask myself, that I admit to my poetry classes, who have always praised my enthusiasm for the subject, that I never read poetry for enjoyment? Maybe a hot dog stand isn't the answer, but surely, I began to think, there is some job out there that would be a better fit.

But these fantasies of escape began in earnest some four or five years ago, and yet I'm still here in academia, even as I've followed my wife to a new job back in the Midwest. This fact has a lot to do with fatherhood. You may have noticed, if you are part of the academy, that there is a fair bit of flexibility in our work. You may have noticed, too, the large expanses of time when school is not in session. These things are unequivocally wonderful, whether you have a family or not. (If you are not a part of the academy, you may have noticed that your professor friends are strangely defensive about this: "Well," they tell you, "it's not free time." I know that there are research expectations and classes to plan, and that some academics are genuinely overworked. But, please: The next time your professor friends insist that they don't have summers off, be sure to roll your eyes.) This flexibility and time are wonderful because they mean that I can pick up my kids early from daycare or drop them off late; that we can all go—without stress—to visit my folks' cottage for a couple of weeks every summer, and take another summer trip or two to boot; that we don't miss family holidays; and that it's never more than eleven weeks before at least a week-long break from the routine. In short, being part of the college system has made our family life much better—I have much more stress-free time with my kids than I would if I were working nine-to-five.

And that's my dilemma: Should I continue to work in a job that, ambition-wise, feels like a dead end but that provides a comfortable and happy family life? Or should I start a new career that would be exciting for me but would create great stresses on our family life, free time, and finances?

I went to see Wendell Berry address a room full of undergraduates once, and Berry was urging his audience to resist the flight and movement of meritocratic professional life. "But what if I don't have a hometown?" one student asked. "What if my family has already moved enough that I don't feel at home anywhere?" Berry's answer, I thought, was a good one: "Well," he replied, "stop moving." Maybe this is the answer for me: Make a home for myself and my family in this town, a place I had never given a moment's thought to before three years ago, even as I drove through it multiple times a year. Instead of building an identity around my importance and visibility, or my essays and books, or even my contribution to my society, I should stop moving, and stop thinking about moving, and simply locate my self in my relationships with family and friends.

When I think this way, it seems so obvious to me that I should reconcile myself to my work life—I should cleanse myself of any residual bitterness at academic life, purge myself of my ambition to be "accomplished," and enjoy the privileged personal life that I have. But then other thoughts inevitably creep in. I talk a lot about vocation when I teach my first-year writing classes, and my college expresses its Protestant roots mostly in its devotion to ideas of service and vocation. And I believe this stuff. Deeply compelled by a vision of a productive and contributive work life, teaching these courses forces me to repeatedly face the fact that my work no longer seems to me a vocation. If I could be a mechanical engineer, I mull, maybe working on wind or solar energy—why then, then, I could be devoted to my work, certain of its value, eager to leave the house in the morning!

If this is a foolish thought, it is no less compelling for its foolishness. A friend of mine earned a doctorate working on models of artificial intelligence and computer language recognition; he is divorced, without children, living in a new town, in many ways alone—but he is doing innovative work and is devoted to his job. I wouldn't think of separating myself from my family, or trading places with him, but I envy him: How great to be doing something genuinely exciting! How great to be doing work suited directly to one's natural talents, all in the cause of social progress! And the truth is I could follow that lead: I could take some physics and math classes over the next couple of years, return to school for another four or five after that, and remake my career. I could be that mechanical engineer.

But at what cost? Well, there is the fear that after all that work re-creating my career, I'd end up redesigning toothbrushes instead of solar panels. And there's the financial hit my family would take with me in school and out of work for years, and the stresses that would inevitably attend this. But the biggest loss would be time with my family: not only the time that would be required by returning to school, and the time required by less flexible workplaces, but also the time that a new vocation would require of me. If I took the time to enter a new career, I feel like I'd have to do so with the kind of energy I brought to this one—which is to say, I would need to identify myself fully with my new work. I'd be up late at night working through problems, and scribbling equations in the dirt at my kids' baseball games. This, I'm sure, would be deeply energizing to me. But wouldn't it also mean investing myself less fully as a father and a husband?

Sure, this is not a zero-sum game: I know that a man can be both a committed worker and a dad. But given my experience in the first five years of fatherhood, I have a hard time believing I would not experience this change as a loss of connection and contact with my kids. The academic world does provide a tremendous opportunity to balance family and work life, particularly, as in my case, if you are not terribly committed (anymore) to production and promotion. Starting another career while fully immersed in family life would certainly upset that balance.

So I float along, taking the middle course always: not ready to quit and become a stay-at-home dad, not yet ready to break a new path, not ready to devote myself again to academic ambitions. Every time that I seem to make a decision that charts a more certain future, that certainty slips away like a dream fading from memory. Two years ago, I received a tenure-track offer, at a solid liberal arts school a little more than an hour away: Here, after all these years, was the golden ring. And yet I turned it down, knowing that we could never have a third child if I was on the road for over two hours a day. Am I a father or a fool?

But if that decision seemed to indicate some embrace of my identity as a father, I then tacked back toward ambition. This winter my dean asked me to take a position as the director of advising. The job offered some, if not all, of the daily flexibility of a teaching position, but it also required work through much of the summer. The job description, though, matched my skills more exactly than teaching does—my deep love for organizational charts would find fulfillment in such a position, and I would be overjoyed that, after years of holding back the desire to snatch essays from students' hands and rewrite them myself, I could now edit documents as I please. And finally, in such a position, I would no longer be "visiting" my own workplace. After some hand-wringing about the diminishment of glorious summer, I took the job.

But taking this new job—like my decision to turn down the tenure-track job, and like my dream of the discovered workshop—has created certainty only for a moment. In truth, my dilemma continues: I do not know where this job leads, nor where I want it to lead. On the one hand, I have no wish to slide into professional mediocrity, keeping a position like this for decades, doing the same thing year after year; on the other, I don't particularly envy the jobs of my higher-ups, with their midnight e-mails and 7:30 A.M. meetings. My daily life continues to feel pleasant and privileged; my future, uncertain and unsettling. Struggling to understand how I will balance fatherhood and ambition, I continue to muddle along in the middle.

Making a Home for Family and Scholarship

TING MAN TSAO

Babies Should Always Be Wrapped

It was freezing in New York, where we were vacationing in my parents' house. I had to take Zaizai ("little son" in Cantonese) out to buy groceries. He was only a few months old. To protect him from the sleet and wind, I carried Zaizai in a soft baby carrier in front. I put the carrier inside my oversized down parka and zipped it up to keep him doubly warm. Then I walked to the deli with Joyce, my wife. A young man saw the bulk on my chest and asked curiously, "Is it a puppy?" "You bet!" I said, blushing, and continued on.

Spring. I was at my studio near SUNY Stony Brook, where I was working toward a PhD in English and a certificate in women's studies. Seasonal change had brought about warmth and sunshine. Joyce was, as usual, at work in the city. Tired of writing my dissertation, I wanted to enjoy the weather outside with Zaizai. I put him in a stroller. As we were about to start our afternoon walk, a woman living next door saw us and commented, "You should put a blanket over your baby." "It's warm," I explained. But my kind-hearted neighbor was not convinced: "Babies should always be wrapped." She walked away, knitting her brows.

Few people around me trusted that I could take care of a baby full-time. Why on earth does a young man stay home with a newborn? Does he know what he is doing? When we were kids, my brother and I were in the care of Yenyen ("grandmother" in Taisanese). After learning Joyce was pregnant, my father suggested that we should look for a nanny. He said that every family he knew hired someone to take care of a newborn so that the parents could work. When we told him that I would care for the baby, we met with great resistance.

We once stayed over at my parents' house when Zaizai was a few weeks old. He was too little to sleep through the night, and so he cried. My father was concerned: "Did you do anything wrong?" as though it weren't normal for newborns to wake up and cry. But Joyce and I didn't want any outside help at that time. As Joyce found a job in the city after I began studying at Stony Brook, we thought the "best" babysitter for Zaizai was me. My coursework was almost over, and I could stay home and look after the baby while working on my dissertation. Since I had only a tuition waiver from women's studies, this arrangement made sense economically. It also made sense philosophically: Joyce and I think that taking care of kids ourselves when they are small facilitates bonding.

My father's worries were not without reasons, though. I didn't have a clue how to take care of Zaizai at the beginning. I vividly remember the first time I changed his diaper at the hospital. Zaizai started shivering, but Joyce and I didn't know why. I rang for the nurse. She came and found that I hadn't wrapped him tightly enough in the receiving blanket. Eventually I learned how to do better, and when I did, I felt insulted that people didn't have confidence in my baby care judgment. As Zaizai grew up day by day, month by month, I finally won the trust of relatives and families, both in New York and in Hong Kong. Just before he died, my father praised me for being "a model father." At that time, Zaizai was already thirteen, bigger and taller than I. Given the fact that my father had never known any other stay-at-home dads, I cherish this compliment.

The Moon at Cornell

Isolation was the price that I had to pay for staying home and taking care of Zaizai. I wasn't the most sociable or active student in the university; nor was I politically savvy. I had no idea how to climb the academic ladder, or even how to keep what little I had achieved. I hadn't been awarded a TA line by Stony Brook, which, like many other public universities, faced extreme financial hardship in the early 1990s. The prospect of the academic job market was so gloomy that a sympathetic professor began his orientation speech to new graduate students by saying, "You guys are very brave to pursue a PhD in English at a time like this." He emphasized the increasing competition for tenure-track jobs, explaining that it was not uncommon to expect students to have published two or three articles before finishing the degree and entering the job market. But I didn't have the faintest clue how the academy worked. I felt quite alien from all the talk about joining professional organizations, going to conferences, inquiring about publication, and preparing dossiers.

Before entering Stony Brook, I had a career in social work. I left because of my passion for reading and studying. I was a bit resistant to the idea of academia as a marketplace in which you plot every book you read, essay you write, and connection you make with established people in the department and beyond. This seemed too much, especially when my first priority was to make sure Zaizai finished his formula or that dinner was ready (or almost ready) when Joyce returned from the Long Island Rail Road. I wasn't eager to attend student and faculty meetings, let alone MLA conferences. I had a whole other world away from the university, a world I felt more comfortable in than Stony Brook or MLA.

Such distance from the academic network cost me my tuition waiver without my even knowing it. Later, I would discover that an administrative error had been made and that I had been accidentally dropped from the list. But the professor in charge wouldn't admit it. Over the phone, she coldly reprimanded me for not acting like a "real" participant in the program. She became quiet when I explained that I was homebound because of Zaizai. Nevertheless, it was my fault for losing the waiver, she insisted.

Losing the waiver meant I would be in debt, for I had already registered for a full load of self-study credits, which I didn't actually need and wouldn't have signed up for had I known about the error. My advisor helped me take the case to the dean and get my tuition covered for that semester. But I lost any future waivers. When the women's studies program had new people in charge, they kindly offered me a much-sought-after TA line, which I refused. At that moment, taking care of Zaizai took priority over adding another make-or-break line on my CV.

Isolation might have contributed to the loss of my waiver, but it brought me a sense of freedom in the writing of the thesis. I didn't worry about the job market or journal publications. I didn't even have a deadline. Time seemed to be on my side. It took time to raise Zaizai. Caring for him was a twenty-four-hour job. Fortunately, Zaizai was an easy, healthy baby. I could steal moments for my own use in the morning and afternoon (evenings, when Joyce was home, were devoted to family). And it took time to research the history of British imperialism in nineteenth-century China. I followed every lead, created an endless bibliography, and gathered materials, many of them quite rare and obscure.

After exhausting all interlibrary loan materials, I wanted to collect some sources from national research libraries. We combined our vacations with my research creatively. A trip to Boston included all the sightseeing spots that a four-year-old would enjoy. But it also included a few hours of walking near Boston Public Library, from which I could quickly get a copy of a rare book; a day in Salem, where I could see the China trade exhibits; and a few evenings in Harvard's Widener and Theological libraries, where I could browse volumes of Victorian periodicals. I did similar things when attending my first MLA conference in Washington, D.C. (a very late introduction to this ritual).

But the most memorable trip was to Cornell. We strolled around the lakes, waterfalls, farms, and parks until we all got very tired. Then in the evening, after dinner, I walked to the Kroch Library while my son was watching Cartoon Network for the first time at the hotel room with Joyce (we didn't have cable TV at home). I found in the library a series of useful pamphlets and periodicals, which became the backbone of my dissertation and later my articles on the British Empire. By midnight, I had harvested enough materials. I headed out and was on my way back to the hotel. The air was refreshing. I heard a crystal clear rippling under my feet. I turned my head and looked down; it was a waterfall with a stream. I looked up; the moon was full. Joyce and Zaizai were sound asleep when I sneaked back into the hotel room with the bulky copies.

But I could not research at Cornell, Harvard, or New York Public Library forever. Zaizai was growing faster than my dissertation. I got stuck; I had no control over the tons of material I had been collecting. My thesis was too murky. My chapters had no organization. In isolation, I had no one nearby to guide me. As Zaizai began going to school and became less dependent on me, I thought I could make better use of my time. Instead of staying at home, I decided to work. Although bad news of the academic job market kept coming, the economy in general became better and better (Bill Clinton was president). I thought that if I could land a decent position, I would not need to worry after getting the PhD.

After trial and error I found a "perfect" grant-writing job at a small, community-based organization. The agency gave me flexibility so that I could drop Zaizai off at school and pick him up. This meant my regular schedule was from nine thirty to three, instead of nine to five. In exchange, I would take home some work to finish, and I would also work overtime at the agency whenever there was a rush to meet grant deadlines.

This position offered me something more. As an unforeseen bonus, it gave me the discipline in writing that I had lacked as a stay-home father-scholar. Grant writing was goal-oriented. I had to write to a specific audience to achieve a purpose (money—always money). There were always guidelines to follow and results to yield. In a fast-paced, growth-oriented agency, I also had to work under pressure. This profession made me more disciplined in writing, and I began to apply the same regimen to my own scholarship. Though working full-time and caring for Zaizai, I finished all of my dissertation chapters in half a year, and used a few more months for submission, revision, defense, and manuscript preparation. After I submitted the thesis, we took a long vacation in Hong Kong. Returning home, I found the diploma in the mailbox. Staying home with Zaizai, I spent a total of six years to complete my dissertation. By comparison, other Stony Brook doctoral candidates who were TAing and were either single or married but with no childcare duty took two to three years.

Muimui and the Tenure-Track Job

"Do you want a little sister or brother?" I asked Zaizai one day. The seven-year-old said yes. I had gotten tired of working in the nonprofit world, and my wife had always wanted a second child so that Zaizai had company. We decided that I would care for our second baby in the same way that I had for Zaizai. History often repeats itself, but not in this case. To my surprise, I found a job too good to turn down, a professorial position at a community college to which I could comfortably commute. Muimui ("little sister" in Cantonese) was born in my first month at the college. This changed our plan, but it did not change our commitment to taking care of children ourselves for as long as we could. Instead of my staying home, Joyce took a leave without pay to look after Muimui. She was entitled to five years of leave, and by then, Muimui would be big enough for kindergarten.

My first two years of teaching were unimaginably tough. I had to get used to everything, both at home and at work. Muimui exhausted Joyce, who did most of the household and childcare chores. I helped out to give her a break whenever I had time and energy. Joyce had higher expectations than I as a homemaker. She did a lot of things I hadn't done (or hadn't done so well) when I stayed home. She made bread by hand, and I used to make bread (if at all) by a machine. She cooked three-course meals; I used to dump everything into a pot and dinner was ready. She cleaned up the house; I left the house dirty until either Joyce or I couldn't bear it anymore (mostly she was the one who first reacted to the messiness). She took Muimui out to some children's library programs; I used to read to Zaizai in the afternoon before his nap (midway through a book, I usually fell asleep earlier than Zaizai). Doing all this day after day, Joyce felt the homemaker's monotony—busy but dull. "It's like you've done nothing after doing so much," explained Joyce.

However, I didn't have much time and energy to help out or simply cheer her up. With an annual teaching load of twenty-seven credit hours, I had too many papers to grade, too many lessons to prepare. And in the first few years of my tenure clock, I also had too many departmental and college-wide meetings to attend, too many committee duties to complete. In addition, my college, unlike some other two-year institutions, requires scholarship for tenure and promotion. I spent a lot of time writing, or thinking about writing if I was not doing so. In my untenured mentality, I found myself not quick enough to grab career-building opportunities, let alone to say no to requests and demands. So I was busy seven days a week.

At one point, I got overwhelmed and forgot about Joyce's medical appointment. She had told me about it many times; on the appointment day, she had reminded me. I was to go home immediately after class to accompany the children so that Joyce could go to the clinic herself. But the whole thing was lost in my mind, as I was preoccupied with this meeting and that meeting. I didn't return home on time, and Joyce missed her appointment.

I regretted this lapse so much I made up my mind that I was not going to let senseless college obligations interfere with our family life. I said no for the first time to certain "busywork" that I didn't think would lead to advancement. I no longer did "everything" and began to select "niches" in which I not only excelled but also excelled visibly. Equally important, I chose commitments that could complement, rather than compete with, one another. I turned, for instance, some of my special teaching projects into scholarship; preparing for the pedagogical projects prepared me at the same time for scholarly publications.

But writing still took time, and I didn't just write about teaching, I was also revising parts of my thesis into articles. I nonetheless persisted, following the pattern of teaching, reflection, and scholarship. By the third year, I already had a track record of pedagogical achievements and publications. I was cautiously confident about getting tenure (my college had a five-year tenure clock at that time).

Yet life is complicated with children. Just when I had found ways to harmonize family and work, Joyce couldn't stand the homebound boredom and isolation anymore. Muimui was over two years old. We agreed it was time for Joyce to cut short her leave and resume working. This meant we needed a perfect daycare situation that would be educative and meet our needs as working parents. We had to think about drop-off and pick-up schedules in addition to transportation. We had to consider holiday arrangements (some good schools have too many religious holidays). Fortunately, we found one in the neighborhood that matched all of our needs. It was very expensive, but we had no choice.

We had to make special arrangements. I rearranged my teaching sched-ule for late mornings, and was responsible for dropping Muimui off for the extended morning service by car. I left the car at the daycare center and ran (rather than walked) to the subway station for the college. After some adjustment, Zaizai was confident enough to go to school on his own. In the late afternoon, Joyce was responsible for picking up Muimui from the extended day service, using the car I had parked at the center. This arrangement worked only when all parties cooperated. One missing link meant trouble. Once, the daycare center canceled the extended morning service without notifying me. As a result, I was late for school. I angrily called the principal. She apologized and resumed extended morning hours. In the following semester, however, I further delayed my teaching schedule till noon so that Muimui didn't have to depend on the unreliable early morning service.

The Economics of Simply Being There

Looking back on the past sixteen years, I feel that making space for both childrearing and scholarly pursuit has been an expensive but worthwhile endeavor. The creation and maintenance of that space has required, first and foremost, Joyce's full support, with which I have been fortunately blessed. We are both committed to caring for the kids ourselves for as long as possible, although this has meant surviving on a single income in one of the most expensive regions in the nation. Joyce has also fully supported my scholarship even though it is not economically rewarding, and even though she has no interest in it (any discussion of my research puts her to sleep immediately). I value such support all the more in light of our background from Hong Kong, a ferociously pragmatic financial center.

Most of our college friends there didn't choose what we chose to do. They didn't take years to pursue a PhD and a less than lucrative academic career. Nor did they stay at home with their kids. They hired nannies and domestic servants to avoid any interruption in their careers. They now earn enviable salaries and own spacious apartments. Pursuing the life that Joyce and I decided to pursue, we have neither. Don't get me wrong, though: We respect our friends' decisions. Using domestic help, they tell us, doesn't make parenting easier, but just barely possible for working couples striving to better their lives in a metropolis where the costs of living make the one-income family the exception rather than the norm.

Therefore, despite the challenges we face, we feel especially thankful for the circumstances under which our childcare plans have worked out. One of us was always home with Zaizai and Muimui, witnessing and participating in the most important period of their growth. Bonding developed as we did the most mundane things—rocking the crib, bathing, talking, pillow fighting, and, simply, being there. It may be too early to gauge the impact of the presence of a father-scholar in the house. But Zaizai and Muimui are both avid readers. They love school. When they are sick, Joyce and I have to force them to stay home. They are independent and, more importantly, happy learners.

Yet stay-at-home parenting is hard to pull off in America, which promotes "family values" rhetorically without providing people with tangible support to grow and sustain families. Joyce and I were lucky to be able to stay home with our kids. The price we paid was earning less money and retarding our careers: a small price for the well-being of children. But not every couple can afford this luxury even when they are willing. And some colleagues I know decide to forgo having children altogether—for economic, personal, or professional reasons. I once had a chat with a junior colleague who seemed to be a happy bachelor. He lived by himself, and had all the time in the world to write and build his career. With both family and college obligations, I said I envied him. But he put things into perspective: "Look at it this way. After getting tenured and promoted in several years, I'll have nothing but a bunch of papers in my filing cabinet. But you'll have a family." Yes, Joyce and I are still on the family track.

Change Is Here, but
We Need to Talk about It

Reflections on Black Fatherhood in the Academy

JEFFREY B. LEAK

> "I am an invisible man. No, I am not a spook like those who haunted Edgar Allan Poe; nor am I one of your Hollywood-movie ectoplasms. I am a man of substance, of flesh and bone, fiber and liquids—and I might even be said to possess a mind."
>
> —RALPH ELLISON, *Invisible Man*

Ralph Ellison's exploration of black masculinity continues to serve as a foundational metaphor for understanding the historical construction of black masculinity. And while issues of invisibility and examples of black male maladjustment abound in contemporary American culture, we cannot deny the successful integration of certain black men into the American mainstream. If there is any doubt about this assertion, the election of Barack Obama as the forty-fourth president of the United States speaks to this literal and symbolic reality in theorizing black masculinity.

But the aspect of President Obama's narrative—as much as I admire his personal and professional journey—that departs from my experience as an African American man is fatherhood. Here I am not questioning our president's commitment to fatherhood, but I am suggesting that his particular model is rooted in the traditional role as provider, with his wife and mother-in-law providing the day-to-day guidance for their daughters. As I consider the life of the most popular black father in the world, I am reminded of our different locations on the map of fatherhood.

For men in general and black men in particular, the social visibility of men who are hands-on fathers (that is, men who are involved in their children's lives beyond a kiss in the morning and a kiss at night) is minuscule. For black men, too many of us are fixated on the model of manhood and success signified in President Obama's example; in this model we have a black man who is the primary provider for his family, a black man with un-precedented access to white institutions of power and privilege. If Obama were white, his story would be interesting but not a phenomenon unto itself. Because the history of white American manhood revolves around a narrow conception of what constitutes manhood, the Obama model res-onates with many black men. In other words, the primary tenet of white supremacy was the emasculation of black men. No wonder, then, that many black men have focused on attaining the power accorded to white men, without critiquing the notion of white manhood.

In the case of Obama's rather traditional role as father, this model works for his family, but some of us have not comprehended the most important aspect of the Obama model: that it is one of numerous options, that black fatherhood presents multiple possibilities. What I mean here is that most men, even in the moderately progressive professoriate, do not exercise the family leave option that is guaranteed by law in the Family and Medical Leave Act. Having done it twice, first with our daughter in 2001, and most recently with our son in 2009, I find that I inhabit a social zone that ren-ders me, alas, invisible. Try showing up at a noontime reading class at the public library with your infant, and you are the only man present in a room with mostly white women and maybe a few black women. Or better yet, attend an infant swim class and share the pool with women ranging in age from thirty to forty-five. In all of these moments, which take place during the weekdays, everyone wants to know, in the lingua franca of W.E.B. Du Bois, "How does it feel to be a problem?" Inevitably, a woman will inquire about my wife. "Are you giving your wife a day off?" "Is she ill?" "Your child is actually with you for most of the day?" Really, what they really want to ask is "Why are you here?"

Men and women, even those who define themselves as progressive, struggle with this alternative social scenario. We are not at the point in our culture where it is expected that men spend substantive, not just symbolic, periods of time with their children. For those who do, the professional and social implications have yet to be determined. How many men could take a leave of absence from their profession to provide childcare for their family and return to their profession years later? Such a proposition is not always easy for women, but because women are still often expected to postpone professional development for the sake of family, they, ironically, appear to have more flexibility in this narrow sense. To make my point, imagine the Obamas in reverse: Mrs. Obama as president, with Mr. Obama slowing down his career to provide primary parenting for their daughters.

Let me be clear here: I am not arguing that every new father needs to become the primary caregiver of a newborn or adopted child. My point is that for those men who, either formally or informally, embrace a more active place in the lives of their children, American society has not quite caught up with this shift in social evolution. My commitment to fatherhood may be appreciated by family and friends, especially in light of the deep social challenges confronting far too many African American families, but this transformation does come with a price. Before I proceed further, I want to state that I am not seeking to equate the sacrifices of father-hood with those of motherhood—although there are singular cases that can prove such a correlation—but I am compelled to articulate the social and professional implications for men whose commitment to fatherhood extends beyond financial stability and occasional moments of extended interaction. And this commitment, in terms of law, social expectations, and professional responsibility, presents a set of challenges that will need to be addressed.

To begin with, upon the births of our children, fatigue was a frequent visitor to our home. New mothers need abundant rest at the very time this new life is drawing energy and attention from them. For women in the professoriate, the saving grace is that during their semester of leave, their clock, whether for tenure or promotion, stops. (We should note here that women in the sciences who may run labs or research groups often cannot afford to be absent for an entire semester.) But for men who invoke FMLA and use that semester to be with their child, the clock keeps running. Regardless of the fact that I was up late into the night with my daughter and often prepared dinner (in addition to other things), my tenure clock (which started in 1998) kept right on ticking in 2001, and I earned tenure in 2004. Needless to say, I was not the most productive during the semesters (or even years) during which our children were born, but I managed consid-erable productivity before their arrival, providing a cushion during these periods in which I had limited energy.

In other words, for fathers in the professoriate just thirty years ago, the responsibility of childcare fell largely on their wives. The English or biol-ogy professor, for example, continued his teaching, research, and lab work with minimal interruption. His wife and their extended families took care of home, and he provided the income—at least that is the dominant narra-tive most often associated with previous generations. Today, as more men in the faculty ranks attempt to be more present in the lives of their families, their teaching, research, and administrative work may be impacted.

Even with this likelihood, we still have not had meaningful conversations in the academy about how to adjust to the increasing number of male colleagues who wish to be more present in the lives of their children. As an African American father, there are other racial and cultural issues that inform what I have discussed here; namely, the complex and convoluted issues that often hover over black gender relations. But if we are going to raise the bar for fatherhood in our culture, men and women will need to understand that sacrifices are imperative. As men, we may have to calibrate our fast-track ambitions, in order to be a presence in the home. If such is the case, women will no longer be in a position to expect men to be primary providers all the time. This latter point will probably prove moot, as the world economy makes two-income households a necessity, and as women continue to outpace men in education and the professions.

Until then, I will not live with the suppressed anger that roils Ellison's Invisible Man; at least the law of the land acknowledges my right to a more expanded idea of fatherhood, but attitudes and perception change slowly. Nonetheless, in those moments when people respond to me with polite incredulity, all I need to think about are those magical, mysterious words: Da, Da Da, and Daddy. Whatever the iteration, my world moves into proper balance.

Vocabularies and Their Subversion

A Reminiscence

JOHN DOMINI

Curriculum Vita, c. 1995: First writing, mostly journalism; then teaching writing; then mélange of both, slightly better paid; then writing for money, PR etc., much better paid.

This much well into midlife. For someone with my set of skills, the combinations aren't uncommon. A comparable sequence could be filleted from many an author's or professor's biography. But in my case, no single career emerges. Midlife, I arrive at mid-lives. Never mind that in the early 1990s, the adaptations I made proved an evolutionary miracle. The PR work brought in the fattest paychecks I've yet to cash, and I saved the farm. Saved the tomato and basil in the backyard, anyway, in a walk-worthy neighborhood of Portland, Oregon. I gleaned a few last kernels of domestic bliss for my wife, my daughter, and myself. Yet then when I lost the farm—when my marriage collapsed, c. 1995—chief among my resolutions was to get a doctorate, literature or creative writing, ideally both. I committed to an academic vocation.

As I looked back over the juggling I'd done, it was the balls I'd recently put in play, the ones wrapped in money, that appeared to have accomplished the least. I'd rescued the family only to see it go to smithereens. What better demonstration could I have for the hypocrisy, the false promise, that lay at the heart of advertising and PR? What better proof of the risk in dealing in lies? Even my status as parent had been downgraded to "joint custody." To earn a PhD seemed like juggling more substantial materials, good honest bricks of book learning. If I learned to handle those bricks, I might yet build an enduring home.

But these are metaphors. That's in my set of skills, the metaphor, and it will do for an essay. It gets across what I was thinking when I decided to go for a doctorate. But then as now, I had no hermeneutic that would explain away the odds I was up against. On my actual CV, in incontrovertible black-on-beige, my bachelor's carried a date from decades before. I had wattles, crow's feet. Then there were the logistics, even more unpromising. My Portland had nothing by way of doctoral studies in my area. The nearest half-decent opportunity required several hours' drive. Time and distance and growing old—no tricks of semantics. Especially when the pain and difficulty of earning my PhD weren't mine alone.

❧ ❧

Concepts of addiction therapy, in dialectic: Al-Anon versus AA; medication versus dependence; personal counseling versus 12-Step sessions; "compulsive lying" versus "a fearless moral inventory."

My daughter (she's asked me to not to use her name for this piece) was entering her teens as her mother and I divorced. The worst time for a kid to see her family destroyed. She suffered the hormones and fragility of her own midlife, middle school. Not that the girl didn't have resources, a deep account of childhood happiness banked against the tragedy. Likewise Mom and Pop had worked through counseling, salvaging a couple of better years out of the decline and fall. We'd finished up with a legal mediator rather than going lawyer versus lawyer. "A good divorce," I learned to call it, this ritual scarring of my late-life initiation. I accepted, too, how my ex now claimed certain areas of our daughter's interests, while I was relegated to others. My special province was that of my higher learning: culture and the arts.

Music, for one, provided the girl and me the same connection as it had since elementary school. We'd jammed together a bit, starting out on guitar and recorder. But by the time the marriage broke down, my playing couldn't keep pace with hers. Rather, in my two-bedroom bachelor space as in my former home, we would boogie to the rock 'n' roll that my daughter had discovered for me. Nine times out of ten this meant hard-hitting women, voices and rhythms burly with a turmoil she must've found sympathetic. This meant Madonna, most famously, but also first-wave women rappers like Mary J. Blige and Salt-N-Pepa, plus the rage-metal of early Alanis and L7. The evening of her thirteenth birthday, I treated her and three Best Female Friends to L7, playing in a club.

One of those nights. One of those moments amid the wreckage, when it felt like my life might be reassembled into some form of contentment. I knew the sweetness of the city, its comfortable drizzle, its neighborhood venues and their generous all-ages arrangements. I reveled in the antiglamour and total command of the four women onstage, the crowd-surfing frenzy they triggered with an anti-anthem like "Pretend We're Dead." My mental scrapbook still carries whole pages from that night, my daughter and her BFFs, now dancing, now chattering.

The girl and I enjoyed quieter pleasures. We would prowl the stacks of Powell's Books, then winnow through our selections in the coffee shop. When Madeleine L'Engle came to town, my daughter not only accompanied me to the reading, but also stood up with a question. She wanted to know more about the heroine of *A Wrinkle in Time*. Also we took in movies. One of her favorites was Todd Haynes's debut, *Superstar: The Karen Carpenter Story*, quite the idiosyncratic choice. Performed entirely by Barbie dolls, *Karen Carpenter* enacts a mocking gay fantasia of the biopic.

Our shared interests, that is, could leave us miles apart. Much as I connected with the L7 experience, my own feelings don't overlap with hers. She's let me know, since, that she and one of her friends had begun sneaking out to clubs before that night. I see no reason to doubt her, or doubt that adolescents need risk, as self-assertion. Back in '96 and '97, what was I up to, if not a middle-aged version of the same? What did my new reading have to teach, much of it anyway, if not that identity's riddled with ambiguity and forever under construction? But the self that my daughter now began to cobble together revealed some disturbing stress points.

For months following the divorce, she left her room in my apartment barren. I don't mean only that I found next to nothing in her bureau, when I gave the drawers a fatherly check. Her wardrobe had shrunk to a few boyish bits and pieces anyway. Maybe the last time I'd seen my daughter in a dress was at the funeral for my Boston grandmother. Far more unsettling, here in Papa's Portland place, was the stark white nakedness of her bedroom walls. Back in what was now her mother's home, she'd strewn her space with party colors. A cornucopia: CD covers, plasticware, headlines and artwork, ads and souvenirs. The girl was forever asking for a fresh roll of tape. But in my apartment she wouldn't even put up a poster. I bought her two to start with, a Madonna and a Marilyn Monroe, the latter in a butch pose, on a weight bench pumping iron. But she left both rolled up in a corner.

For weeks I held my peace. Then came the breakdown, a classic, the first Thanksgiving without a family. The bawling out of control, the role reversal as daughter comforts father. By New Year's, the walls of her second bedroom were brightly littered. She even got more color into her wardrobe, a bandanna at her wrist. But no decoration could express the grief and terror she must've been feeling, storms that must've surged up worse when she saw me express the same, over uneaten turkey and potatoes. It wasn't much later that, during a fatherly check of her backpack, I discovered it reeking of marijuana. In a side pocket, I turned up pills.

New vocabulary, first semesters of doctoral reading: heteroglossia; metanarrative and its subversion; enabling as artistic process; gender and its subversion.

Whatever's riddled with ambiguity and forever in process, as I say, made up most of my curriculum. High-level literary discourse, at my turn of the millennium, prized transgression and breaking down differences. Everywhere, established strata were shown to bleed into one another. Learning to make sense of that interactivity, the way it subverted the worn-out and enabled the fresh, struck me as fascinating. I was born postmodern, I suppose. My course of study had to be interdisciplinary, all about po-mo cross-pollination. So when such a curriculum turned up in a program that was at once fully accredited and low-residency—a program that wouldn't require me to leave town—I got busy. Evening after evening I sat through the screechy dial-up that e-mail then required.

Nowadays, it's worth noting, everything about the process has streamlined. Even Ivy League universities have embraced the interdisciplinary dissertation, which combines a research essay with an artistic project. Low-residency programs too have multiplied. In the mid-nineties, however, my choices were few and my double-dissertation loomed scarily. My critical vocabulary lagged decades behind, and my proposed creative project, a novel, had thus far proven beyond me. To be sure, these shortcomings had something to do with my failed marriage. But if I now pinned my frustrations on my ex, wouldn't the sharp end go right through her and on into my daughter? Wasn't it safer to huddle within the buffers of a "good divorce"? As I entered the thickets of recent literary theory, the Lacanian doubling and Derridean punning, I had to stay out of any such briar patch of the heart. If some passage set me shouting at the bookshelves, I had to notice the echo, the hollow echo. On my desk and table, a jerry-built wraparound, I built a protective wall of papier-mâché. Materials ranged from the *Brittanica* to the Post-it, at first in seeming compensation for my daughter's desolate bedroom. In among the reading, too, was always my most important personal model. An impossible figure for comparison, but I can't make sense of this sea-change half decade without him. Not without Dante Alighieri and *The Divine Comedy.*

I'd known from the first that the epic had to be part of my learning. Inter-disciplinarity had to include the language and culture of my immigrant father. And once my program got under way, early signs of progress included grants and assignments that took me to Italian New York and even to Naples and Rome. I traveled in steerage and burdened with multiple tasks, but the trips mattered so much that they suggest a wholly different essay. I could instead celebrate my renewed bond with my heritage. Italian Americans like W. S. Di Piero have become a primary subject for scholar-ship, and Naples has figured prominently in two of my novels. All well and good, but all another story. Another Lacanian mirror, reflecting a happy image out of a troubled time. For my journeys also tasted distinctly of Dante's "bitter exile," as each left me more out of touch with my daughter. We found our connection tattered before I was halfway to the doctorate.

Counseling and AA, structures you'd think would help me reach the girl, instead wound up as additional branches of my research. In Al-Anon, the parents' group, I learned to spot less obvious symptoms of drug abuse, as well as recognize addictive patterns in the parents' families. I picked up the term "high-functioning alcoholic" and discovered it applied to one of my uncles. But when I wanted simply to sit and talk with my daughter, a meeting room or a psychiatrist's office could function like a protective wall of her own. She preferred it back there, something else that turned up in my research. Avoidance behavior, check. So too I was braced for the ugly suggestion that I'd abused her. One counselor after another tried to paste that bright label over the case, no matter how my daughter and I pushed it away. Yes, she'd broken with the norms of family connection. Yes, she needed to quit the drugs—her most terrifying combination was alcohol and amphetamines. But she and I both knew there hadn't been any abuse in the home. The root problem might elude us too, but we knew it wasn't any-thing so simple. Anyway, I suffered guilt enough as it was; I'd moved two time zones away.

Before I was halfway to my doctorate, I stubbed up against its cost. Tuition too is impervious to metaphor, especially for a man also saddled with the expenses of therapy. And this after I'd turned my back on writing for money. Yet the money came through, salary and benefits. In a turn of events that prompts dizzy hyperbole, "beyond my wildest dreams," I landed one of the country's best visiting appointments in creative writing. The position included full family medical, and if I worked up at the level of wildest dream, it would last four years. It seemed I'd saved the farm again. Except in this case the farm, the job, was in Chicago.

Thus the crux of this essay, a schism that won't be bridged no matter how snugly I hook together my concepts and phonemes. The more perfect expression is the howl I fell into the morning I moved, half an hour and more of wailing helplessness in a corner of the room that had been my daughter's, under Sheetrock once again stripped bare. The same truth came babbling out of me throughout the coming year, every time I headed to my Chicago office. I walked to work and, throughout the first year, along the way I'd make a resignation speech. I'd tell my chairperson that I had to leave, my daughter needed me, though this came out more in patterns of sound than actual words. Murmurs, prayers, moans—not much different from my daughter's evasions—such stuff is central to what I'm getting at. For if there was a consistent exception, if there was something the girl and I could talk about openly and frankly, it had to do with my doctoral work. We talked about Dante and his *Comedy*.

Naturally we found other neutral arenas, beyond the little plot of experience I'm trying to harvest here. My daughter had sober enthusiasms, from riding horses to assembling a band. Still, few subjects opened up for us like this one. Terza rima took us to the thrice-closing word *stelle*, and circles of Hell to spirals of Purgatory. One of the few even-tempered conversations I recall from my daughter's high school days took place before the poetry shelves of Powell's, as we looked over a few translations. We enjoyed something like ten minutes of shared goodwill, a long time for us in those days.

Books mailed to my daughter at the "transition home": Inferno, *Dante, trans. Robert Pinsky;* The Scarlet Letter, *Nathaniel Hawthorne;* Cosmicomics, *Italo Calvino;* The Women of Brewster Place, *Gloria Naylor.*

A piece of writing grooms a small plot of experience, but events and feelings spill in as many directions as a stash of X spilled across a bedroom floor. L7 in a Portland club was one thing to me and another to my daughter. So too her eventual commitment to sobriety extends its tangles far outside my boxes and rows. Nevertheless, from where I sit, the catalyst was writing. Three pieces of writing, composed as I began the fourth year of my Chicago appointment. One piece was for my doctoral committee, the second for my daughter, and the third for her mother and therapist. With the ex and the doctor I communicated via e-mail, to the girl I wrote longhand, and for my dissertation's context essay I had the full array of pertinent software.

My novel was finished (though it would go through more drafts before publication) and my coursework had all been approved. Only the context

essay remained, a 150-page reconfiguration of the vocabulary and references over which I'd now gained command. Yet when I turned from my
smudged keyboard to the yellow legal pad, when I dashed off a letter for my
daughter hardly lifting my pen, the hours of picking academic nits felt as
if they'd helped. They'd delivered me to a greater flexibility of mind. That's
the word, flexibility. A Latinate but not too highfalutin', it'll do as well for
what I needed at the end of these same exhausting days. Midnight sometimes found me patching together an e-mail for my daughter's mother and
therapist. A legal brief, almost, this piece argued that my daughter's cure
had to be found in our own messy world. To live drug-free meant little in
an artificial environment, under close supervision. For that was where she
found herself now, in the semi-arid Oregon outback, sharing a rehab facility with other teenagers. The confinement seemed a draconian measure
and I said so. Careful—flexible—I suggested alternatives.

As for the letters, I'd mail those off with a book or some other small gift.
Never a financial gift, forbidden under house rules, just as phone calls from
parents were restricted to Sunday afternoons. So my daughter's response
to what I wrote only reached me in bits and pieces. At the time, once again
she opened up most about her reading, the books I sent. She devoted much
of one phone conversation to a rave review of *The Scarlet Letter*. Otherwise,
a bristling distance still yawned between us, and my letters were written
toward an image: the best I could summon up for our eventual relationship as adults. I called on the best I might yet become, an interdisciplinary
effort that put everything I'd learned to use. Some of this was 12-Step work,
acknowledgments of fault and making amends. But the strata of blame kept
bleeding into better, into strengths of her character and, even, mine. What
were characters like Dimmesdale and Prynne, I wrote, if not spirits who'd
achieved wholeness only after they embraced what had previously appeared
monstrous about them? What had I been trying to accomplish for five years
now, if not to move beyond a monolithic sense of self? I'd subscribed to
false concepts, the Breadwinner as opposed to the Artist-Scholar. But now
I could see these elements in dialogue. Now I could write, in plain English,
about my daughter's sexuality. She was gay, yes. She was gay, and it made
no difference. However she defined her gender, she was loved. All this I got
down on paper at last.

That summer, as I say, I heard little by way of reply. I lived instead with
an often-discouraging heteroglossia. I'd begun to circulate my vita, and I
was hearing a lot of *No*. But I also got word that the dean had signed off
on my doctorate and my daughter had moved back up to Portland. She

reenrolled in high school and in AA, and over the months that followed she stuck it out with both. The next substantial exchange between the two of us was a long time coming, almost a year after my final letter to the "home." But that talk, when it came, was a miracle.

Dialogue c. 2001, between John Domini, PhD, and his daughter, AA, DJ:
    Gosh, I'm so sorry my work took me away from you at such a hard time.
    Pop, the worst that happened would've happened anyway.
    Maybe, but my not being there made it harder.
    Maybe, Pop. But maybe seeing how you worked on yourself made it easier. Because you got somewhere.

Well, actually, I did and I didn't. Over the last decade, the stinginess of the academic marketplace has asserted itself. I've never found a tenure-track slot. My novels, though, have made it onto estimable presses. I've a got a memoir under way, a book that will have to include both this story and a number of happier developments. In particular there's my new wife and my daughter's own good luck in love. Her partner's another Sober Soldier and an artistic type, so sweet a match that the two have spoken of marriage. That's grounds for a bit of ribbing, marriage. Where I live, unlike benighted Oregon, gays have the right.

But mostly my daughter and I talk about music. She's spoken of her furtive early clubgoing. She's explained her work as a DJ, a creative endeavor. All about the "mash-ups." A successful DJ has to comb through tracks of all kinds and combine them in ear-catching new ways. She puts Stevie Nicks '77 over Atlanta crunk from 2005, with electronic obbligato from early '90s Herbie Hancock. I could say it's a bit like a writer's gift combined with higher learning to arrive at an enlarged capacity for love. But just now, I'd like to keep dancing.

Balancing Diapers and a Doctorate

The Adventures of a Single Dad in Grad School

CHARLES BANE

"Me make a mess." These were the words my two-year-old son, Geoffrey, said as he stood over the toilet with a feather duster in one hand and a ten-dollar bottle of Bausch & Lomb ReNu® Multi-Purpose Solution in the other on one bright, and otherwise cheery, Saturday in April. Three completely separate thoughts ran through my head. One, "That's an absolutely brilliant example of alliteration. He's obviously got the heart of a poet." Two, "That's just a ten-ounce bottle; why the hell is there so much water on the floor?" And three, "You're not the only one, kid."

The first thought is a mixture of wishful thinking and literary analysis of which only a PhD candidate in English can conceive. A sort of "Of course my child is a poet. How could he not be!" jumbled up with the uncontrollable urge to view every incident of the day as a text to be analyzed. After long consideration (it's taken me six years to come to grips with this), I don't believe I was witnessing a fledgling Whitman in the earliest stages of his career (however, I do believe the soul of an artist resides in the inner recesses of my son's chest). It's more likely that I was witnessing the confession of a two-year-old who has been caught in the act.

The second thought, and possibly most important question raised by this incident, will be answered a little later. As for the third thought, there were times during my grad school stretch that I believed that I had truly made a mess of my life. However, it was generally one of my children, and incidents like Geoffrey and the toilet bowl, that brought clarity to the moment.

Just over a year earlier, I had been a married junior high English teacher who was completing his MA degree. I had a home, a cat, and three wonderful children: Ericka, Katie, and the aforementioned Geoffrey. And then something happened. In the spring semester of 2002 (as anyone in academia knows, it's easiest to remember one's life in terms of semesters) I accepted an offer from Louisiana State University to enter the PhD program in English. Two weeks later, I was served with divorce papers from my soon-to-be ex-wife. Granted, it wasn't a complete shock; we had been separated for a few months, but I honestly believed we were in the "we can work it out" phase of the relationship. I sat on the floor of my seventies-style (not retro, mind you; the décor simply had not been updated for thirty years) studio apartment, contemplating what to do with my life.

A PhD was the dream, but I was a father of three. If I chose to let the offer lapse, I could continue teaching eighth-grade English or possibly land a job at the local community college, teaching five sections of composition. If I followed through with the PhD, I had to leave my children behind. They were not coming with me. So, I did what I generally did (and still do) when life presented me with a difficult situation: I called my dad.

My father was the first in the family to go to college. He had a BSE in math and science and master's degrees in math, counseling, and administration. He had spent over thirty years of his life in the public school system. He understood the complexities of family and school life and did always seem to know the best solution to the problem. After a lengthy discussion, we decided that I had to pursue the degree and that we would just have to work out some sort of system for being with the kids on some sort of regular basis. Eventually, this regular basis would turn out to be every other weekend and school breaks. Geoffrey, because he was not yet in school, could visit a little more often and stay for longer periods.

And so, this is how I found myself in a 645-square-foot graduate student apartment on Nicholson Street in Baton Rouge, Louisiana. The apartment was a three-bedroom, one-bath unit with a linen-closet-sized kitchen. The floors were industrial tile, and the walls were cinder block, painted in a lovely Drizzling Mist Gray. The smallest of the three bedrooms was eight feet square and contained the only air-conditioning unit in the apartment. This is important. In Baton Rouge, the humidity is so high that mold forms everywhere. So, as per the housing contract with the school, tenants had to promise to keep the window unit running every day, year-round. Since this was the smallest room in the apartment, I used it as an office; since it had the window unit that was cooling the entire apartment, the temperature in the room hovered around fifty-five degrees on any given day.

The week of the toilet incident had been one of my "good weeks," meaning that I had spent the previous weekend with my daughters and Geoffrey, and since he was not in school, he was staying with me for an entire week. He had recently woken up from a nap and was having a snack while I was putting the finishing touches on what I believed to be a brilliant Freudian analysis of David Lynch's *Mulholland Dr.* Then, the silence began. I'm often asked by friends and colleagues who don't have children how I can get any work done with all the noise. As any parent knows, it's the silences you have to worry about. I left my igloo to search for the two-year-old, a task that should not be difficult in a 645-square-foot apartment. I found him in the bathroom, standing over the toilet with his chosen tools for the day. When he saw me, he happily dropped the feather duster and began squirting the precious contact fluid into the toilet while saying, "Me make a mess." I complimented him on his alliteration and stepped into the bathroom. As my foot came down, there was an audible splash accompanied by a soaking sensation in my sock. "That's just a ten-ounce bottle; why the hell is there so much water on the floor?" The answer was simple. Geoffrey had used the feather duster to scoop the water out of the toilet and was using the contact solution in a futile attempt to refill it.

It was incidents like this that helped me get through graduate school. I know it sounds completely insane, but having kids actually helped me succeed where others were struggling. While at LSU I was surrounded by single men and women, a few married couples, and others who were in "serious relationships." But almost none of them—I can only think of two besides me—had children. In fact, most of them swore that they would never have children because they did not want to put their careers, and therefore their lives, on hold. A choice had to be made. Career or children? PhD or poopie diapers? One could not have both. This mentality was reiterated constantly by the graduate faculty in advising situations, at monthly job talks, or simply in the hallway. Children meant the death of your career. It was only once someone had completed school, landed a job, and published extensively enough to guarantee tenure that one could even begin to consider the possibility of having children. This was made abundantly clear to me by one of my committee members who upon finding out that I had accepted an additional class for a little more money scolded me for not focusing on my research. When I told him that I needed the additional pay, he asked, "What for?" I answered, "I've got three kids." To which he replied, "You need to get your priorities straight. You're here to get a PhD." Having Geoffrey empty the toilet bowl with a feather duster helped me learn to prioritize. Freud and Lynch were going to have to wait. The bathroom needed to be mopped, and someone obviously wanted to play.

The most important lesson I learned in my studies at LSU didn't come from a seminar, or a conference, or even a book. The most important lesson had nothing to do with deconstruction, semiotics, or voiced bilabial stops. The most important lesson I learned was about balance. When you've convinced yourself that you have to stay focused on the goal and every waking moment must be focused on the goal, you eventually crack from the pressure of obtaining the goal. And how do you deal with this pressure? You go on ridiculous shopping sprees for shit you don't really want or need. You veg for hours watching the latest reality TV show. You spend way too much time at the bar. But when there is something else competing for your focus, for example, a diaper that must—*must*—be changed, you change the diaper. Shopping sprees and reality TV can wait, and the bars will always be open. The diaper will not wait. Trust me, if there is any delay, the contents of the diaper will find its way onto the child's fingers and eventually onto the Drizzling Mist Gray cinder-block wall.

Having Geoffrey around kept me out of the bars and away from the television. I read, studied, and wrote while he slept. Because I wanted him to be healthy, I ate better meals than most of my colleagues. Rather than making late-night runs to IHOP or Jack in the Box, we sustained ourselves on home-cooked vegetables. Because I had someone around who needed me for his very survival, I learned to balance the goals I wanted to accomplish. I wanted a PhD, but Geoffrey needed a father.

Having Geoffrey around seemed to teach those around me about balance as well. I couldn't afford childcare, and my schedule wasn't rigid enough to demand it anyway. I taught class three days a week and attended class only two days and one night a week. I was physically around most of the day, so I called on my friends and colleagues to help out. Shelisa was more than willing to watch Geoffrey for an hour while I taught freshman comp. Though I sometimes worried that I was cutting into Shelisa's time, I think she, too, learned about balance. Jessie Redmon Fauset was a worthwhile scholarly pursuit, but reading *Miss Mary Mack* (Mack, Mack, all dressed in black, black, black) to a two-year-old, though not as intellectually stimulating, was worthwhile in its own way. And though Sean loved to delve into the brilliant metaphysical conceits of John Donne's poetry, he also enjoyed teaching a little boy to scream, "HULK SMASH PUNY HUMAN!"

After watching this process, several of my friends who swore they would never have children now do. Others are "thinking about it." As for me, I finished the degree in just over four years (I'm told it's a record at LSU). I have a tenure-track job in a respectable and growing university in the same town where my three children live. Every other weekend has been replaced by three and a half days every week. I see my children all the time. We continue to grow together and to learn from each other. And I continue to learn about balance. I want to further my career, but Geoffrey needs a soccer coach. Some things just have to wait.

One other bright and cheery Saturday in April, Geoffrey was outside drawing on the sidewalk with chalk. It was a year later, and we had moved to the front half of a home on Ivanhoe Street. Several other grad students in the English program lived on the same street. Geoffrey's normal routine when he draws is to strip to the waist, take off his shoes, and sit cross-legged in the middle of his canvas. He looks like a cross between a fledgling Picasso and Buddha. On this particular day, my friend Scott wandered up and asked Geoffrey what he was doing. Geoffrey responded, "I'm drawing my name." Scott looked at me with a sense of wonder and amazement and said something like "Did you hear that? He didn't say he was writing his name. He said he was drawing his name. It took me an entire semester on semiotic theory to understand the arbitrary nature of the signs that we choose to represent our language. He's three and he already gets it. You could learn a lot from this kid."

Scott, you have no idea.

It's a Chapter-Book, Huh

Teaching, Writing, and Early Fatherhood

ALEX VERNON

Though unaware of this fact until after my daughter's birth, I could not have chosen a better career for balancing professional fulfillment and fatherhood. The time demands of faculty life, for example, are onerous, but controllable—except when I am in class or a meeting, I can take her to the doctor or pick her up from school as needed, and even exercise my stress and last night's dessert away. If I work as hard as most serious professionals eight months of the year, the other four months belong to me. I frankly don't know how civilians cope, year in, year out, with only a couple of weeks each year of respite. In our line of work the light at the end of the tunnel is never far away, and shines big and bright.

I teach at a small liberal arts college in the South. In the fall of 2002, I was the first expectant father in its over 150-year history to request parental accommodation. I did not ask for much: a week of no classes after her spring semester birth, a Monday-Wednesday-Friday class schedule the following fall, and no committee work that first year. After her April birth, I returned a week later to finish the semester; in midsummer, when my wife returned to work, I stayed at home with our baby girl for another six weeks. The next few years, before kindergarten, she continued attending daycare over the winter and summer breaks, but I dropped her off later, fetched her earlier, and some days did not take her at all: time to write, time to read and think about my classes, and time with her. My first sabbatical semester coincided with her first kindergarten semester, enabling me in that stressful time to walk her to school, chaperone a field trip, carve watermelons for a class party, attend all her daytime events, and organize a class after-school park event. Her mother, on the other hand, a small-city tall-building attorney, has had much more trouble getting away. When she does find herself with more time on her hands, it means she isn't billing enough hours, risks an income drop, and feels like she isn't pulling her weight at the firm.

That with elementary school comes no summer or winter daycare, and so far less time to research and write, I don't mind. I have tenure now, and have established myself sufficiently as a scholar and writer. My pace can relax. I am less urgent about my writing. Teaching and writing are serious play, but not nearly as delightful or profound as watching my little girl believe she's training our dogs to give a high-five.

The balance I strive to strike necessarily leans me away from some institutional obligations. Having a child and living thirty miles from campus, I do not participate as much as I would like in after-hours campus life, a real problem in a school that prides itself on its community. Scheduling, be it of meetings or classes, is difficult. Because of her school schedule, I cannot arrive to teach first period classes, and four o'clock is the latest I can stay on campus most days of the week. I could not manage it without the understanding and kindness of my departmental colleagues. As a dear friend from the Math Department once said, with what struck me—perhaps I am being too self-congratulatory—as a mix of criticism and envy, "Between work and family, your priority is made abundantly clear." And having only one child probably makes life easier.

I am clearly fortunate. A 3/3 load with relatively small class sizes of up to twenty-five students makes for a healthier pedagogical life than what many of us must survive, with larger classes and a 4/4 load. Ever since my first term as an assistant professor, I have designed my own courses and taught a good mix of introductory and upper-level literature courses, and writing courses. The professional development component of faculty evaluation includes publication only as one possible method of fulfillment (I believe the lack of a strict publication schedule has made me more productive, by freeing me from the pressure and letting my curiosity go where it will). The compensation leaves something to be desired—less, for example, than my sister-in-law, who teaches public middle school and is not still paying off loans from nearly a decade of graduate school—but we also face less pressure to save for our daughter's college education. It has afforded me several cool trips, to Spain, Hawaii, Key West, Vietnam, and I hope Switzerland soon. It has supported some of my research, and has brought to campus writers whose company I kept: Tim O'Brien, Richard Ford, Miller Williams, Maxine Hong Kingston, Barry Lopez, Jorie Graham.

Raising a child has made me a better teacher, both in the way I think about my students (as sons and daughters) and, through expanding my own experience of life and love, in my understanding of literature. When in *Beloved* Paul D tells Sethe "You your own best thing," intending to cure her of her destructive if understandable overinvestment in motherhood, of ownership of this former slave's own flesh and blood, I can better appreciate the gap between Sethe's life and my own. My child is my best thing, which no one need tell me; then again, my story is not Sethe's. I also suspect that ten, fifteen, and even twenty years from now I will command a knowledge of my students' cultural lives far more than today, thanks to my now five-year-old daughter (excuse me: five and a half.). From the truism that students teach us as much as we teach them it follows that they can mentor us too, certainly those of us learning to be parents: When they volunteer their experiences growing up, in conversation or a piece of creative nonfiction, I sit up and take serious note. Rarely but blessedly I hit the jackpot: an only child, a young woman, whose parents also divorced when she was quite young, and who likes to talk.

Just as interesting, perhaps, is the way fatherhood intersects with my second and associated career as a writer. One of my books is a memoir composed of essays—an essay cycle? a composite memoir?—that charts my days as a West Point cadet and a Gulf War veteran become fresh academic and brand-new father while watching the second Iraq war come to be. It ends with my daughter's birth a few days after my old division rolled into Baghdad. Well-trained liberal academic that I am, I still sometimes wonder about my right to tell her story. The book is dedicated to her, the final line belongs to her—about my peace sign tattoo: "Daddy, what's that?"—and she joins me in the back flap author's photo.

Shortly after the book's release, flipping through a collection of essays on the American literature of the U.S. war in Vietnam, I ran across a line observing how many narratives by and about veterans locate their recovery not with homecoming, or with romantic love, but with fatherhood. I think I laughed aloud in my office. Studying literature, in our era of constructed identities, tells me intellectually that everyone is in some measure a cliché or amalgam of clichés. Reading that line effected my acceptance of my own clichéd self. And becoming a parent, remembering my childhood perception of my parents—how they embarrassed me so!—and imagining how much I will embarrass and disappoint her, and knowing viscerally just what it means to be the daddy in the "daddy's girl" formulation, has only reinforced my acceptance that it's okay to be a cliché. My premature absentmindedness and frayed attire are okay too.

⋞ ⋟

During my pre-divorce separation, more nights than not our very young child stayed with me, asleep early in the evening. I couldn't leave the house physically, but at least a part of me could escape to the jungle. Lonely nights meant time on my hands. Lonely nights meant a freely sauntering mind, and eventually a book: *On Tarzan*.

Freedom. That's one way I imagine others imaging a connection between the subject of my writing and the state of my being, with Tarzan an objective correlative for autonomous, nondomestic manhood restored, perhaps tinged with vicarious anger through Tarzan's ferocity and the misogyny that characterizes the universe of Tarzan narratives in book, film, and comic form. Burroughs and Hollywood both tried to kill off Jane—in *Tarzan the Untamed* and *Tarzan Finds a Son!*—but settled for omitting her from most of the stories (the misogyny hardly ends there; the threat of rape, for example, by ape-creatures and even by Tarzan, pervades).

I sense things differently. I sense a correspondence not with my child's mother, living in an apartment a couple of miles away, but with her. Experiencing this little creature needing, and moving in the world, and expressing herself physically and then verbally, corresponded to reflecting on little Tarzan doing the same. And through her I came to understand the animal nature of love. Hers for me, mine for her. Sometimes it feels like the entire universe was set into motion in order to someday produce this child. That's not just a way of expressing a truth. As far as my body is concerned, as far as my genes are concerned, it's the truth of truths.

Tarzan's ape-mother personifies such love. Burroughs tried his damnedest, in an age fighting desperately to keep its women child-rearing and stove-tending, to gender such love naturally feminine. Yet Burroughs had two small children himself when he wrote *Tarzan of the Apes*. Surely he felt something of what I feel; surely the past century of progress has not so thoroughly reconfigured our emotional lives. When the book finally came out, and she flipped through the pages, she inquisitively declared, "It's a chapter-book, huh."

❈ ❈

It's the New Year as I write. The tax-man cometh. When I buy a book, or subscribe to a journal, do I treat it as a 1040 professional deduction or a Schedule C business expense? Cable television, Netflix DVD service, the Internet—how do I accurately split these bills among personal life and my two professional lives? In the Tarzan book I write about Disney's *Tarzan* and *Tarzan II*, and DreamWorks' *Madagascar*, even as I purchased these

DVDs for my child. Indeed I could never have written that page about *Madagascar*, or that line about Curious George and the man with the yellow hat, were it not for time spent with her. A writer friend considers travel to see his grandchildren as a legitimate business expense on his Schedule C, and my dissertation advisor passed along the legend that novelist Jerzy Kosinski counted every penny he spent on anything as a writing expense: "He deducted his entire life." The three parts of my life—teaching, writing, and fatherhood—overlap, but I don't go that far.

The rest of the year I worry about less material matters. I worry that she will read some of my books, my memoirs especially, before she can really understand them. Those two books document my failure to come to terms with my first career as a soldier. How old does one need to be to develop a sympathetic appreciation of soldiering? How mature must one be to recognize those failures as productive and artful?

I worry because that's what parents do.

Most of all, I hope she'll be proud of me. For my teaching, for my writing, for bringing her a custom-made *ao dai* from Vietnam, but not just for these things. For providing enough—a roof, if one in need of replacing, and no trips to Disney World anytime soon—and for being able to be there as many fathers' careers do not enable them to be (even when I have put down the crayon for a few seconds to scribble a note in a draft's margin). I don't claim to have figured it all out. I have been extraordinarily fortunate. No foresight or planning placed me in a career and especially an institution within that career easily synched with parenthood. I know full well how odds-defyingly lucky I was, having sent sixty-some applications that job-search cycle and landing only one interview that somehow turned into an offer. No foresight at all: Sometimes I think I chose a career as a reaction against my army career, hanging with students in a classroom quite far away from taking a shit beside a tank in a nowhere desert. So many things frustrate and disappoint. Life outside of home, school, and writing suffers. The balance is always tipped a little too much in one direction. On any given day I neglect a student, or my writing, or a friend, or my parents or brothers, or my child. I don't even have time to read as much as I'd like. To read—the very foundation of my professional identities. We manage. On good days, we more than manage.

I have always cringed when my parents speak of their pride in me. I get it now. Everything Anna Cay does fills me with pride—even when she tells me she won't be my friend anymore, even when she stopped letting me kiss her when I dropped her off at school, even when this five-year-old sounds like a fifteen-year-old: "Whatever. Duh. What's the big deal anyway, guys?" But still it feels perfunctory. Parental pride: Duh. A parent's pride in a child is a given; a child's pride in a parent, it seems to me, is as it must be, which is to say: Earned. When I recently read from and spoke about the Tarzan chapter-book, Anna Cay sat with her mother in the audience. My talk about the miscegenation subtext must have sounded to her like the wha-whan-blanh-whan of the adults in the *Peanuts* shows. But she endured it, and every once in a while this little trooper perked up to report, "Mommy, he made them laugh!" That was a good day.

Pitcher This

An Academic Dad's Award-Winning Attempt
to Be in Two Places at Once

COLIN IRVINE

Recently, a few weeks after successfully negotiating the tenure-gauntlet—having managed to maneuver my way through it for six years—I found myself leaning against the island in the middle of our kitchen exhausted. It was late afternoon and I had commuted home from the college where I teach, one that's fifty miles north of the small town where we live. For several nights, I had stayed up long past when I should and hours after grading and prepping for classes in order to work on what I hoped would be the first of many pieces of creative writing I would produce now that I could, now that I was not feeling the publish-or-perish pressure. To be sure, this earned exhaustion and this kind of writing was my reward to myself for having, finally, been granted tenure and for having made other sacrifices that made this creative work possible and, in my mind, permissible, at least from a professional standpoint. Personally, I wasn't sure how to feel about this newfound freedom or the urge to redirect my energies toward pursuits I had been putting off since long before having kids, going to graduate school, or getting married.

Standing there with both hands on the counter, I looked and felt like I had just finished a marathon—and as anyone who has finished such a race knows, that's not a look of exhilaration, inspiration, or even relief. It's simply a look of exhaustion, plain and simple. But then, things began to change, if only slightly.

I heard somebody at the back door, and then I heard what sounded like rustling bags and heavy breathing. Two seconds later, my seven-year-old son, Caleb, came bounding up the six steps and scrambling excitedly into the kitchen. Smiling, he slipped out of his backpack in one fluid, practiced motion, dropped the bag to the floor, and pulled out of it a hard yellow folder taped with some odd blue kind of electrical tape. "Here," he said,

handing it to my wife while still grinning at me. As she does when opening presents, she carefully peeled back the tape. "What is this?" she asked
him, smiling. "What did you do?" Her tone gave her away, and I could tell
she knew more than she was letting on, which was much more than I
knew. She slid from out of the folder a certificate, four tickets to a Minnesota Twins baseball game, and a packet of some kind. She held up the
official-looking, embossed document and, in a formal voice, read, "Congratulations, Caleb Irvine. Second Grade Runner-up. Father-of-the-Year
Essay Contest." Cal turned to me, his expression showing how he thrilled
he was to have won this award and how pleased he was to report that it was
for an essay about his dad. And as for me, I was beyond proud (I don't
know what I was more excited about—the fact that my buddy had won an
essay contest or the fact that it was for a paper about why he was glad to
have me as his dad).

There was, however, a catch, as there almost always is, it seems. Because
Cal's essay had been selected as one of sixty out of nearly twenty-three thousand entries, I was, in turn, invited to participate in the Father-of-the-Year
Contest. This would, I soon discovered when reading through the packet
of materials that accompanied Cal's award, entail answering online questions about fatherhood, and then—should I be deemed fatherly enough—
participating in an interview. After the interview stage, a select group of
five finalists would be invited first to the state capitol for an afternoon with
the governor and then to the Metrodome a week later for an evening at
the Minnesota Twins baseball game, where the five fathers and their kids
would be part of a Father's Day ceremony and where the winner would get
to throw out the first pitch.

Burdened by the piles of ungraded essay exams and boxes of freshman
comp portfolios that had accumulated during the final few weeks of the
tenure-review process, I did not have time to participate in this contest, or
in anything else non-work-related, for that matter. If I was going to sit and
write anything, it was going to be comments on student papers, responses
to e-mails blackening my in-box, or, in the wee hours when these things
were done, another draft of an essay unlikely to make it out of an editor's
in-box. So, of course, having learned to say yes to everything for the previous six years as an assistant professor, I sat down and wrote my responses
to the online questions, a ten-minute task that took the better part of three
hours, one that had me smiling again and again in my office and among
my work piles as I thought about the years I had spent with Cal and with
Caroline, his younger sister.

I must've said the right things and pushed the right buttons when answering the questions, because a couple of weeks later, I was participating in my first phone interview since going on the job market.

Midway through the interview, I was asked, "If you could offer any advice to a new father about what he should give to his children, what would you tell him?" Without hesitating I said, "Time."

"Can you say a little more about that? What do you mean, exactly, by giving your kids 'time'?" the interviewer asked.

What follows is not, of course, what I said; it's what I would've said if I had had more time to think about it. Ironically, it is what I wrote when I—the allegedly effective and caring father—wasn't spending time with my wife and kids. And there's the rub. To be an effective academic, a caring father, and an aspiring writer, one apparently has to choose at times between living life with family and re-living it, alone. In fact, I feel lately like a writer on his honeymoon trying to steal a few hours here and there to hammer out a romance novel, or like a father shushing his kids so that he can write clever responses to questions about what it means to be a good dad.

Anyway, here's what I would've said—

A week or so ago, an unexpected letter arrived from a friend in Milwaukee, where my wife and I lived for five years when I was working on my PhD at Marquette. Along with a note updating us on some of our close friends and favorite places was a picture of my wife, my son, and me the week before we moved west to Minneapolis so that I could take a tenure-track job. There in the picture was my little Caleb, just three months shy of his second birthday and sporting his yellow-and-brown sweater and his bunched-up brown corduroys. He was proudly wearing the soft, fuzzy blue socks that he wore so often when I would hold his two feet cupped in my one hand while carrying him easily in the crook of my other arm, and he was looking at me here in the present from there in the past.

It was strange. As I stood there in the dining room staring at the picture, I found that I missed that friend of mine, even though the older version was lying on the living room floor not more than twenty feet away, a lanky, beautiful young man counting down the days until summer and the time when he can boast of being a "third grader."

It was more than déjà vu, the way I felt when I looked at that picture of my boy, my wife, and my younger self there on the front end of something different, a new life maybe. I could feel again how I felt so often during those weeks and months leading up to that moment, those times when I had napped with Cal on a random Tuesday, had rolled a ball across the rug to him in the flat-light afternoon of an otherwise insignificant Friday in February, and had bounced him in the middle of the night on my hip in the cold kitchen of our Milwaukee apartment while mixing yet another bottle. I remembered with clarity much of what led to that time, back in the beginning when things were still pretty simple—when there were only two of us to worry about—and when I was still incredibly naïve about what was coming.

Having been awarded a year-long research fellowship, I had planned to write my dissertation and take care of Caleb. My plan, as I recall it, was to work at my desk while he hung out in the swing and took naps and cooed (yes, I really was thinking in terms of "cooing"). It would be perfect, almost romantic even. And, practically speaking, it would help us face our financial problems, which stemmed from my modest income of 12K a year.

My older sisters—who between them had seven kids—laughed at me when I told them my plans. "You're gonna what?!" they said, before offering the "good luck with that" curse, which worked like magic. Caleb did not, as it turns out, follow any of the guidelines laid down in the standard literature concerning infants and their sleeping and eating patterns. Unlike the children referenced in those parenting books, he did not "sleep 16–18 hours a day in the first four weeks," nor did he sleep "14–18 hours a day in the subsequent months." Instead, he slept about nine or ten hours a day, and never for more than an hour or two at a time.

Frustrated and exhausted a couple of weeks into our undertaking, I wanted to find and beat the person who coined the phrase "sleeping like a baby," and I had less and less tolerance for our friends and fellow parents, the people who took their tiny infants out to restaurants, the perfect parents with perfect kids who made offhand comments such as "She'll sleep all day, if we let her" and "He didn't sleep through the night for the first two weeks, but now we've usually got him down by six." It's important, they would explain in response to our blank stares that they no doubt misinterpreted, to get them on a schedule early. "I'll give you a schedule," I would think to myself, and my wife would look at me sternly, warning me not to say anything.

Had I not been working against the clock and wrestling with all sorts of questions regarding who I was, what I was doing (and not doing), and what I would do next, I would've likely settled into my strange routine with Caleb and enjoyed living life on his schedule. But I had work to do. I was on an open-ended ticket to graduate school with no guaranteed flight back to reality. And, looking back, I realize now that I was bothered by those casual graduate students who haunted the academic halls where we had our offices. These were individuals, almost all single from what I could tell, who had apparently settled serenely into the strange rhythms of graduate school. Hip grad students—not the supposed nerds everyone outside of academics associates with the people who take five or six years to finish up the dissertation—these were the people in the worn jeans with the edgy glasses, the young/old twenty-somethings who made secondhand sport coats look trendy when worn with tall black boots or threadbare T-shirts. These were the grad students who, though we were living in Milwaukee, always made me wonder if they had just returned from Vegas or Santa Cruz or Taos, people who got away with references to Bakhtin and the Diaspora during lunch at Jimmy John's.

These people—or, really, the thought of becoming one of these people—terrified me. I was married. I was thirty-three years old. I had lived and worked in the real world, the place my wife spent the better part of her day with other bona-fide adults doing important, billable-hours kinds of things.

Against the backdrop of these fears were all the worries concomitant with being a new father in this particular dialogic Diaspora (that was about my best effort right there). I couldn't just hang around and hold on and hope for the best. I had to make things happen. I had to get stuff done, chapters written, things in the mail.

Meanwhile, Caleb kept screaming and fussing. He couldn't care less about who I was or who I wanted to be or needed to be. His stomach hurt, and he wasn't shy about sharing this fact within anyone in our apartment or the one above it. So, with the computer monitor displaying the often incoherent, unfinished page or paragraph I was working on, I would stand in the spare room of our duplex holding him and bouncing—the only thing that seemed to soothe him—while trying to read and hunch and type with one hand.

This lasted about a month before my wife and I agreed that we needed to try something else, something different. Hence, as people are wont to do in such dire situations, we hatched a plan. We decided that while my wife worked from eight to five, I would take care of Cal. Then, after dropping him off at her office at precisely five o'clock, I would go to campus and set up office on the fourth floor near the loud, humming fans of the Cudahay classroom building, which had the feel of a corporate headquarters with its gray/red industrial carpet, its open atrium all the way up to the glass roof, its fluorescent lights, and its secure entranceways that required an ID card for access.

Out in the hall at a small table tucked back into a corner near the stair-way exit, I sat there each night writing and reading almost frantically, tak-ing breaks when my eyes hurt or my hand cramped to look out the large windows to my left at the view of the world to the west, with the eclectic campus skyline of spires, flat-topped buildings, and treetops.

If things went well, I would work until midnight before packing up, hurrying to the car parked in the lot below the tangle of freeways, and head-ing home, where I would try to log two more hours, which would make eight for the day, my goal. But sometimes, the cell phone there on the table to the right of my stack of notes would ring relatively early in the night, at around nine or ten, and my wife would be calling. "How's it going?" she'd ask, and I'd panic. I could tell by something in her voice that she was worn out, done for the day and done with all of this that we were trying to do. Quickly, I would try to think of the right answer—if I said, "Great," she'd ask if I could come home a little early and help out with Cal. If I said, "Not so great," she'd suggest I take a break, maybe start fresh tomorrow. But I couldn't quit early. I needed something to show for my efforts. I needed to get to that place in the process that Ernest Hemingway described, when I knew I was on a roll and could come back to the writing a day or week later and pick up where I left off. "Hon," she'd say with Caleb screaming there by the phone, "can you come home? Honestly, I'm beat, and I have a meet-ing in the morning with Fred that I need to get ready for." "Yes," I'd say and suddenly feel better, knowing what I needed to do.

The weeks went by in a blur and the days crawled along. In the morn-ings, Cal and I would go through our routine: breakfast of toast and coffee for me and a bottle for him, bouncing in the kitchen and bouncing in the bedroom and down the hall, then a bath with the foam yellow sponge in the warm water beneath his bald head and smooth, slick, and soapy back and bottom, in the late morning. Then we'd hang out in the small and comfy living room on the big rug in front of the TV for a while. At first, until he was a few months old, he would lie there on the red-and-white-and-black padded blanket under the toy with the dangling, jingling plastic parts Velcro'd to it, and I would slide in by him, my head by his, his hands in my hair and on my face. Later, when he was almost crawling, he would sit propped up against some cushions, and we would play at whatever for as long as he liked. And sometimes during those days and weeks and months I would be right there with him. I would reach out and rub his warm little head with the wispy blond curls, and I would squeeze his fat hands and hold his little feet in those soft light blue socks.

Some of the best times I spent at home that year with Caleb were nap-times, when we would lie on top of the down comforter in the queen bed and he'd rest his head in the crook of my arm and up under my shoulder. Cuddled in next to me with his blanket covering all of him and half of me, he'd sleep deeply there by his dad. I would think to myself, "This is the best day of my life. It will never get better than this right now." Then I'd fall asleep and wake up an hour so later and ruin the rest of the day by turning it into a four-hour layover between then and my work later that night.

And despite that I was doing what I had always wanted to do as both a parent and as a professional, and despite the many moments of bliss I was enjoying with Caleb that year, those were tough times. Tough on my wife, tough on me, tough on our marriage, and, I suppose, tough on Cal. And it was during this year that we first began to get hints of what it would be like to live in two overlapping time-spaces as parents and professionals.

The hard work paid off, I suppose. I finished the dissertation in what my director assured me was record time and graduated in May of that fourth year, right at the finish line of my fellowship—never did a grant-giver get more bang for his buck than did Arthur J. Schmitt.

With my parents watching from high up in the box seats in the Bradley Center (home to the Milwaukee Bucks), which my wife's boss had graciously offered to us for the occasion, I sat on the stage wearing the black robe that felt so heavy and important on my shoulders and looking out over the undergrads and the professional studies students. Sitting on my right, shoulder to shoulder with me, was the keynote speaker, Stephen Covey, who talked about deposits and withdrawals as they relate to our relationships at our work, in our families, and with our friends. I could feel my wife up there watching, and I knew we were both thinking the same thing: I had been making a lot of withdrawals and far too few deposits during the past four years, and maybe it was time for a change.

But things didn't change and neither did I, not when it came to living more in the moment and thinking less of me and my future, habits of the head my profession seemed intent on turning into well-worn grooves in my life and relationships.

As an adjunct instructor that next fall, I took on eight classes at three different schools while pursuing the job of getting a job. This new routine meant the end of our tag-team approach to parenting. It also meant that we would be putting Cal in daycare four days a week, a decision we could not not make, of course, at least not if I was going to keep moving forward toward our shared goal of my securing a tenure-track job at a liberal arts college.

Shopping around for daycares made me wonder, though, how badly I wanted to get on this train and leave Caleb there, alone, at the station for the rest of his life. We visited in-house (in-basement) daycares. We visited places connected to churches, places where the kids slept on cots in the closets and where they played in kid kennels covered in asphalt and surrounded by chain link. And each time we drove away from one of these visits, having looked into the blank stares and studied the snotty faces of all those kids in their dirtied shirts and saggy pants, we said nothing for a long time, both of us wanting to get home as soon as possible and get Cal out of his car seat and hold him. Finally, though, we found a "daycare center" that we could live with. The initial "interview" with the "director" was a bit odd, as she spoke to my wife the entire time in an imperious, lecturing way that suggested we had done all sorts of damage that she and "her staff" would be forced to counter through the use of various strategies, including helping the children to "define and defend their personal space" and, of course, constant exposure to "sensory experiences" that would help Caleb develop his "gross motor skills," a phrase people who run daycares are apparently instructed to use in every third sentence.

While the woman talked to my wife, I held Cal up and away from the other kids, standing, I suppose, in a way that suggested that they were infectious and he was the rightful heir to the throne. "Go ahead and put him down and let him explore his environment," the woman instructed, adding, "and we," meaning she and my wife, "can go to the office to take care of the paperwork." I sat him down bottom first, rubbed his head, and told him, "Be back in a minute, buddy." He didn't cry, but he did look confused. I, on the other hand, who knew what was going on, barely kept it together. Walking down the sterile hall of tile floors and aluminum-lined interior windows toward the office in what used to be an elementary school, I felt my wife's hand slip into mine and she gave me a squeeze to reassure me he was fine, we were fine, everything was fine.

And it was.

A year later, a month before Cal turned two, we moved to Minnesota, where I commenced my work in the English Department at an urban college in Minneapolis bordered on its southern flank by the interstate, 444 miles west on the same interstate that throbs along the edge of Marquette's equally metropolitan campus. There, as a full-fledged assistant professor (a paradox to be sure) and no longer a TA or adjunct, I began working at a crazy pace all over again, teaching seven and soon eight classes while spending my nights and weekends writing and submitting anything and everything I could for publication.

Aside from the way that time and life picked up speed after I began my pursuit of tenure, what was most surprising about the move into the academy was the way that my work so often positioned me against my wife and our son and, soon, our daughter. This positioning was nobody's fault—unless, maybe, it was mine. It was simply a consequence of the fact that colleges and universities—with their always-evolving daily and weekly and yearly calendars—move at different tempos than does the world my wife and kids inhabit. Add to this scenario wherein one's work life is out of step with one's home life the demands and expectations associated with pursuing tenure and you have a recipe for real stress. I soon discovered that the tenure-track assistant professor must demonstrate on a regular basis his commitment to serving his students, his college, and his colleagues. And because one cannot possibly be in two places at once (e-mail doesn't count), a person in this untenable situation must, I learned again and again, pick one or the other—work or family—and he or she must do so often. The result: I found myself wishing I could say no in response to a request made by somebody above me; and no, one gets the sense when negotiating the academy as an assistant, probationary professor, is not a good answer to give when trying to convince the tenure and review committee to eventually say yes.

But, then, all of a sudden, when I came up for air one nondescript afternoon in late January—after nearly six short years of long, exhausting days, and after weeks of waiting for the final verdict from the tenure and promotion committee—I learned that the powers that be had said yes and thus granted me tenure. And in that instant everything changed, except my life, which I apparently cannot seem to transform completely. Sure, there was a moment when, after opening the envelope and reading the letter from the dean while standing there in the kitchen with my wife looking over my shoulder, I felt a kind gratitude that illuminated the rest of my wonderful life the way the lights do when turned on at a surprise party. But, for better or worse, my always-unsettled self pushed this other person—this newly tenured, smiling and appreciated father and husband—aside. This artistic (or maybe just egotistic), driven person inside of me saw an opening, a chance at long last to write fiction and creative nonfiction, to produce something from nothing, to say, "Look, I wrote that." It was a case of two steps forward and one or two or maybe more backward. We'll see, as they are fond of saying here in Minnesota.

I hope that in this next chapter, as my kids move from toddling to running and from running to running around with friends, and as I attempt to teach and parent and write and live in these overlapping worlds, I will get better at being where I am, at being present as a professor and, most importantly, as a parent. Who knows? Perhaps I'll learn to manage things so that on my last day of work I do not look back when my office books are boxed up and the house on the other end of the commute empty and wonder what happened. Maybe I will even find a way to capture this time in writing without having to miss it.

After I announced that, thanks to his essay, we were now in the running for the big award and would find out the winner at the capitol in about a week, Cal asked, "What if you don't win? Will you be disappointed?"

"Of course not," I told him, adding the expected, "I've already won. I've got you."

"Ugh, Dad!" he groaned. "That is so corny." As was the case when I found out that he was already an award-winning writer, I didn't know if it was the professor or father in me who was more excited and proud. Maybe it was both.

Now, sitting prominently on the file cabinet in my office is an 8 × 10 framed picture of Cal and me standing on the pitcher's mound at the Metrodome. He's wearing jeans, a brown-and-yellow shirt, his favorite sneakers, and, in my imagination, fuzzy blue socks. Handsome and happy, his head just below the height of my shoulder—there where it used to be when we napped on the big bed in Milwaukee—he's grinning big-toothed at the camera, two days from his eighth birthday. And me? I, too, am smiling and proud and truly present, my arm around my best boy and my life paused, perfect. I am, for the time being, content.

The pitch, by the way, was a strike, I hope.

Odd Quirks

CHRIS GABBARD

My son, August, has a number of odd quirks that distinguish him from the typically developing ten-year-old. He lives with cerebral palsy, is a spastic quadriplegic, has cortical visual impairment (meaning he is legally blind), is completely nonverbal and cognitively disabled, has a microcephalic head, and must wear a diaper. Moreover, he is immobile—he can't crawl or scoot around or hold himself up or even sit in a chair without being strapped in it. If someone were to put him on the floor and leave him there, he would still be in the same location hours later, give or take a foot.

At home, in the eyes of my wife, Ilene, and me and our seven-year-old daughter, Clio, August seems a little eccentric, possessor of a few odd quirks, as I said. We don't think about him as being different; he is August, just another member of an already quirky family. Although he cannot play with his sister, she loves him. Without being prompted, she recently made pipe-cleaner wheelchairs for her dolls and rendered her wooden doll house ADA-compliant by retrofitting it with ramps. Now the dolls wheel freely in and out. For family bike rides we have a specially built bicycle with a Tumble Forms chair attached to the front for him to ride in. I feed August his meals (he cannot feed himself), change his diapers, place him in the super-sized jogger when I go running, and put him to bed. He and I have a good relationship: he laughs at my attempts at humor, which consist of making odd sounds or putting him face up on the rug, holding his feet and legs up high, and rocking him swiftly back and forth. He seems to enjoy my company, and I most certainly enjoy his.

Outside of our home, my wife and I and Clio are constantly reminded of how unusual he must appear to other people. We assume he appears odd because he elicits responses ranging from aversion to "the stare." We understand that his drooling stems from his cerebral palsy—the spasticity in the muscles of the mouth prevents him from being able to control saliva.

No connection exists between mental disability and drooling, but, in the public imagination, this association has long been established. In the eyes of some, August answers to stereotypical images such as the cartoon character "Zippy the Pinhead." Yet, likening my son, and other people who have microcephalic heads, to Zippy, is about as relevant as likening African Americans to their blackface caricatures. In the eyes of others, August answers to Terri Schiavo, who, for the secular educated, triggers the fearful response of "better off dead than disabled." Many of these well-meaning people would like to put an end to August's suffering, but they do not stop to consider whether he actually is suffering. At times he is uncomfortable, yes, but the only real pain here seems to be the pain of those who cannot bear the thought that people like August exist. For many of these folks, someone with August's caliber of cognitive and physical disability raises the question of where humanity leaves off and animality begins. But this animal-human divide is spurious, a faulty "either-or." And then there are the Christians, who see in August a child of God. Given the educated alternative I just sketched out, this response seems a relief. Here in the South, they come up and say, "God bless!" to which, depending on the occasion and the person, I sometimes respond, "This is my beloved son, in whom I am well pleased." For almost everyone, August signifies one of the great tragedies that can befall a family.

After his birth, we ourselves lived in the tragic mode, but we soon grew tired of it. August brings us joy, as does his sister. Admittedly, the parenting commitment takes time from my career teaching English at the University of North Florida (UNF) in Jacksonville, where I am a tenured professor. And caring for August requires more time than does attending to Clio. Because August is a spastic quadriplegic, he necessitates the consuming regimen of daily full body care. Each morning I lift him from his bed, put him on a table, change his diaper, and wash and dress him. Next I carry him up to the breakfast room, strap him into his wheelchair, hand-feed him breakfast, wash his hands and face, brush his teeth, wheel him out to the van, and drive him to his school. On regular school days, this morning preparation can take up to two hours to perform. In the late afternoon and evenings I follow a similar routine: I drive through heavy traffic from campus to the only after-school facility in Jacksonville equipped to handle children like August. Once there, I lift him into the van, bring him home, hand-feed him dinner (his food must be puréed and otherwise specially prepared so that he won't choke on it), find something to occupy him after dinner, and finally prepare him for bed. All of this activity takes between two and three hours. Often in the evenings my wife and I hire people to help us so that we can get our work done and take care of our daughter. However, we cannot just hire the fifteen-year-old down the street to babysit: to take care of him properly, a caregiver requires at least a week of training. At my campus we have had good luck finding nursing and physical therapy students, but we must pay more than the customary seven dollars an hour.

On the days that I teach and August's school is out of session or his after-school facility shuts down, my wife and I must scramble to cover him. We cannot afford for my wife, a self-employed physical therapist and Pilates instructor, to give up a day of patients and clients. Other types of daycare facilities and the usual programs for typically developing ten-year-olds cannot accommodate a boy with spastic quadriplegia. I used to take him with me to the university, but he has now grown too large for that, and besides, he can be temperamentally unpredictable, making teaching difficult. Just recently, our family experienced an additional ripple of difficulty. My wife suffered a herniated disk in her neck, brought on in part by lifting August. An artificial disk was inserted, and, once she is fully recovered, the new disk will limit her to lifting no more than fifty pounds. Unfortunately, August now weights at least seventy. Because we moved from San Francisco to Jacksonville so that I could take my tenure-track job, we have no family in the vicinity to help us. Even worse, we have no rich uncles in the offing. As a result, almost all of the caregiving responsibilities have fallen on me. My wife and I have plans—but at present not the money—to remedy the situation: procure a Rifton lift (for inside the home) as well as a van with a wheelchair ramp. (Yes, August has the Florida Medicaid waiver, and we have a PPO through the university, but when we make requests for his needs, the wheels turn slowly and sometimes not at all.) In the meantime, I cannot leave the house for more than about eight hours; every day, morning and evening, I must be on hand to perform the routines. In sum, I cannot travel at all, even overnight. Hence, in the near future I do not foresee going to conferences, traveling to do research, or applying for the tempting academic opportunities that entail going abroad, or, for that matter, going anywhere. In a sense, I am as stranded as Robinson Crusoe on his island. Just a few weeks ago someone in the university offered me an additional job with a small pay increase. However, the job necessitated spending three days' training in nearby Orlando, so I had to turn it down.

While August has limited what I can accomplish in my academic career, he also has broadened my teaching and scholarship. In order to explain how he has done so, I have to go back to my grade school years in Palo Alto,

California. For the most part I was a good student and a nice boy, nice, that is, except when I was bullying Peter, the lone kid in the class who had learning disabilities. Perceiving him to be the bearer of stigma, my fellows and I trailed after Peter, calling him idiot, moron, imbecile, stupid, and cretin. Our *Lord of the Flies* vehemence at least respected the boundary of not physically harming him, though our psychological abuse must have damaged him. As I grew older, I was inspired by Socrates' statement that "the unexamined life is not worth living." Similarly, Aristotle's dictum that "man is the animal having *logos*" impressed me. The notion that the human being is a rational animal made sense, and I internalized it as a basic assumption, as I also did Socrates' pronouncement. At San Francisco State University I became intrigued by the Enlightenment. John Locke, David Hume, and Immanuel Kant fascinated me. Who would not want to be enlightened? Who in his or her right mind would choose in favor of a benighted past of superstition, ignorance, and blind faith in custom? I put my faith in reason. Eventually, I obtained my doctorate at Stanford in eighteenth-century British literature—the age of reason: Anne Finch, Alexander Pope, Jonathan Swift, Samuel Johnson.

In sum, I grew up prizing intellectual aptitude and detesting "poor mental function." Not that I am a candidate for Mensa, but perhaps what helped make me revere intelligence was growing up in Palo Alto, with Stanford less than half a mile away and a number of Nobel Prize winners and famous and wealthy technology innovators living all around me. People in my immediate vicinity had good brains, and that meant money, respect, and international influence. Given, then, my nearly metaphysical attachment to intelligence, imagine my surprise when in March 1999, at my first child's birth, he failed to breathe and consequently suffered severe brain damage. The delivery was taking place at an internationally prestigious teaching hospital, one that, I later learned, was attempting to reduce the number of cesarean sections performed because a belief had emerged that American medicine was relying too heavily on the procedure. After his birth, as I scrubbed, put on a mask, and was being led through very wide double doors into the intensive care nursery, I was deeply ambivalent, having been persuaded by Princeton philosopher Peter Singer's advocacy for expanding reproductive choice to include infanticide. But there was my son, asleep or unconscious, on a ventilator, motionless under a heat lamp, tubes and wires everywhere, monitors alongside his steel and transparent plastic crib. What most stirred me was the way he resembled me. Nothing had prepared me for this, the shock of recognition, for he was the boy in my own baby pictures, the image of me when I was an infant. Eight months after the birth, a doctor commented, after viewing the results of a CT scan, that his brain looked like "Swiss cheese," it was so full of dead patches. So I had to wrestle with the reality of his condition. Martin Luther was of the opinion that, because a child such as August was a "changeling," merely a mass of flesh, a *massa carnis*, with no soul, he should be drowned. And Singer reasonably would maintain that my son would not qualify as a "person" because he would have no consciousness of himself in time and space.

Days later at the hospital consult, the doctors tried to explain what had gone awry but without yielding any information that might provide the basis for a malpractice suit. Because nothing significant was disclosed, my wife and I secured a lawyer to find out what had happened. A medical expert reviewing the records reported back that malpractice had occurred. In the meantime, we had discovered that the expense of caring for August over his lifetime would likely exceed hundreds of thousands of dollars— a van with a lift, a lift in the house, thousands of hours of attendant care, lost wages, etc., all on an educator's and a physical therapist's salaries. Then the first lawyer mysteriously dropped out, and lawyer after lawyer looked over the records and passed on the case: a series of serious medical mis-judgments had been made, but no single "smoking gun" instance of mal-practice certain to convince a jury was likely to turn up.

My son's birth initially cast me into a wilderness of perplexity, doubt, and discontent. This was part of my wife's and my tragic mode, as I men-tioned. My formerly complacent assumptions began coming apart, and over the next few years they crumbled. I had seen the dark side of medicine— the quintessence of the Enlightenment—and firm ground slipped out from under me. Then came the Terri Schiavo case six years to the month after his birth. That a Florida court would order the deliberate starvation and dehydration of a woman whose mental disability differed not that much from my son's struck me as what Judith Butler terms "an enabling viola-tion." Schiavo's death served as a turning point, and new interests, beliefs, and curiosities began to coalesce.

In my teaching and scholarship I now interrogate some of the ideas that once informed my assumptions, and the questions I ask fit awkwardly into the academic landscape. Is it really true that the unexamined life is not worth living? And is it accurate to say that the possession of logos qualifies an entity for human status? For me, Socrates' and Aristotle's monumental truths gave way to questions for which I still do not have answers. And yet,

I concluded Luther was wrong, and I arrived at sufficient resolution to join a group called "Not Dead Yet" and to pass out leaflets on its behalf when Singer spoke on the UNF campus. I do not know how far I wish to go in demystifying logos: after all, I would not want to encourage my students to make unintelligent choices, leave their potential unexplored, or write irrational essays. What I do want to do, though, is bring forward to my students, colleagues, and readers what should have been obvious to me all along: namely, that the Peters of the world are as much members of our human tribe as any of us are. Especially in an academic environment that privileges being smart, how do I broach the idea that people with intellectual disabilities are fully equal? We academics advance in our careers by demonstrating how clever we can be, and because so much depends on flaunting intelligence, it is harder for us than for most to steer clear of prejudice. In posing my awkward questions, I have focused on teaching literature and cultural disability studies courses and writing articles that examine the rhetoric and representation of intellectual disability.

My commitment to bringing cognitive disability into the foreground in the humanities can be glimpsed in the way I teach Toni Morrison's short story, "Recitatif." I teach it every chance I get. Overall, the story illustrates how irrational frustration can well up even in sympathetic characters, compelling them to seek scapegoats. This story helped me begin to understand how my own troubles at home many years ago played a part in my abusive actions toward Peter. If I did not have August in my life, I probably never would have reconsidered my behavior toward Peter, or read this story carefully, let alone begun to teach it.

To admit how August has changed me is not to assert that what he has given me compensates for what he, my wife, my daughter, and I have lost on account of the poor decisions made by the hospital where he was born. There is no getting back what we have lost. Compensation is just a trope, and belief in compensation is as superstitious as belief in the medieval notion of correspondences. Besides, nothing can compensate for what all of us have had to give up. It would be better for everyone if he could run around and shout intelligible language. And I agree with Rabbi Harold Kushner when he writes and talks about bad things happening to good people: August's disability does not form a part of "God's plan" and does not serve as a tool for God to teach me or anyone else wisdom. What kind of a God would it be, anyway, to deprive my boy of speech and movement just to instruct me? A cruel and arbitrary God. August's disabilities are not a blessing; but then, neither are they a divine curse. To traffic in a cosmic economy of blessings and curses is to revert to an ancient prejudice. Indeed, even though August's disabilities offer ample opportunity for public interpretation, they do not mean anything at all in and of themselves—they have no intrinsic significance. They simply are what they are. This is not to deny that August, along with my daughter and my wife, is the most amazing and wonderful thing that ever happened to me, for he has allowed me an additional opportunity to profoundly love another human being. A person such as Singer well may conclude, reasonably, that I have become mystified by parental sentiment. So be it. I can live with that. There are limits to reason.

The Precarious Private Life of Professor Father Fiction Chef and Other Possible Poignancies

GARY H. MCCULLOUGH

Of course you wanted to be a rock star. What red-blooded American male growing up in the eighties didn't? You played the electric guitar at five hundred decibels (all distortion) and decided with tears in your eyes you had a true gift and intended to share it with the entire world, especially chicks. And while you were live at Dreamfest 1985, you decided you could be a screenwriter, too. You could write your own musical scores and direct them, as well. Go on tour with the band between films. Like Pink Floyd, only better. Write a few novels on the side that become bestsellers and buy the perfect writer's house in the Smoky Mountains overlooking what used to be a beautiful valley but now has Dollywood, racetracks, and enough airbrushed T-shirts to parachute the planet into the hell it deserves for screwing up your plans.

But, to be fair, plans do change. Even for Generation Xers.

They must. Between then and now run miles and miles of highway reality. Exit signs read "Fall in Love Here," "Have Children Here," "You Suck at Guitar and Sing like a Dying Quail Here," "Get a Job You Can Actually Earn Money At Here," and, of course, your favorite, "Starbucks, Next Right." Nothing to make you stop and rethink life like a double-shot low-fat mocha latte. "What was I thinking?" you ask yourself as your hand reaches conscientiously past the sugar jar for a solo packet of Splenda. Who wants to ride around on a stupid tour bus all the time anyway? Smoky nightclubs really bother your allergies.

It's not possible to piece together life's entire roadmap to determine how you arrived at your current locale. Even GPS can't display all the back roads and crossroads and side roads of life. And who would want it to? Imagine the nagging computerized version of your mother's voice: *Recalculating route; turn left two years ago and don't ask out Charlotte Mayberry.* Yeah, okay; sure. But it did seem like a good idea at the time. So did Milli Vanilli.

Change is good.

Along the way you get inspired by a few "rock star" teachers, experience the thrill as a doctoral student of writing and directing your own research projects, which might improve people's lives, and find the perfect little house at the foot of those Smoky Mountains (not Pigeon Forge), near a beautiful college campus where the leaves turn brilliant colors and young minds seek sculptors. Finally, and most importantly, you fall in love with not one but three girls: your wife and two daughters (not necessarily, though preferably, in that order). Turns out . . . they need "rock stars," too.

You stare out across the green expanse of the main campus lawn in October, the leaves just beginning to color, the sky a deep blue with a smattering of white clouds loitering in billows; the marching band is practicing in the distance, and you remember the home football game this Saturday: one of approximately twelve your university will lose by New Year's Day. "Hey, this isn't half bad, eighties boy," you realize aloud. You're one of the guys you totally thought was a loser a decade ago, but who cares? It is a pretty decent gig . . . for a "job." Sure, you have to deal with the comments from friends and family: "I forget, does academia have eighteen or twenty-seven holes?" Get it? It's so laid-back it's like a golf course. Hysterical! LOL. "Twenty-seven," you tell them, "which is the number of years I stayed in school and accrued student loan debts in order to get this job." And who knows when you'll pay the money back. Your friend who keeps teasing you just graduated from medical school. He paid his loans back by the end of his second month at work. And he really does play golf!

Another favorite . . ."Do you have to wear patches on the sleeves of your corduroy jacket, or can you get tenure without them?" Truth is, you don't know. You have patches, so you're covered either way. That's the kind of logical thinking that earned you a PhD in the first place. You made fun of the jackets when you were a cool student in the eighties, dressing so flash. And what amazing hair you had then. But there is something about the job of professor that begs for corduroy and a pipe, though it's now a non-smoking campus and there's really no need to start a bad habit you made it all the way through high school and college without (like dating). If you'd only had the corduroy jacket back then . . . with the hair and Milli Vanilli playing in the background . . .

Big-time!

Ten minutes pass before you realize you're doing exactly what you've been accused of in academia: nothing. But it doesn't last. As soon as you sit down in the grass to relax with your latte from the new Starbucks conveniently attached to the campus library, the cell phone rings: one of your doctoral students panicking about a research subject and the end of the world as she knows it. She has to meet with you now. Which reminds you of the class in grant writing you teach in thirty minutes and for which you haven't finished grading the tests. The elementary school beeps in and tells you your daughter is sick and has to be picked up immediately. Your wife is in an all-day meeting with the faculty senate (yes, she, too, has a PhD and must endure meetings void of and, ironically, filled with agenda). And you suddenly remember why you were walking across campus in the first place: a meeting with the dean for which you're now seven minutes late.

So here's the good part. While rushing back to your office you tell your doctoral student to be creative and exercise her problem-solving skills, stick a note on the door canceling class (which can only elevate your teaching evaluations), and fire off a quick e-mail to the dean explaining the sudden illness. In fifteen minutes you're at home on the couch watching *Hannah Montana* with your daughter. Try that one in the middle of surgery, MD boy!

Back to the bad part. This doesn't exactly help your hardworking academic image. Say . . . How many PhDs does it take to change a light bulb? Nobody knows. The committee tabled the issue and appointed a subcommittee to gather data from other universities around the country and investigate the possibility of some videoconferences prior to calling for a vote. Okay, true (no, seriously, true); but subcommittees take up a lot of time. And videoconferencing is very unreliable. Moreover, in the end, the dean will most likely turn down the request for a new light bulb on budgetary grounds.

What most fail to recognize is there is a great deal more to academia than meets the eye. Just because you don't have to work 8:00 A.M. to 6:00 P.M. like everyone else doesn't mean you're free to smoke dope and dream about liberal concepts . . . like peace. But if you could turn it into a learning experience . . . No! You have to actually work. You have to teach classes, meet with students, write research grants (and get them funded), publish papers and books (if you want to actually keep the job, that is), attend faculty meetings where most issues really are tabled and handed to subcommittees for further review. It's a job. And it's more than forty hours per week. Typically much more. But you also have the freedom to schedule some of your own classes, some of your appointments with students and other faculty. You can grade your papers and write grants and submit articles after the sun goes down and bats take to flight, as long as you own a Gaggia espresso machine and stock Illy espresso (fine grind only). "Did

Vlad Dracula have a PhD?" He was definitely productive at night. Check his corduroy jacket for patches. You can also check for gray hair and bags under the eyes, which are other common side effects of academia and family.

Because while academia can wait, it never ends. (You see a bumper sticker in your future.)

Truth is, you can leave your job in the middle of the day if you have to and no one will die. In fact, most won't even notice. There is no need to argue this essential truth. But after watching *Hannah Montana* and tending to your daughter, cooking dinner, feeding everyone, giving baths, reading something involving Junie B. Jones, and tucking two little girls in thirty-two times (which research suggests is actually how many times it takes [$p \leq .05$]), you eventually have to sit down and finish the work you left without the shadow of a thought some seven or eight hours ago. You call your doctoral student (though she would prefer you Twitter or use Facebook, you're just too old); you grade the papers and post the grades online for your class, who, in the age of rapid technology (see first part of sentence), expects immediate information. You e-mail the dean to reschedule your appointment, and then, around 11:00 P.M., decide to do what you actually want to do for yourself. Could be *The Daily Show* and *The Colbert Report*. Perhaps a good replay of a game on ESPN Classic. For you, it's giving in to the nagging desire to be a writer you haven't been able to quell over the past two decades. Did you mention the necessity of an espresso machine? Many outstanding novels have been written by sleep-deprived individuals. Though you have no definitive examples and are too tired to look them up, you're certain this is true. And even if it's not, you have a PhD, which is, in fact, a license to make up information when you do not have it readily available. And while the pages of your fiction don't always flow like aimless rhetoric in faculty meetings (read *Straight Man* by Richard Russo for additional information), academia is a job that provides opportunity for at least a few minutes a day to pursue, in addition to family, whatever else it is you want to pursue (really shouldn't be co-eds). You simply have to make choices: *Monday Night Football* or work on your novel. Fortunately, it's Thursday and April and life becomes blessedly simple. You can sit down with the novel as soon as you crank out 2,500 words for some essay about having a PhD and children, both of which you should have to *earn*.

A retired individual once said to you about work (no joke), "Enjoy it while you've got it, because it won't always be there." Three points came to mind. First, is this an episode of *The Twilight Zone* where everything is suddenly bassackwards? Second, this was obviously before the demise of the 401(k), as no one can retire anymore. And, third, you're not concerned in the slightest. Sure, you enjoy your work. College campuses live, breathe, and thrive; and all you have to do is walk across one to know this. It's good. But not having this one day is not your greatest fear.

In an age when men often have no idea they even have families, much less whether or not it's gymnastics day or piano day, male academicians are able to not only know but participate. You never miss a party at your youngest daughter's preschool. You eat lunch once a week with your oldest. You know what makes them laugh, as well as cry (tickling does both if you're persistent). You know their favorite TV shows and can actually watch/screen them. Your youngest loves puzzles and games. Your oldest: clothes, Barbies, and chase. And you want to chase her, because one day you just won't catch up. And that really is your greatest fear. That's what you will miss.

As a father who wants to actually be a father, the benefits of academia, be it eighteen or twenty-seven holes, far outweigh the risks associated with insomnia, vampire bites, or tired, baseless comments about not having a real job. Show me a man who drops off his daughter at eight and picks her up at three, takes her to seventy-five after-school activities, and makes it home in time to cook Tomato Basil Risotto with Scallops (see appendix A), a dish that has earned him the title of executive household chef, and I'll show you a college professor. And when your daughters walk down the aisle at their weddings, releasing your hand for the last time to take someone else's, they'll remember how hard you worked. They'll know it wasn't on a golf course, too. It will be worth the late nights and the insincere comments, and even the faculty meetings.

You'll trade the midnight oil for the three o'clock smile any day of the week. After all, that's your job: professor father fiction chef. And you wouldn't have it any other way.

Appendix A: Tomato Basil Risotto with Scallops

Ingredients

White wine (any kind you are willing to drink)
6 cups of chicken (or seafood) broth
1 (16-ounce) can of diced tomatoes
¼ cup olive oil
Sea salt
1 red onion, diced

Enough garlic to ward off those vampires (keep extra in office at all times)

2 cups of Arborio rice

A couple good handfuls of fresh basil leaves

Parmigiano Reggiano

Butter (not as much as Paula Deen would use)

1 ½ to 2 pounds of fresh bay scallops (can substitute regular scallops at will)

Salt and pepper to taste

Instructions

Fill glass of wine and begin to drink.

Meanwhile, in a medium-sized pot, heat 6 cups of chicken broth (seafood broth would totally rock if you have it) and 1 or 2 cups of tomato juice from your can of tomatoes. In a large nonstick skillet, heat olive oil and add onion and sea salt. Stir and cook for 2 to 3 minutes. Add garlic and cook for another 1 to 2 minutes. Add Arborio rice, stir, and cook 2 to 3 minutes. Add about a cup of white wine (not the one you're drinking). Allow wine to cook down by half. Begin adding broth one ladle at a time, allowing each ladle to soak into the rice and then stirring. Once broth is reduced by half, add the next ladle. In about 10 minutes, add in the tomatoes and basil. Continue adding broth and stirring as before for another 10 minutes or until risotto is al dente. Add salt and pepper to taste. A few minutes before risotto is done, grate fresh Parmigiano Reggiano (until it feels real good) into the rice and stir.

In a separate skillet, melt butter, then add scallops (salted and peppered— could blacken, too: mmm). Brown scallops everywhere you can possibly brown them over high heat for just 2 or 3 minutes, and add a little white wine so you can scrape up the amazing bits that stick. Remove scallops from heat to a plate. Place risotto in bowls to serve immediately; top with scallops. Add a little herbs de Provence or fresh parsley for additional kick.

Optional: After-dinner double shot of Illy espresso (or your baby's love).

Notes on Contributors

Mike Augspurger received his PhD from the American Studies Department at the University of Iowa. After spending seven years visiting English, history, and American Studies departments at the University of Central Arkansas, the University of Regensburg (Germany), and Augustana College (Illinois), he has settled down into the role of director of advising at Augustana. He is the author of *An Economy of Abundant Beauty: "Fortune" Magazine and Depression America* and has published essays on Sinclair Lewis, Archibald MacLeish, Henry Luce, and Robert Penn Warren, among others.

Charles Bane has lived in numerous places all over the country and has worked variously as a country music disc jockey, an oil refinery demolition specialist, a movie critic, and an eighth-grade English teacher. He earned his doctorate in twentieth-century literature and film with a minor in comparative literature from Louisiana State University in 2006. He now lives with his wife, Paulette, and his three children, Ericka, Katherine, and Geoffrey, in Conway, where he is an assistant professor of literature and director of English education at the University of Central Arkansas.

Kevin G. Barnhurst (PhD, University of Amsterdam, 1997) teaches theory and research methods as a professor of communication at the University of Illinois at Chicago. He is the award-winning author of *Seeing the Newspaper*, coauthor (with John Nerone) of *The Form of News: A History*, and editor of *Media Queered* (Peter Lang, Inc.) and has published more than one hundred articles on the ideology of news, visual communication, and the sociological life histories of young adult audience members. Besides the Fulbright to Peru and the fellowship at Columbia described here, he was a Shorenstein Fellow at Harvard, a Fulbright Distinguished Chair in Italy, and a Faculty Scholar at the Great Cities Institute in Chicago. The product of a Korean War affair, he lost his mother when he was nine and never met his natural father, who in family lore was a Jew who converted to Mormonism and became a bishop in Salt Lake City.

David Haven Blake is a professor of English at the College of New Jersey, where he teaches courses in American literature, film, and creative nonfiction. He is the author of *Walt Whitman and the Culture of American Celebrity* and the coeditor of *Walt Whitman, Where the Future Becomes Present*. His political and cultural essays have appeared in *Epoch*, *Virginia Quarterly Review*, the *Chronicle Review*, and the *Huffington Post*. He is currently writing a book on the convergence of politics and celebrity in Dwight Eisenhower's presidential campaigns.

John Bryant, a professor of English at Hofstra University, has written on Herman Melville, related writers of the nineteenth century, and textual scholarship; he is also editor of *Leviathan: A Journal of Melville Studies*. His recent book *Melville Unfolding: Sexuality, Politics, and the Versions of Typee* is based on his online fluid-text edition, titled *Herman Melville's Typee*, appearing in the Rotunda electronic imprint (University of Virginia, 2006). His books include *A Companion to Melville Studies*, *Melville and Repose: The Rhetoric of Humor in the American Renaissance*, and *The Fluid Text: A Theory of Revision and Editing for Book and Screen*. He has edited several editions of Melville works, including *Typee*, *The Confidence-Man*, *Melville's Tales, Poems, and Other Writings*, and the Longman Critical Edition of *Moby-Dick*. He is currently working on a critical biography, *Herman Melville: A Half-Known Life*, and the Melville Electronic Library (MEL), an online archive.

David G. Campbell, a professor of biology at Grinnell College, is a scientist, teacher, and author. He may be the only biologist to have research sites in those antitheses of diversity, the Amazon and Antarctica. After coming to Grinnell College in 1991, Campbell began a long-term project in Belize on the Maya forest and its people. The author of numerous professional papers, Campbell is also a writer of literary nonfiction. His works include *The Ephemeral Islands* (1977), a natural history of the Bahama Islands; *The Crystal Desert* (1993), a reminiscence on three summers in Antarctica (chosen as one of the notable books of 1993 by the *New York Times Book Review*); *Islands in Space and Time* (1996), an exploration of ten wilderness areas from Palau to Paraguay; and *Land of Ghosts* (2005), a personal essay on Amazonian diversity, biotic as well as human.

Stanford W. Carpenter is a cultural anthropologist and assistant professor in the Department of Critical & Visual Studies at the School of the Art Institute of Chicago. Carpenter conducts ethnographic research among artists and media makers in order to address the construction and depiction of identity and community. He uses his ethnographic research both for scholarly manuscripts and for arts-based projects.

Lennard J. Davis is a professor in the English Department in the School of Arts and Sciences at the University of Illinois at Chicago. In addition, he is a professor of disability and human development in UIC's School of Applied Health Sciences, as well as a professor of medical education in the College of Medicine. Davis is the author of two works on the novel—*Factual Fictions: The Origins of the English Novel* (1983) and *Resisting Novels: Fiction and Ideology* (1987)—and coeditor of *Left Politics and the Literary Profession*. His works on disability include *Enforcing Normalcy: Disability, Deafness, and the Body* (1995), which won the 1996 Gustavus Myers Center for the Study of Bigotry and Human Rights annual award, and *The Disability Studies Reader* (1996). His memoir *My Sense of Silence* (2000) was selected an Editor's Choice Book by the *Chicago Tribune*, submitted for the National Book Award for 2000, and nominated for the National Book Critics Circle Award for 2000.

John Domini has won awards in fiction, the essay, and poetry. These include a fellowship from the National Endowment for the Arts. His last novel, *A Tomb on the Periphery*, was praised in *Bookslut* and elsewhere; the Emerging Writers Network called that book and the 2007 novel *Earthquake I.D.* "back-to-back stunners." *Earthquake I.D.*, in Italian translation, was runner-up for the Domenico Rea Prize. Short stories have appeared in *Paris Review*, *Ploughshares*, and anthologies. Criticism and essays have appeared in the *New York Times*, *Ninth Letter*, and elsewhere. His doctorate is from Union Institute and University, and he has held visiting positions at Northwestern, Lewis & Clark, Harvard, and elsewhere. He still doesn't have a real job.

Eric H. du Plessis is a professor of French studies at Radford University. He received his PhD at the University of Virginia. His literary translations include *Balzac's Wann-Chlore* (2005), *Balzac's The Last Fay* (1996), and *The*

Nightcharmer and Other Tales of Claude Seignolle. He is also the author of *Nietzsche en France, 1891–1915,* and his articles on literature, history, and cultural studies have appeared in *Revue de Littérature Comparée, Poe Studies, European Studies Journal, Dalhousie French Studies, SSC: Short Story Criticism, The World Education Encyclopedia, ALFA,* and the *World Press Encyclopedia.*

Chris Gabbard earned his PhD from Stanford University and now serves as an associate professor of English at the University of North Florida. His articles have appeared in *PMLA* and *Eighteenth-Century Studies,* among others. He currently is at work on *Idiocy and Wit: Mental Dis/Ability in Eighteenth-Century Representation.*

Joseph Gelfer is an honorary research associate at the School of Political and Social Inquiry, Monash University, Australia. He is founding and current editor of *Journal of Men, Masculinities and Spirituality* and author of *Numen, Old Men: Contemporary Masculine Spiritualities and the Problem of Patriarchy* (2009).

Robert Gray is a writer and a professor of film and screenwriting at the University of New Brunswick in Fredericton, Canada. His essay about becoming and being a donor dad will appear in the forthcoming anthology *And Baby Makes More: Known Donors, Queer Parents, and Our Unexpected Families.* His first collection of short stories, *Crisp,* is forthcoming in early 2010.

Andrew Hazucha is a professor of English and department chair at Ottawa University in Ottawa, Kansas. An eighteenth-century scholar by training, he has published essays in a variety of other areas, including William Wordsworth, Nelson Algren, contemporary Irish poetry, the 1977 Chicago L-train crash, and the Chicago Cubs. His most recent publication is a collection of essays that he coedited with Gerald Wood entitled *Northsiders: Essays on the History and Culture of the Chicago Cubs* (2008).

Colin Irvine is an associate professor of English and environmental studies at Augsburg College in Minneapolis, Minnesota. He enjoys hanging out with his wonderful kids, Caleb and Caroline, spending time with his lovely and supportive wife, Kelly, and teaching courses in American literature, English education methods, and environmental literature. He recently edited a collection of essays titled *Teaching the Novel across the Curriculum: A Handbook for Educators* (2007) and is currently at work on an annotated edition of Aldo Leopold's *A Sand County Almanac* (1949). And, in what was a shock to everyone who knows him, he was named the 2009 Minnesota Twins Father of the Year.

Amitava Kumar is the author of *Husband of a Fanatic* (2005), *Bombay–London–New York* (2002), and *Passport Photos* (2000). His novel *Home Products* (2007) was short-listed for India's premier literary prize, the Crossword Book Award. His latest book, *A Foreigner Carrying in the Crook of His Arm a Tiny Bomb*, is a writer's report on the global war on terror (forthcoming). Kumar is a professor of English at Vassar College, where he teaches courses in literature and creative writing.

Jeffrey B. Leak is an associate professor of English and African American literature at the University of North Carolina at Charlotte. The author of *Racial Myths and Masculinity in African American Literature*, he is currently working on a biography of Henry Dumas, a writer often associated with the Black Arts Movement of the 1960s.

Mary Ruth Marotte, PhD, is an assistant professor of English and the director of Graduate Studies in English at the University of Central Arkansas, where she specializes in women's studies and critical theory. Her book, *Captive Bodies: American Women Writers Redefine Pregnancy and Childbirth*, was released in October 2008. She has written a chapter to be included in *The Palin Factor* and has contributed to the *Encyclopedia of Motherhood*, both due out in the spring of 2010. She lives in Conway, Arkansas, with her husband and three children.

William Marsiglio is a professor of sociology at the University of Florida and a fellow of the National Council on Family Relations. He has written extensively on the social psychology of fathering and men's sexuality, fertility, reproductive health, and mentoring of children. He has lectured at national and international conferences on fatherhood and consulted on national surveys about male sexuality and fatherhood. He has published seven books including, most recently, *Men on a Mission: Valuing Youth Work in Our Communities* (2008), *Situated Fathering: A Focus on Physical and Social Spaces* (2005), and *Stepdads: Stories of Love, Hope, and Repair* (2004).

Robert Mayer is currently an assistant professor at the College of Southern Idaho in Twin Falls, where he teaches English composition and literature courses. Prior to becoming a full-time faculty member in 2002, Mayer had spent seven years as a newspaper reporter covering a myriad of beats for a small-town newspaper in nearby Burley, where he has lived since 1992. Married to his wife, Shannan, since 1994, Mayer is the father of three sons, ages eighteen, seventeen, and four. A native of the Pacific Northwest, Robert holds a BA from Brigham Young University–Utah and an MA in English from Idaho State University.

Gary H. McCullough received his PhD from Vanderbilt University in 1997. He is currently an associate professor at the University of Central Arkansas in Conway. He has served on program committees and best practice guideline committees for the American Speech-Language-Hearing Association as well as the international Dysphagia Research Society and has been awarded research grants by the National Institutes of Health and the Department of Veterans Affairs to investigate evaluation and treatment tools for individuals who suffer from swallowing problems post-stroke. He has fifteen years' experience as a clinician, researcher, and teacher. He has nine years' experience as a husband, eight as a father, seven as a chef, and twelve as a writer of fiction. Being a husband and a father has been, by far, the most enjoyable and successful.

Mark Montgomery is Donald L. Wilson Professor of Enterprise and Leadership, and a professor of economics, at Grinnell College, in Iowa. His research has appeared in such journals as the *Review of Economics and Statistics, Economic Inquiry*, the *Industrial and Labor Relations Review*, the *Review of Economic Dynamics and Control, Land Economics*, the *Journal of Environmental Economics and Management*, the *Quarterly Review of Economics and Finance*, and a number of others. He is coauthor (with Tinker Powell) of a mystery novel, *Theoretically Dead* (2001). His essays have been published in the *Chronicle of Higher Education*, the *Des Moines Register*, the *Dallas Morning News*, the *Cedar Rapids Gazette*, the *Mystery Readers Journal*, the *American* (online), and the *Imperfect Parent* (online). His commentary has been heard on Public Radio International.

Gregory Orfalea currently teaches Arab American literature at Georgetown University. Richard Rodriguez called Orfalea's 2009 memoir, *Angeleno Days*, "delightful and wise." The author of two acclaimed histories, *The Arab Americans: A History* and *Messengers of the Lost Battalion*, Orfalea has also published two books of poetry, and edited, with Sharif Elmusa, *Grape*

Leaves: A Century of Arab American Poetry. In 2010, he published his first collection of short stories, *The Man Who Guarded the Bomb*. Orfalea's work has been widely anthologized in such places as *The Norton Introduction to Poetry*, *Imagining America*, and *Multiculturalism in the United States*, and he has won several awards and grants for his writing. He and his wife have three sons; he divides his time between Washington, D.C., and Los Angeles.

Mark Osteen is a professor of English and film studies at Loyola University Maryland. He is the author of *The Economy of Ulysses: Making Both Ends Meet* (1995) and *American Magic and Dread: Don DeLillo's Dialogue with Culture* (2000), and the editor of *The Question of the Gift* (2002) and coeditor of *The New Economic Criticism* (with Martha Woodmansee; 1999). In 2008, his edited collection *Autism and Representation* was published by Routledge. Osteen has completed a memoir, *One of Us: A Family's Life with Autism*, and is currently at work on a study entitled *The Big Night: Film Noir and American Dreams*.

F. D. Reeve earned his doctorate in Slavic languages at Columbia, where he taught for ten years before moving to Wesleyan for forty and switching from professor of Russian to professor of letters, retiring in 2002. He was a visiting teacher at Oxford, Columbia, and Yale. Besides a dozen and a half translations, he has published five novels, two books of short stories, and eight volumes of poems, most recently *The Toy Soldier* (2007) and *The Blue Cat Walks the Earth* (2007), poems designed for jazz accompaniment and so presented. He served as vice president of the Poetry Society of America, founded the *Poetry Review*, was the Poets House secretary in its formative years, and is on the board of directors of the *New York Quarterly*. In 2007, he was keynote speaker at the Moscow International Conference of Translators of Russian.

Paige Martin Reynolds is an assistant professor of English at the University of Central Arkansas, where she teaches Shakespeare, Renaissance drama, eighteenth-century and Restoration drama, and world literature. Her research interests include studies in early modern drama, performance, gender, and Elizabeth I. She has authored articles published or forthcoming in *SEL: Studies in English Literature, 1500–1900*, *ANQ: American Notes and Queries*, and *1650–1850: Ideas, Aesthetics, and Inquiries in the Early Modern Era*. Reynolds is also a professional voiceover artist and stage actor, most recently portraying Lady Macbeth with the Arkansas Shakespeare Theatre in 2009. She lives in Little Rock, Arkansas, with her husband, Bert, and daughter, Anna.

Ralph James Savarese teaches American literature, disability studies, and creative writing at Grinnell College. He is the author of *Reasonable People: A Memoir of Autism and Adoption* (2007), which *Newsweek* called a "real life love story and a passionate manifesto for the rights of people with neurological disabilities." He is also the winner of the Herman Melville Society's Hennig Cohen Prize for an "Outstanding Contribution to Melville Scholarship." His scholarship, essays, poems, and opinion pieces have appeared, among other places, in *Prose Studies, Leviathan: A Journal of Melville Studies, Disability Studies Quarterly*, the *Journal of Literary and Cultural Disability, Politics & Culture, Southern Humanities Review, New England Review, Sewanee Review, Southwest Review, American Poetry Review, Modern Poetry in Translation, Rattle*, the *New York Times*, the *LA Times*, the *Houston Chronicle*, the *Atlanta Journal Constitution*, the *Huffington Post*, and the *Des Moines Register*.

J. Aaron Simmons received his PhD in philosophy from Vanderbilt University in 2006. He is currently a visiting assistant professor at Hendrix College in Conway, Arkansas. Specializing in Continental philosophy of religion and political philosophy, Simmons is the coeditor of *Kierkegaard and Levinas: Ethics, Politics, and Religion* and the author of numerous essays in academic journals. At present, Simmons is coediting a volume entitled *Religion with Religion* and finishing two book manuscripts: *God and the Other: Ethics and Politics after the "Theological Turn"* and *Heavenly Minded and Earthly Good: On the Evangelical Turn to the Environment*.

Ira L. Strauber is a professor of political science (Senior Faculty Status), Grinnell College, Iowa. He has a BA from Queens College (CUNY, '63), an MA from Northwestern University ('68), and a PhD from Brown University ('73). He taught constitutional law and politics (and political theory) at Grinnell College. His *Neglected Policies: Constitutional Law and Legal Commentary as Civic Education* received the C. Herman Pritchett Award, Law & Courts Section of the American Political Science Association, for Best Book on Law and Courts published by a political scientist, 2002. Among his most recent publications are "When the Law Speaks: US Constitutional Law, Acts of Intolerance, & Threats to Self-Identity" in *Diversity and Tolerance in Socio-Legal Contexts Explorations in the Semiotics of Law* (edited by Ann Wagner and Vijay Bhatia, 2009) and "An Indifference Thesis: Constitutional Law and Politics in an Era of 'Conservative Domination' of the Judiciary," *Studies in Law, Politics, and Society* (2008).

Jason Thompson is in his first year as an assistant professor of English at the University of Wyoming, where he teaches the rhetoric of video games, technical writing, and composition. He has most recently published a collaborative essay, "Portrait of the Profession: The 2007 Survey of Doctoral Programs in Rhetoric and Composition," in the *Rhetoric Review*. His research interests include new media, game studies, digital archiving, classical rhetoric, and Kenneth Burke. His poetry has been published in *Prairie Schooner*, *Phoebe*, and others; this is his first nonfiction essay.

Ting Man Tsao is an associate professor of English, teaching composition and literature at LaGuardia Community College of the City University of New York. In addition to teaching, he facilitates the following faculty development seminars at LaGuardia: the Faculty Scholars Publication Workshop and the Carnegie Seminar on Teaching, Integration and Scholarship. With a native fluency in Chinese, he majored in English at Hong Kong Shue Yan College. He holds an MA in comparative literature from the University of Washington at Seattle and a PhD in English from the State University of New York at Stony Brook. His dissertation is titled "Representing China to the British Public in the Age of Free Trade, c. 1833–1844." He has published in the following journals: *Peer English*, the *History Teacher*, *In Transit*, *Nursing Education Perspectives*, *Teaching English in the Two-Year College*, *Victorians Institute Journal*, and *Writing Macao*. His book chapters appear in *Asian Crossings: Travel Writing on China, Japan and Southeast Asia* and *Illness in the Academy: A Collection of Pathographies by Academics*, and *Pirates and Mutineers in Nineteenth-Century Literature*.

Alex Vernon is an associate professor of English and department chair at Hendrix College in Conway, Arkansas. He is author or editor of six books: *Approaches to Teaching the Works of Tim O'Brien* (2009); *On Tarzan* (2008); *Most Succinctly Bred* (2006); *Arms and the Self: War, the Military, and Autobiographical Writing* (2005); *Soldiers Once and Still: Ernest Hemingway, James Salter, and Tim O'Brien* (2004); and *The Eyes of Orion: Five Tank Lieutenants in the Persian Gulf War* (1999).

Jerald Walker is an associate professor of creative writing at Emerson College in Massachusetts. He is a graduate of the Iowa Writers' Workshop, where he was a Teaching/Writing Fellow and a James A. Michener Fellow, and he holds a PhD in interdisciplinary studies from the University of Iowa. His work has appeared in numerous publications, including *The Best American Essays* (2007 and 2009), *Best African American Essays* (2009), *Mother Jones*, the *Oxford American*, the *North American Review*, the *Missouri Review*, the *Chronicle of Higher Education*, the *Barcelona Review*, the *Iowa Review*, and *Brothers: 26 Stories of Love and Rivalry*. His book, *Street Shadows: A Memoir of Race, Rebellion and Redemption*, was published in January 2010.

John W. Wells served as a faculty member for twelve years, teaching courses in American history and political theory. He has served as a department head, division dean, provost, and interim college president. He is the author of numerous articles on civil liberties, academic administration, and the role of religion and politics in American life. Along with David Cohen, he is the coeditor of *American National Security and Civil Liberties in an Era of Terrorism*. He is currently the vice president for academic affairs at Mars Hill College and lives in Asheville, North Carolina, with his family.